DYNAMICS OF GENDER PLANNING AND POPULATION

DYNAMICS OF GENDER PLANNING AND POPULATION

Issues and Challenges

Edited by

K.B. DATTA

AKANSHA PUBLISHING HOUSE

NEW DELHI-110 059 (INDIA)

AKANSHA PUBLISHING HOUSE
R 37-B, Vani Vihar, Uttam Nagar
New Delhi - 110 059
e-mail : ektabooks@yahoo.com

Dynamics of Gender Planning and Population

First Edition 2002

ISBN 81-87606-29-0

PRINTED IN INDIA

Published by M.P. Misra for Akansha Publishing House, New Delhi and Printed at Tarun Offset Printers, (Delhi) Ph.: 2910794

Contents

Acknowledgements

In preparation of this work, I have drawn material from various sources i.e. magazines, Reports, abstracts, journals, book reviews, etc. Hence the credit goes to all the scholars of great eminence devoted to study of gender planning, population and other related issues. I am deeply beholden to those all whose works and opinions are cited and substantially used herein. I am equally indebted to all the editors and publishers and copyright holders of the different sources cited here.

Finally I owe a sense of admiration to my publisher Mr. M.P. Misra for his motivating attitude and also for materializing my endeavour to reality.

—KBD

Introduction

Gender planning includes several critical characteristics. It is both political and technical in nature. It assumes conflict in the planning process. It involves transformative processes. It characterizes planning as 'debate'.

Analysis of the underlying reasons for current planning assumptions relates to the roles and needs of women and men in society. This highlights the overtly political nature of gender planning. It challenges outright the view that a gender planning methodology can simply adopt an existing 'neutral' and universally applicable set of technical procedures. It also raises the question as to the extent to which planners themselves play a role in shaping people's demands. The separation of values and facts allows for the precise distinction between client and expert. However, in reality planners are experts providing 'value-laden' advice, and, along with other actors, cannot be neutral (Healey 1989). Furthermore, given that the goal of gender planning is the emancipation of women, the political nature of the planning tradition is explicit. the rationale for the planning process then requires 'negotiation' as the basis for its agenda. Rational comprehensive planning techniques, appropriate for planning traditions based on consensus, are, therefore, inadequate as the methodology for gender planning. It requires a methodology in which the political dimension of negotiation is its key concern.

In identifying such a methodology, two recently articulated methodologies can contribute to gender planning. One of these is the political economy approach to planning, which focuses on the redistribution of resources through structural change. Based on a conflict model of society, it argues that the unequal distribution of resources is the inevitable outcome of fundamental class conflict. The role of the state is often one of an integrating mechanism, designed to preserve its own interests. Thus, the state is not neutral but a major actors in the conflict inherent in the planning process. This allows for the distinction between two sets of planning needs. The planning methodology required to meet practical gender needs is essentially 'technical' in nature; it simply requires the development of the necessary tools and techniques to help women do better what they are already doing. In contrast, the planning methodology required to meet strategic gender needs is clearly 'political' in nature. Strategic gender needs derive out of the subordination of women to men in society. From the perspective of a political economy approach such redistribution of power and resources between men and women requires structural transformations.

Although the political economy approach has successfully incorporated conflict into planning, as a model it has been criticized as explaining rather than developing an appropriate planning process. Healey (1989) argues that *planning as debate,* a further recent planning methodology, provides the basis for a planning methodology with a political economy approach. This recognizes that planning is neither just a technical process, nor merely political, with its real concern the interaction between the two. The central premise of this model is that, in a plural society with a diversity of interests, often in conflict, the democratic mode of collective action has to proceed through debate.

> "Planning as debate has the potential to confront those who 'currently' hold power at the level of ideology and philosophy as well as materially. It in effect changes the locus of exercise of power from the wielding of material resources, to association with a convincing argument....Its challenge is to address rather than ignore tensions."

Planning as debate provides useful guidelines for the elaboration of the gender planning process. For, unlike physical planning traditions with their clear-cut operational methodologies, obviously 'subordination' or 'emancipation' cannot be operationalised as such. The goal of gender planning refers ultimately to changes in the relationships between groups in societies, more specifically between men and women. Therefore, the planning methodology must place emphasis on planning as an iterative process. The premium is on process, identified as the institutional mechanisms and operational procedures through which interests and needs are 'mediated' into strategies, policies, programmes and projects.

Gender planning is concerned with transformative processes that are highly political and can be assumed to involve conflict. This requires a planning methodology that emphasises debate, negotiation and conflict resolution. The underlying assumptions that such a process may not necessarily be either rational or comprehensive. Planning as debate comes closest to this form of planning process. However, not only do the details of the methodology remain to be developed, but ultimately this may only happen through debate, decision and practice. Consequently, the following description of gender planning methodology can only be tentative and exploratory.

Where the planning tradition defines the objectives, purpose and agenda of gender planning, the planning methodology outlines both the planning process and the organisational structure that implement it. As a new planning tradition, the focus of gender planning is obviously on gender—that is, the social relations of inequality between men and women. The knowledge base for this new planning tradition comes from many sources. The most important are the feminist debates from both the First and Third World, and the more recent WID/GAD debates. The objective of this planning traditions to achieve both strategic and practical gender needs. Its goal is to emancipate women from their subordination, and to embrace equality, equity and empowerment. Its agenda is the specific strategic gender needs of women, which relate contextually to social relations such as class, ethnicity, 'race', religion and location. It is important to stress that the agenda of gender planning is not solely concerned with achieving practical gender needs of women. Practical gender needs are critical, but above all as instruments to achieve strategic gender needs.

Planning frameworks comprise several procedures. Ideally these identify a logical sequence of stages that describe the necessary number of actions required to complete the planning process. It would make gender planning easy to undertake if its planning process contained a number of finite stages of logical progression, such as the straightforward linear procedures of blueprint planning and rational comprehensive planning. However, where the purpose is a change in attitudes rather than to produce products, solutions are not so simple. Whereas gender-aware planning may be able to adopt rational comprehensive planning procedures, gender planning cannot. As Huxley (1988), for instance, so aptly comments, 'Neighbourhood houses and the design of communal kitchens will not, in and of themselves, change the social relations of patriarchy':

The focus of gender planning on social transformation means that its process relate to processes of negotiation and debate. These are concerned with the redistribution of power and resources within households, civil society, the state and the global system. The fact that there are very real problems in ''operationalising' subordination means that the epistemology of this type of planning process is difficult to articulate. Also, much of the methodology relating to the procedures through which interests and needs are mediated into strategies, policies, programmes and projects is context-specific. It cannot be determined a priori.

For reasons such as these, the gender planning process does not consist of a logical sequence of stages in an a priori defined process. It consists of an iterative process made up of a number of procedures, which constitute steps that are 'ongoing and overlapping'. Each of these procedures utilises and incorporate a number of *methodological tools,* deriving out of gender planning principles. These iterative procedures, in turn, are integrated into the four different components of gender planning practice.

These three interlinked elements—methodological tools, gender planning procedures and components of gender planning practice—in total constitute the gender planning framework.

Methodological Tools

In order to inform the manner in which planning is undertaken, these are translated into tools for planning practice, as illustrated gender planning as a planning tradition many of the more 'technical tools' easily identified in physical planning traditions do not exist. The goal of gender planning, to overcome subordination, is not easily susceptible to spatial and, physical interventions. These refer to changes in the relationship between men and women. Consequently, many of these tools are essentially *performance indicator,* designed to measure changing processes rather than technical interventions. The following six principles can be identified, with their associated planning tools described.

Gender Roles and Gender Roles Identification

The first principle relates to gender roles. Existing gender divisions of labour manifest themselves through the different roles played by men and women. Obviously the concept of the triple role is simplification of the complexities of the social contruction of gender relations and divisions of labour in specific socio-economic contexts, and their changing dynamics move time. For planners, however, this provides the first key principle for a gender planning methodology that enable them to translate gender-awareness into a tool for planning practice.

Above all, *gender roles identification* is a tool that makes visible previously invisible work. Most women live in a situation in which only their productive work, by virtue of its exchange value, is valued as work. Reproductive and community managing work, because they are both seen as 'natural' and non-productive, are not valued. This has serious consequences for women. It means that often the majority, if not all, of the work that they undertake is invisible. Neither men in the community nor those planners whose job it is to assess different needs within low-income communities recognise it as work. In contrast, most men's work is valued, either directly through paid remuneration, or indirectly through status and political power. The purpose, therefore, of gender roles identification is not only to separate out the different tasks both men and women, and boys and girls do. It is also to ensure the equal valuing of these tasks through the identification of reproductive, productive, community managing and community politics roles.

Gender Needs and Gender Needs Assessment

The second principle relates to gender needs, and the assessment of those that are practical and strategic in nature. The planning tool for this is gender needs assessment. Its purpose is to recognise women as active participants in development (practical gender needs). It also recognizes that women do not participate in development on equal terms with men because of their subordinate position (*strategic gender needs*).

Gender needs assessment classifies planning interventions in term of those that meet practical gender needs—that is, the needs identified to help women in their existing subordinate position in society—and strategic gender needs—namely, the needs identified to transform existing subordinate relationships between men and women. Because it deals directly with the issue of subordination, this planning tool is the crux of the framework for a gender planning methodology. As such, gender needs assessment is a tool by which it is possible to measure changes.

Intra-household Resource allocation

The third principle concerns intra-household resource allocation in terms of ensuring equal control over resources and power of decision-making between men and women within the household. The widespread popularity of the household as the unit of planning derives from the fact that it is analytically simple as a unit of analysis for economic decision-making than is the individual. In addition, it is much easier for planners to direct resources flows and benefits to the household as a unit. But the welfare of family members cannot be read off from the socio-economic characteristic and economic choices made by the household head. Neither does the distribution of resources at the household level guarantee that the benefits will trickle down. Assessments of poverty based only on household income many thus conceal much hidden poverty. Equally, resources allocation policy focused at household level does not necessarily deliver benefits to all members of the household. Women and children are often chronically under-resourced relative to men in many poor households. Once intra-household allocation is viewed as the outcome of bargaining processes, then planners can recognise that the individual to whom the resources are directed most frequently decides the control over allocation. Gender-based responsibilities in most societies show that it is more efficient to allocated benefits directly to women if children's welfare is the main priority.

Then necessary planning tool here is desegregated data at the intra-household level. Its purpose is to ensure that planning equal benefits all members of the household by allowing women access to and control over resource allocations. It will, ensure that planning interventions benefit women by reaching their practical gender needs.

Balancing of Roles and Inter-sectoral linked Planning

The fourth principle relates to the balancing of roles, which derives from gender roles identification. For women, this relates to the coordination of their triple role. Women experience competing demands between *reproductive, productive* and *consumption* activities. Productive work has to fit round family and community-level responsibilities. It is therefore often part-time or carried out at home. For women the key problem is the relationship between wage agricultural, child-care or community managing work. The fact that the burden of simultaneously balancing these roles severely constrains women is ignored. Hence, traditional sectoral-based planning is often unhelpful for women. Planning which focuses, for example, on provision of transport or services, or any sector on its own, does not consider links with other sectors. Thus it does not realise the constraints influencing women's use of goods and services provided by planning initiatives.

There is a need, therefore, for *intersectoral linked planning* that links different activities and scales of planning, such as home and transport or workplace and environment. This will ensure that the goods and services provided can be utilized by women to balance their tasks better within the existing gender divisions of labour.

The Relationship between Roles and Needs and the WID/ GAD Policy Matrix

The fifth principle relates to the relationship between roles and needs. The five different policy approaches to WID that have been identified all differ in terms of the triple roles of women that they recognize. They also differ in terms of the practical or strategic gender needs they meet, and the extent to which they include participatory planning procedures. This provides the conceptual rationale for a further principle of gender planning, which relates to the relationship between roles, needs and planning processes, and the fact that meeting strategic gender needs changes existing gender roles. The relevant planning tool is the WID/ GAD policy matrix. This is a performance indicator to measure the extent to which different planning interventions transform the subordinate positon of women by meeting both practical and strategic gender needs.

Equality and Incorporation in the Planning Process

The sixth principle relates to *equality between men and women* in the planning process. While the participation of local women in the planning process may result in greater control over the allocation of specific resources, it may not reduce intra-household inequalities. There are significant constraints arising from different perceptions of needs between men and women, and this has implications in terms of intra-household entitlements. These constraints suggest that changes in women's outlook and increases in their freedom with in and beyond the family unit require further planning principles and planning tools.

Access to productive work can help women, changes in household dynamics are often more influenced by extra-household experiences of collective action. In this respect women's solidarity groups play critical role in providing women with the space and opportunity to question their subordinate status. Such groups empower them to confront and transform the oppressive aspects of intra-family and household relations. The planning tool for this purpose is the *incorporation of women, gender-aware organizations and planners into planning*. This aims to ensure that real, as against perceived, practical and strategic gender needs are identified and incorporated into planning processes.

These tools of gender planning challenge current planning stereotypes. They can be utilized in planning practice to help planners appraises and evaluate ongoing planning interventions. Tools such as the triple role, gender needs assessment, the WID/GAD matrix and gendered participatory planning can also help them to formulate and implement gendered proposals at policy, programme or project level.

General Planning Procedures

Methodological tools are not only important for planning generally. In addition, they are fundamental inputs for incorporation in to planning procedures specific to the gender planning framework. Following Levy, these are identified as gender diagnosis, gender objective, gender monitoring, gender consultation and participation, and gender entry strategy. As mentioned above, these procedures are not stages in a logical planning framework, but are iterative overlapping procedures that can be incorporated at any stage of the planning process.

Gender Diagnosis

As is obvious from the name, gender diagnosis is concerned to identify the particular implications of contextually specific problems of development for men and women, and the relationship between them. Levy identifies two stages in such diagnosis. First, analysis of the problem using methodological tools such as gender roles identification, gender needs assessment and the WID/GAD policy matrix. The second stage is the organization of problems into a cause and effect hierarchy to establish a gender aware perspective on the dominant problems. She comments that gender diagnosis is an ongoing activity that is carried out at all key points of an organisation's planning cycle.

While undertaking gender diagnosis at the planning stage it is important to identify the socio-economic information on gender roles already available, and what needs collecting. At a minimum, gender diagnoses usually requires data on the following issues: the division of labour in productive activities; the division of labour, by age and sex within the household, including seasonal difference; the structure and size of households, and stage in the life cycle; sources of household income, including off-farm activities; control and decision-making within the household over cash, land and other resources; the structure and composition by age and sex of community-level decision-making bodies; local-and national-level political structures.

Gender diagnosis integrated gender planning tools such as gender roles identification and desegregated data at the household level. The use of such tools often requires the collection of accurate gendered reformation. Implicitly, such critical questions as how 'objective' are the data, who collects the data, and who has access to the data have to be addressed. Obviously, all planning methodologies require that planners have accurate and reliable information. However, if people are to be involved in decision-making and debate throughout the planning process, they also require access to information, and this is not always so obvious.

The assumption that data are objective and 'value-free' is particularly problematic for a planning tradition concerned with transformation, and the redistribution of power and resources within society. So much of the bias in data collection has been the result of the very biases of researchers. This makes it important for women to participate in the collection of data concerned with gender issues, for the manner in which questions are asked and the sex of the researcher can decide research outcomes. In many societies, unless women speak, data will only reflect men's view of the world. Therefore, a precondition of *gender diagnosis is the involvement of women researchers in data collection.* In addition, it includes consultation with community women and with local, progressive, gender-aware organisations, in which women themselves are the source of this information.

Within specific planning contexts gender diagnosis questions current statistical research stereotypes about the household as the unit of analysis, and th e male breadwinner as the household head. Both have had important implications for the invisibility of women. One of its objective, therefore, is to identify the gender biases in data analysis. This requires the identification of the roles and needs of both women and men in the household and the community, as well as difference in household structures and in intrahousehold control over resources and power. Among the extensive number of questions addressed are those concerning the assumptions made about tthe roles of men and women in society. Are these explicit? Are they realistic? Within their roles, across societies, men and women can be involved in different activities. Since gender relations are socially constructed, they are contextually specific and often change in response to altering economic circumstances.

In the second stage of gender diagnosis, where *because* and *effect* are identified, the most critical tool is often gender needs assessment; that is, the gender-specific understanding of what is causing subordination and the barriers preventing its elimination. It is this that leads into the identification of gender objectives.

Gender Objectives

Gender objective are a guide to action at particular points in the process of making policies, programmes and projects more gender aware. Gender objectives are redefined as the process proceeds, responding to changes brought about either by actions to make interventions more gender-aware, or by other factors external to the process.

Gender objectives provide the basis for a specific agenda that identifies which gender needs are to be selected,and the strategies to accomplish this. Gender objectives like gender diagnosis, then become an interactive process leading to the re-identification, adjustment and refinement of practical and strategic gender needs, thus ensuring that they can be introduced into any stage of the planning process.

Gender Monitoring

Gender diagnosis provides the performance criteria to appraise and evaluate the extent to which actions and interventions achieve gender objectives. Again these are iterative processes, used at different stages in any planning cycle to assist in the redefinition of gender objectives. Monitoring and evaluation can be undertaken with specific questions using gender planning tools.

(a) what will be the impact on women in their productive role?

(b) What will be the impact on women in their reproductive role?

(c) What will be the impact on women's ability to balance their triple role?

Gendered Consultation and Participation

In a planning methodology that emphasizes debate,

negotiation and conflict resolution, gendered consultation and participation is the most critical yet complex gender planning procedure. Although theoretically 'participation' in planning is genially considered a 'good thing', clear consensus still does not exist as to what it means in practice—and throughout the ensuing text the term 'participation' is used generacally to include consultation. A large number of definitions reflects the ideological range of interpretations of development and different approaches to planning, which have themselves changed over time. The more the rhetoric of participatory planning is evoked the greater is the diversity of interpretations as to what it means. The distinction between the four questions of why participation, when to participate, whose participation and how to participate provides a useful framework for understanding some complexities of this issue. These are identified generally as well as specifically in terms of gendered participation in planning. This question refers, obviously, to the reasons for and causes of participation. One useful general definition of the objectives of participation in development projects is that of Paul (1987), who identifies as fivefold continuum. This ranges from the objective of participation for empowerment, to capacity-building, through increasing project effectiveness, to improving project efficiency and, finally, to project cost-sharing. Central to the debate about participation is the issue whether participation includes an element of empowerment. Where participation is a means, it generally becomes a form of mobilization to get things done. This can equally be state-directed, top-down mobilization, sometimes enforced, to achieve specific objectives, or bottom-up 'voluntary' community-based mobilisation to obtain a larger share of resources. Where participation is identified as an end in itself, the objective is not a field, quantified development goal, but a process, the outcome of which is an increasingly 'meaningful' participation in the development process.

This is particularly significant for gendered participation and the active consultation of women in the development process. Projects frequently rely on women's participation as a means to ensure project success. However, they far less frequently recognise that for women as much as for other groups in society, participations an end in itself. The first objective identified below relates to empowerment; the second concerns participation as a means to achieve efficiency, effectiveness and cost recovery; the third objective of woman's participation focuses on capacity-building.

(a) Women's participation is an end in itself. Women as much as men have the right and duty to participate in the execution of projects which profoundly affect their lives. Since women accept primary responsibility for child-bearing and rearing, they are affected most by housing and settlement projects. Women should, therefore, be involved in the planning and decision-making as well as the implementation and management of projects that relate particularly to their lives.

(b) Women's participation is a means to improve project results. Since women have particular responsibility for the welfare of the household, they are more aware than men of the needs for infrastructure and services and are also more committed to the success of a project that improves living conditions. The *exclusion of women can negatively affect the outcome of a project, while their active involvement can often help its success.*

(c) Participation in housing activities stimulates women's participation in other spheres of life. Through active involvement in housing projects women may be encouraged to participate full in the community. Participation in projects has been seen as an important mechanism to 'overcome apathy' and 'lack of confidence' and it can make women visible in the community. By coming out of their houses and showing them the potential of self-help solutions it may raise awareness that women can play an important role in solving problems in the community.

(b) *When to do gendered participation?*

It refers not only to the gender analysis stage, described

above, but also the whole planning process. In project planning, for instance, this is most commonly identified as decision-making, implement at in, financing and managing. However, it also includes a number of other phases depending on the project type.

The extent to which planners block or adopt a gender planning methodology depends on whether there is participation by women in the identification phase when general policy directions and goals are decided. Much of the planning for WID, for instance, totally ignores this stage, but this is when it is necessary to discuss the nature of gender subordination in the prevailing system, or structure of society. This sets the framework for what is essentially a highly political process.

The basis of such a framework is the distinction between whether the issues identified is one of 'gender' or women. Is the issue seen a strategic, relating to the fact that women are subordinated? Or is it decided as practical, relating to female marginality due, for example, to lower educational levels or unequal access to employment? This distinction determines whether a gender planning or gender-aware planning approach will be adopted. It is the former planning approach that specifies its genderal goal as the emancipation of women.

(c) *Whose gendered participation?*

In identifying who gains access to the debate about the gender planning process and on what terms, planners havea responsibility to argue for a broad-based approach including different interests and attitudes (Healey 1989). Once the notion of a single public interest or a coherent political consensus disappears, an inclusionist approach must be advocated. For any participatory planning process this also includes identifying who controls the process of the identification of goals and objectives. Whose judgments are use about what is necessary or satisfactory? These questions refer not only to whether it is the planners or the people, but also whether it is men and women, local communities as much as elite groups.

The tendency is to understand 'the community' in homogeneous terms, with further desegregation only done at the household level. This means that the policy level rarely mentions the important role women play in participatory planning. It occurs despite the constant comments from those working on the ground that 'without the women the project would have failed.' The fact that men are more likely to be involved in community politics means that the participation of local women as community manage is frequently either invisible or not valued. However, there is also a negative side to women's participation. While their participation is often crucial for project success, this is based on the assumption that women have 'free time'. Lack of awareness of women's triple role, therefore, can be cause of project failure when women fail to participate, it is not women who are the problem.

(d) *How to do gendered participation?*

It addresses the question of how the dynamics of the participatory process resolve themselves in reality. Here the contradictions between intentions on paper (often lip-service) and the real agenda (often hidden in the planning stage) can become apparent in the practice of gendered participation.

The question of how to do gendered participation focuses directly on the style and procedures of the gender planning debate. For instance, if the decision-making stage includes participation,the methods used and the timing of consultation can influence the target groups reached. In many low-income programs and projects, participatory methods of recruiting beneficiaries often in a dvertently discriminate against or exclude women. This is true of scheme announcement methods, applications, procedures and down-payment requirements. When authorities assume that everyone reads newspapers or public notices, with information distributed in written form, they ofter miss women. In many parts of the world women's access to education is considerably less than that of men. In addition, women are less likely to be exposed to information because of their lack of daily mobility. Even where planners use more direct methods of advertising, such as meeting where eligible applicants are likely to live, domestic responsibilities ofter prevent women from attending. If they attend mixed meetings they generally stand at the back, on the assumption that they will not talk. *Real consultation with women* often demands *house-to-house consultation* or *small-group, all-women gathering rather than large-scale meetings.*

The capacity of women to be involved in such participatory processes requires changes in the ways in which participatory consultation is undertaken. These relate not only to such logistical problems as the hours of meetings; it also includes more fundamental problems relating to female consciousness and its articulation in participatory processes. Where negotiation and debate are critical to the planning process, judgements are made as to what values should govern decisions (Healey 1989). One important issue relate to differences between men and women in their perceptions of personal welfare and self-interest, against family welfare. These result in bargaining disadvantages that feed on themselves generationally through feedback transmission. thus he comments that 'the political agency of women may be particularly important in ncountering the pervasive perception biases that contribute to the neglect of women's needs and claims'.

Participation presupposes a pro-active capacity and willingness to negotiate and debate throughout the planning process. Because of the way that women are so effectively excluded from real decision-making, in reality they often chose to withdraw rather than participate in planning processes. A useful concept that addresses this aspect of gendered participation is the analytical distinction between 'voice' and '*exit*. The capacity to exert voice (pressure to perform) has received far more attention in the literature on gendered participation than has the capacity to find exit (alternative sources of supply). However, they may be equally important in the planning process.

Gender Entry Strategy

Gender diagnosis results in an understanding of the mechanisms of gender bias in terms of the underlying assumptions of sectoral policies and organisaitonal structures. Gendered participation ensures negotiation and debate in the planning process. Gender objectives set the agenda for intervention. None of the these procedures in themselves, however, can ensure that interests and needs are mediated to policies, programmes or projects. Gender planning is inherently a contextually specific political activity. Therefore it requires an entry strategy. An entry strategy is a prioritized and tactical set of actions designed to expand the room-for-manoeuvre at a particular socio-economic and political juncture to overcome constraints which may block or subvert desired gender interventions, and to utilise potential which may provoke a resource or an opportunity to promote them.

Essentially, a gender entry strategy defines what it is possible for gender planning to achieve in a specific context. Entry strategies can be identified as having two phases. First, gender objectives, deriving from gender diagnosis and gendered consultation and participation, can be used to identify the critical points where practical gender needs have the capacity to reach strategic gender needs. The second stage is an assessment of the constraints and opportunities provided by institutional structures and their operational procedures. This is to ensure that the planning agenda can be translated into practice. The identification of entry points involves strategic political choices.

Gender Planning Practice Components

In the recent past gender policy and gendered development policy have made impressive advances. In both cases gender diagnosis and gendered consultation and participation have been important. But WID policies frequently fail to become implemented practice, while the content of WID/GAD policies often changes during the implementation process. The increasing priority for those working on gender issues relates to the inability to translate formulated gender policy into practice. In the complex reality of planning processes it is often difficult to separate out the interrelated factors that influence and decide the implementation process. Nevertheless, if changes are to be made in current procedures it is crucial to identify the constraints and opportunities acting upon them.

The development and adoption of gender planning as a new planning discipline with its particular principles, tools and procedures does not ensure its successful implementation into planning practice. It does not mean that current planning practices operationalise them, that existing organisational structures institutionalise them, or that professionals involved in planning make *gender-aware decisions.* The first three are identified as the institutional structure, operational procedures and behaviour of planners involved in gender planning practice.

This book is designed to discuss various crucial issues pertaining to gender planning process and the poulation challenge. The material contained herein will definitely benefit the policy planners, various govt. agencies, and demographers and women activists besides the academics in the field.

CHAPTER 1

Practical and Strategic Gender Needs

While identifying interests it is useful to differentiate between 'women's interests', strategic gender interests and practical gender interests, following the threefold conceptualisation made by Maxine Molyneux (1985a). Having identified the different interests of women it is possible to translate them into planning needs; in other words, the means by which their concerns may be satisfied.

From a planning perspective this separation is essential because of its focus on the planning process whereby an *interest*, defined here as a 'prioritized concern', translates into a need. This in turn is defined as the 'means by which concerns are satisfied'. One more distinction can then be made concerning women's needs, strategic gender needs and practical gender needs.

Strategic Gender Needs

Strategic gender needs are the needs women identify because of their subordinate position to men in their society. Strategic gender needs vary according to particular contexts. They relate to gender divisions of labour, power and control and may include such issues as legal rights, domestic violence, equal wages and women's control over their bodies. Meeting strategic gender needs helps women to achieve greater equality. It also changes existing roles and therefore challenges women's subordinate position. Strategic gender needs are those needs that are formulated from the analysis of women's subordination to men. Deriving out of this analysis strategic gender interests necessary for an alternative, more equal and satisfactory organization of society than that which exists at present can be identified. This relates both to the structure and nature of relationships between men and women. As will be illustrated, the strategic gender needs identified to overcome women's subordination vary depending on the particular cultural and socio-political context within which they are formulated. Strategic gender needs, as Molyneux has identified, may include all or some of the following:

> The abolition of the sexual division of labour; the alleviation of the burden of domestic labour and child care; the removal of institutionalised forms of discrimination such as rights to own land or property, or access credit; the establishment of political equality; freedom of choice over childbearing; and the adoption of adequate measures against malevolence and control over women. (1985a:233)

Strategic gender needs such as these are often identified as 'feminist', as is the level of consciousness required to struggle effectively for them. Historically, top-down state intervention alone has not removed any of the persistent causes of gender inequality within society.

Practical Gender Needs

Practical gender needs are a response to immediate perceived necessity, identified within a specific context. They are practical in nature and often are concerned with inadequacies in living conditions such as water provision, health care, and employment.

Practical gender needs, in contrast, are those that are formulated from the concrete conditions women experience. These derive from their positions within the gender division of labour, in addition to their practical gender interests for human survival. Unlike strategic gender needs they are formulated directly by women in these positions, rather than through external interventions. Practical needs, therefore, are usually a response to an immediate perceived necessity which is identified by women within a specific context. As Molyneux has written, 'they do not generally entail a strategic goal such as women's emancipation or gender equality...nor do they challenge the prevailing forms of subordination even though they arise directly out of them'.

The gender division of labour within the household gives women primary responsibility not only for domestic work involving child care, family health and food provision, but also for the community managing of housing and basic services, along with the capacity to earn an income through productive work. Therefore, in planning terms, policies to meet practical gender needs have to focus on the domestic arena, on income-earning activities, and also on community-level requirements of housing and basic services. In reality, basic needs such as food, shelter and water are required by all the family, particularly children. Yet they are identified specifically as the practical gender needs of women, not only by policy-makers concerned to achieve developmental objectives, but also by women themselves. Both are, therefore, responsible for preserving and reinforcing the gender division of labour. Since there is often a unity of purpose between the development priorities of intervening agencies and practical gender needs identified at the local level, the two frequently and easily become conflated. This serves the purpose of planners who are then identified as meeting 'women's needs'.

It has become very popular for policy-maker and the media alike to label any policy or programme associated with women as 'feminist' or 'women's liberation'. Such terms are used by many in such a nebulous manner that this provoke a hostile and negative reaction from female and male planner alike. The differentiation between practical and strategic gender needs provides a critical planning tool. This allows practitioners to understand better that planning for the needs of low-income women is not necessarily 'feminist' in content. Indeed, the vast majority of interventions for women world-wide are concerned with them within the existing gender division of labour, as wives and mothers.

These are intended to meet their practical gender needs. No doubt, such interventions are important, they will only become *feminine* in content, if, and when, they are transformed into strategic gender needs.

Gender needs differentiation, therefore, provide a useful tool for planners. Not only does it help in diffusing the criticisms of those who find 'feminism' unacceptable by showing them that working with women is often not 'feminism' unacceptable by showing them that working with women is often responsible for meeting the practical gender needs of women,in assisting their adoption of more 'challenging' solutions. What then defines the 'political space' for addressing different gender needs within specific contexts? Is it the family, civil society or the state? To answer such a question requires an undertanding of the interrelationship of these three levels of social, economic and political organization.

Regulation of Women's Strategic Gender Needs

The extent to which the state mediates relationship not only between state and civil society, but also those within the family between men, women and children, has critical implications for the identification of the 'room for manoevre' to address strategic gender needs. The last few decades have witnessed an important expansion of research on the state and the extent to which it liberates or controls the lives of women through a diversity of social, economic, political and legal policies. In different contexts, marriage laws, legal provisions regarding rape and abortion, and pollution-control policies control female sexuality and fertility. Similarly, state laws governing wages, taxation and social security benefits have combined to reproduce gender divisions of lobour within the family. In the space available a complex topic such as this cannot be reviewed comprehensively. The intention is to provide some very general indications as to the implications in terms of meeting both practical and strategic gender needs.

Just as there are different interpretatons of the origins

and dynamics of female subordination, so too there are different feminist analyses of the state, and the extent to which it controls women. Radical feminists, for instance, identify sexual politics as the central area of struggle, and traditionally have stressed the biological basis of the sexual imbalance of power, thereby often being identified as promoting biological determinism (Hartman 1981). They see the basic motivating force of history as men's striving for domination and power over women, with the physical subjugation of women by men as the most basic form of oppression. Radical feminists emphasize the importance of patriarchy in reinforcing women's subordination, which they define as the system of sexual hierarchy in which men possess superior power and economic privilege. patriarchy is maintained through male control over such arenas of power as politics, industry, religion and the military both within and outside the state.

Marxist feminists, in contrast, see the capitalist state as the root of women's oppression. Capitalism is particularly responsible for women's women commonly form the cheapest, most vulnerable part of the labour force is in the interests of capitalism; the at women, who through their domestic labour, provide services which women otherwise have to be paid for lower the cost of real wages, is also the interest of the state, since it would otherwise have to pay to provide the services necessary to ensure the reproduction of the labour force for capitalism. If capitalism is viewed as oppressing women, has socialism liberated them? It was Engels who first identified women's particular subordination as being derived from their position within the monograms family. Their empancipation from patriarchy and control would come with their entrance into productive work, with their domestic reproductive work to being taken over by the state. This view has dominated thinking in socialist economies where it was envisaged that women would join men in the proletarian struggle to over-throw capitalism.

Molyneus (1981: 1-2) identified three main areas where the aims of capitalist and socialist states in principle do differ. First, socialist states officially recognise women's oppression and identify it as a social and political problem requiring official intervention, typically in the form of strategic gender needs met top-down by the state. This cotrats with capitalist states, where historically even enfranchisement has been a struggle (1981:8); secondly, under socialism, labour-force participation is a normal expectation for every active woman, if not a duty to both the state and their families. Socialist states try to maintain high employment levels (thereby meeting practical gender needs for gainful employment through top-down intervention). By contrast, in capitalist states women are more likely to form a large part of the preserve army; thirdly, socialist states accept a greater responsibility of rt reproduction of labour power and for social welfare, particularly in the support structures for a diverse number of practical gender needs relating to child care, health education and community-level services. Although many such provisions may have been insufficient, the degree of intervention is far greater than in capitalist economies with a comparable level of economic development.

Legal reform has been used in many socialist states to challenge traditional practices through legislation they have introduced top-down strategic gender needs, redefining family relations between both men and women and parents and children. These have included the banning of ploygamy, child marriage and marriage payments. However, despite the existence of legislation with the potential to meet strategic gender needs, men have continued to subordinate women under socialist systems. Women continue to cluster in less-skilled, lower-paid and lower-status jobs. They fail to reach positions of power, and commonly undertaken most of the domestic work, or where this has bene socialised, it remains under-valued 'women's work'. The socialist feminits, who emerged to deal with the 'unhappy marriage' of Marxism and feminism, therefore recognized the pervasiveness and persistence of patriarchy within and cross societies sand classes evening socialist countries.

Why is it that the gender divisions of labour around

human reproduction are so rigid, regardless of state intervention? Socialist feminists argue that this is because the gender allocation of tasks is most crucial for the perpetuation of existing relations of marriage, procreation and filliation. It is within these that male dominance and control over female sexuality is incorporated. Consequently, it is s around human reproduction that gender division, of labour is identified most strongly as 'natural. Any changes are perceived as a serious threat to established forms of masculine and feminine gender identity. Thus the perpetuation of women's subordination lies in the interrelationship between their position in the marriage-based household and in the wage sphere. Women work not only for capital but they also work directly for men. Therefore men have voted interests in women's subordination. In some contexts, both men and women may have wanted to change the exploitaties conditions of capitalism, but they may not be struggling for the same transformations. As is only too well known, national liberation has not necessarily meant women's liberation.

The 1990s has already witnessed the destruction of many socialist and communist state systems as well as the growing influence of religious fundamentalism as the basis for tat elegitimacy. Hence, the simple dichotomy between capitalism and socialism is no longer as useful an analytical tool as it seemed a decade ago. This makes it even more important to deconstruct state policy as it relates to different aspects of women's lives.

State Policy Towards Women

If feminists cannot agree of the degree to which the state oppresses women they concur that it is the family that is the coresite of women's oppression'. For it is the family that is identified as providing the boundary between the public and the private domains; that is, the boundary of state interference in individual existence. Consequently, it is in policy towards the family in which the state intervenes most powerfully in the lives of women. This applies both to legislation and planning interventions, and to countries with very different 'political' systems. For as Molyneux (1985b) has identified, even socialists states did not destroy the family. They sought through their constitutions to create a special family form as the basic unit of society to ensure productive and social stability. State policy towards women within the family, however, is highly complex, because it is not unidirectional. It varies depending on its purpose, alternatively controlling and supporting women.

(a) *Domestic Violence*

At one level the family is seen as a private domain in which the state only interferes in special circumstances. Here state policy concerns the articulation of relationships between the public and private spheres. The concept that family matters are a private business gives husbands licensee to teat wives as they wish behind closed doors. For women this has been particularly problematic over such issues as domestic violence and sexual abuse. Violence is closely linked to unequal family structure and women's economic dependence on men. In addition, social stigma attached to single women frequently forces women to stay married. Urdang (1989) recalls, 'she find it too difficult to go against social attitudes, she is afraid that if she is alone she will be labelled a prostitude by the community'. Because domestic violence occurs in the private sphere of the home, it is most frequently invisible. Even when domestic violence is identified, relatives as much as judges, the courts or the police, are reluctant to interferes. Many statesidentify such strategic gender needs as control over their sexuality and bodies and consequently also lives) as a 'private' family matter between man and wife, and outside their mandate. Even when laws exist on the statute books, police lethargy in its enforcement is common. In 1979 a women's campaign ocurred in Delhi against dowry murders—bride burning of women who had not paid full dowry to their husbands' families.

(b) *Female Fertility and Women's Reproductive Rights*

One of the best-known 'special circumstances' in which

the state is quite willing to intervene inside the family relates to women's reproductive rights including its control over female fertility. Such policies are justified in terms of a number of different reasons. Anti-natalist policies to limit population, in countries such as China (Davin 1987) and India (Editorial Collective 1987), relate to economic growth priorities and the fear that the 'population explosion' could offset this; pro-natalist policies can relate to demands for labour in the economy, as has happened in Eastern Europe and the erstwhile Soviet Union. Nationalism and the concern with the survival or expansion of a particular group, based on ethnic, religious or other criteria, in countries as diverse as Malaysia an Israel, have also resulted in pro-natalist policies. As Yuval-Davis (1987) has described, 'the most important national role of Israeli Jewish women relates to the army, namely as reproducers.

The problem with population policy, whether pro-or anti-natalist, is that it fails to recognise Women's strategic gender need to control their own fertility. If the birth-rate is left to women, it obviously gives them great power. The right to choice is commonly equated with the right to have children or not to have children. While access to education and employment has decreased female fertility, it is clear that men and women have different interests in children.

State intervention varies from attractive incentives to drastic disincentives in its control over women's reproduction. Nowhere is the latter more explicit than in China's one-child family policy, which is also unusual in targeting both parents as responsible. Disincentives for more than one child include fines, salary deductions and job promotion limitations imposed on both patents. nevertheless, the main burden of such policy falls on women in term s of both health effects of multiple abortions and selizeions. In addition, female infanticide increases as parents keep struggling to have sons. This suggests that top-down policy has not changed the traditional devaluation of daughters and preference for sons (Davin 1987). A similar problem has emerged in India.

An active family-planning policy—at times even coercive—in urban areas has resulted in increased amniocentesis and the aborting of female foetuses. The extent to which female children are devalued is illustrated by a 1982 survey by the Women's Centre in Bombay, which found that 7,999 out of 8,000 abortions were of female foetuses. Though late, now the Govt. in India has banned the gender identification, if not in spirit that too in literally.

(c) *The Legal Status of Women in Marriage*

In other contexts, the state view the family as fragile and needing support, with the latter's 'collapse' identified in terms of the 'breakdown' of the 'fabric' of society. State morality can provide the basis for legal control over women's status within the family. The conflation of female sexuality and social order has important implications for women's strategic gender needs relating to control over their lives.

Where religious oppression is institutionalised by the state, as in Iran, this is often manifest in an extreme form. Afshar (1987) maintains that in Iran it is he interpretations of Islam by male religious leaders that is at the root of women's oppression. The Koran itself guarantees certain economic and religious rights to women, even in defining them only as mothers and inferior to men. The religious fundamentalist revival in the post-revolution state of Khomeini after 1979 identified 'women's liberation' as yet another export of western imperialism. This resulted in a severe reduction in women's rights, which include the following; men and women have unequal citizen status, such that women's evidence as witnesses in their own right is not accepted unless corroborated by a man; women's freedom of dress and movements is curtailed with the compulsory reinstantment of the hejab (veil) outside the home, based on the ideology that women are a source of corruption and sexual provocation to men, and therefore must be covered; with the revoking of the 1967 and 1976 Family Protection Acts polygamy of upto four wives is legally permissible, based on the argument that this is a mechanism to prevent women's destitution or prostitution. Afshar argues that in practice polygamy does not protect women, but merely displaces them to make room for other potential mothers, such that 'the husband has become an absolute ruler, entitled to exercise the power of life and death in his home.

It is important to realise that even in countries with highly sophisticated civil legal system, the coexistence of religious and civil law can effectively oppress women. The constitution of India guarantees equality for all, outlaws discrimination on the grounds of race, caste and birth, and promotes equality of opportunity in employment for all. But, despite constitutional rights of all citizens under civil law, religious laws for each religious groups have jurisdiction over all family matters such as marriage, divorce, child custody and dowry A single civil law pertaining to family matter does not exist. The reason is the 'communalist' agreement that such a uniform code would be a interference with the diverse rights of some eight religious groups with their own laws to determine their own personnel matters. However, by also allowing religious autonomy, religious laws can deny women these rights, as well as preventing them from claiming rights under civil law.

(d) *Benefit Rights and Welfare Policy*

Ulimately, the state sees the family as the main organizational structure through which it can reinforce its control over differences in the benefit status of individuals, most specifically in its definition of means. Historically, European patriarchal ideology influenced policy towards the family. The separation of public and private spheres reinforced the model of the dependent family with the male 'breadwinner' and female career, which was then crystallized in legislation and welfare policy. A classic example is provided by the social reformer, Beveridge In his vision about the post-World War II welfare state, he was unequivocal about women's role. "In the next thirty years housewives as mothers have vital work to do in ensuring the adequate continuance of the British race and of British ideals in the world' welfare-state legislations is still salutary today, given the widespread export of british welfare policy to its ex-colonies.

Support of a particular family form meant that the welfare state sustained rather than alleviated the depedency of women on men within marriage through a diversity of policies. As Paschal (1986) has detailed, this status resulted in a separate insurance class of 'housewives, that is married women of working age' most of whom it was assumed would make marriage their sole occupation' Beveridge concluded that the married woman's benefits need not be on th same scale as the solitary woman, because among other things her home is provided for here. Thus married women would have 'contributions made by the husbands. Simultaneously the welfare state failed to reduce women's dependency within the family by recognizing reproductive work through redistributive income and financial maintenance.

State control of women also extends beyond the family to control of their position within the labour market. here the relationship between reproduction and production is at its most explicit with the historic concept of the legally enforced 'family wage'; that is, of a man's wage being sufficient to support two adults and their children. Even where equal pay legislation promises equal pay for women, their wages generally have continued to be depressed. Low pay does not meet strategic gender nees for independent control over resources, but interacts with, and reinformces, women's economic dependence within the family.

Practical Gender Needs and Planning Practice

Given the very real interests of the state, civil society and men in subordinating women through control of their status, bodies and indeed sometimes even their lives, there are widespread constraints in meeting strategic gender needs. Consequently, planners often seek to use practical gender needs as an entry point for more fundamental change. The following examples of inter-ventions in such sectors as employment, housing, rural production, the environment and basic urban services illustrated the potential and limitations of different planning practices to reach both sets of needs within specific planning contexts. However, even in planning for practical gender needs it is necessary to recognise that women require inegrative cross-sectorial planning strategies. For instance, most governments base national planning priorities on a sectorial approach. Employment planning, for instance, is concerned with individuals as paid workers. It assumes a household support system, while women's participation in the labour force is constrained by their triple commitment. Social-welfare planning which concentrates on the child-rearing roles of women, does not adequately take account of their income-earning activities. For example, health facilities in low-income areas are frequently undersubscribed because their opening hours are inappropriate for working mothers. The failure to recognise women's multiple responsibilities may not merely jeopardise the implementation of policy, with programmes frustrating rather than meeting basic needs; perversely, it may in fact worsen the position of women.

Gender Needs in Employment

With the lives of the majority of low-income women dominated by the necessity to generate an income, one fundamental problem faced is the lack of adequate skills. the provision of training, therefore, meets an important practical gender need allowing access to employment. How far it also reaches more strategic gender needs depends not only on whether it increases women's economic independence, but also on the type of training. In many ex-British colonies community development centers for decades have provided women's training courses in home economics, introducing skills intended to assist women become better providers within the household. Such training recognises the reproductive role of women, and can meet practical gender needs relating to basic health and nutrition but does not recognise women's productive role and the important practical gender need to earn an income.

In a recent example from Nigeria, the curriculum in a community development home economic course included new recipes such as angle cakes to be cooked in Western-style ovens (Erinle 1986). The majority of low-income women dropped out of the programme, preferring to cook 'traditional gari (Processed cassava) food for sale. The training recognized the reproductive role of women and might have met nutritional needs, assuming that angle cade had greater nutritional value than the traditional food sfor which it substituted. But it failed to recognise the productive role of women, which was the priority for the women themselves.

By contrast, skills training in primary school teaching, nursing and dress-making often meets income-generating needs. A common type of training is dressmaking, taught throughout the world, at a range of levels from government programmes, through medium-sized NGO projects, to small, self-help groups. In diverse cultures and contexts the underlying rationale for the provision of dressmaking skills is similar; that this is a skill women already know, or should know, and one they can use not only in the home but also to earn an income.

The training of women in areas traditionally identified as 'men's work' may not only widen employment opportunities for women, but may also break down existing occupational segregation, thereby contributing to the strategic gender need to abolish the gender division of labour. Women's training in house-building skills such as masonry and carpentry provides one such example. Although in most societies women tradition all are involved in rural house building, the urban-based development of a female formally skilled labour force for house construction has been prevented by a occupational sex segregation, with construction designated as 'men's work', other than in those contexts, such has India, where women provide unskilled labour (NIUA 1982). Skill training for women in the construction sector often meets with hostility and resistance, precisely because it challenges the existing gender division of labour. As case studies from Jamaica

(Schmink 1984a) and Nicaragua (Vance 187) show, training and the tacit acceptance of male colleagues both assist women construction workers to find work either in existing projects or in the construction sector generally.

For rural women involved in agricultural production and processing, access to credit is often tightly constrained. Frequently, even in credit schemes designed to assist women, there is a tendency to allocate resources at the family or household level, despite the fact that they generally remain in the hands of the male household head. A typical example is a project to provide loans to landless families in Bangladesh to assist household-level rice-processing businesses by enabling the men to buy additional paddy. Although their wives undertook additional productive processing activities, this was simply identified as an extension of reproductive work, and men still 'sold the final product and controlled the earning's. In contrast to this, in a gari processing project in Ghana in which the itroduction of new technology enabled the women to increase their output of gari considerably, the women controlled the marketing. The fact that the project recognized women's productive role meant that they achieved the strategic gender need of keeping control over the resources themselves. In fact they were able to use their additional resources to buy a tractor to assist the men to put more land under cassava cultivation. In this case 'involving th women in the design of the technology undoubtedly contributed to the success of the projects.

Gender Needs in Human Settlements and Housing

In the planning of human settlements and housing the necessity of introducing a gender perspecive is still not widely recognized, despite the fact that women, as wives and mothers, are primary users of spae both in their houses and in the local community. In the planning stage, although consultation with women about housing design would ensure that their spatial needs are met, this rarely occurs. Examples of the detrimental effects of sensitive house design are widespread, particularly where 'modernisation' or 'developmentalism' has resulted in radical design changes. This often affects Muslim women. Because their social life is almost entirely confined to th home, they have special needs for internal space. An example of this in tun is, Tunisia, occurred in two low-income settlements, Mellassine, a squatter upgrading project, and Ib Khalkoun, a planned community (Resources for Action 1982). Women were dissatisfied with house design because of the small size of the inner courtyard. pressure on land, insensitivity to women's needs, and middle-class aspirations to European architecture had resulted in a reduction of inner countryard area, in some cases leading to psychological depression, neuroses and even suicide among women residents.

Because of the need to balance roles, women are often involved in informal sector activities in or around their homes. Where zoning legislation prevents the making and selling of goods from their homes, the only solution is to do so illegally. At the Dandora Site and Service Project, in Nairobi, Keyna, restrictive zoning legislation was identified by women as the main cause of arrears in repaying building loans. Gender-aware changes in zoning legislation to allow household enterprises can therefor meet the practical gender need to women to earn an income.

Women are the principal users of housing does not necessarily mean that they become the owners of either the house or land. Tenure is generally given to men as household heads, even where women de facto have primary household responsibilities. For women, ensure rights are a strategic gender need which ensure protection for themselves and their children in unstable or violent domestic situations. Without land rights women often cannot provide collateral to gain access to credit; since ownership of land represents a form of saving, women may end up without capital in the seven of marital separation. Housing projects that provide for ownership regardless of the sex of the 'household head' may be difficult to design in countries where women do not legally possess rights of ownership. However, in other contexts where it is a consequence of 'tradition; there may be relatively simple means of making land-ownership rights available to women. In an upgrading project in Jordan, for example, it was found that because a woman staff member happened to be in charge of handling the title deeds in the Community Development Office, many men in the community allowed their wives to complete the relevant paperwork. As a result, title deeds tended up in the women's names, thus meeting, if unintentionally, their strategic gender need to own land Examples of rural development schemes which have displaced women from their traditional agricultural work and their control over land are widespread.

Gender Needs in Environmental Planning

In their reproductive role, rural women depend on the resources of wood water and soil for daily survival, and as such are often the primary users of the environment. Yet their practical gender needs are often not recognized by those who utilise the environment as a productive resource. Thus Shiva in her feminist analysis of women and the environment, describes forestry for instance, in the following terms: "There are in India, today, two paradigms of forestry— one ice-enhancing, the other life-destroying. The life enhancing paradigm emerges from the forest and the feminine principle; the life-destryg one from the factory and the markets. The Chipko movement in the Himalayan foothills of India provides a graphic example of this conflict of needs. When the Forestry Development Corporation employing local men sough to cut down the forests for commercial extraction, on the basis that they produce 'profit, resin and timbers. Local women resisted because they identified the forests as bearing 'soil, water and pure air'. The solidarity between local men and women broken down; enwanted felling contracts and the women organised themselves into a cooperative to protect the forests. They provided work for women as guards to ensure that no felling went ahead (Dankelman and Deviation 1988). The community management of SIRDO water recycling in Merida. Mexico, by contrast, was an environmental project, based on a recognition of women's triple roll. In this resource conservation project designed to improve sanitation, water and waste control, women as community managers formed a committee to supervise the operation. This not only increased overall community health which concerned them as mothers an wives, but also allowed women in their productive role to sell the fertilizer produced by the project.

Basic Services and Gender Needs

The delivery of basic services in both rural and urban areas can have fundamental implications in terms of the gender needs. The planning of child-care facilities provides a good example of the way in which differences in location can result in the fulfillment of different gender needs. If located at the woman's workplace it will certainly meet her practical gender need for adequate child-care facilities, essential for her to undertaken waged employment. If located in the community this may encourage a sharing of responsibilities with the family, although if anyone other than the mother delivers the child it is likely to be another female member of the family. If, however, the nursery is located at the father's place of work, this provides the opportunity for meeting both practical and strategic gender needs since it involves the father in taking some of the responsibility for child care, and thereby alleviates the burden of domestic labour for the woman.

The most critical problem faced by women in the transport sector is that transport services are organised to meet the needs of male workforce schedules, wit buses running from the periphery to the centre during morning and evening peak periods. Their daily average travel time was three times longer than that of men. Low-income women often not only use public transport more than men but require it for multiple activities, such as school, shopping and health-related trips, in addition to work trips. Although the provision of adequate off-peak transport meets practical gender needs, it cannot meet strategic gender needs since it does not alleviate women's burden of domestic labor and child care.

Timing of meetings can radically afffect women's attendance in rural communities, and resultantly their capacity to gain access to important information relevant to them in both their productive and reproductive roles. Rural extension workers frequently report that women fail to attend their meeting. In a project in Botswana, for instance, meetings were held in the morning in order to ensure that male farmers, gathering in their productive and community politics role, were sober and attentive. However, this timing automatically excluded women who were bus at this point of the day with necessary reproductive responsibilities. Since information about family planning as well as credit schemes was intended primarily for women, rural extension workers were obliged to reschedule the meeting to a hour later in the day when women had *free* time. The example cited above show the limitations of individual sectorial interventions for low-income women. Because of the necessity to balance their triple role, women require integrative strategies which cut cross sectorial lines. They also reveal that the majority of planning interventions intended for women meet practical gender needs, and do not seek to change existing divisions of labour. Therefore, they are not 'feminist' in content. In reality, practical gender needs remain the only specific policy target for most of those concerned with planning for women.

CHAPTER 2

Gender Planning Strategies and Training

Training has become identified as a critical component in ensuring that organisations successfully integrate gender planning into their work. A proliferation of new 'approaches,' courses and workshops have abounded as different institutions and individuals have sought to fill this need. In many contexts training is now identified as the panaceas, the solution to all problems. It highlights the different components of a gender-training strategy, drawing on a decade of personal experience. Five fundamental questions—*why train, when to train, who provides training, whom to train* and *how to train*—provide the framework for addressing training issues. Gender training is a complex, sensitive and sophisticated field of work, conceptually, methodologically and, above all, in its practice. The 'first generation' of genderationers has already learned through bitter experience that, despite the immense demand for such training, either 'instant fixes' nor 'quick sales' of guidelines, manuals and packages provide the panacea to gender planning problems. Attempt is made here to highlight several important substantive and methodological issues of use for those involved in the development of gender-training strategies.

Training Approaches

Of late along with the development of different conceptual approaches to the issue of women and development, and the varying institutional structures and operational procedures to ensure their implementation, different training strategies and techniques have developed. WID/gender training developed primarily as a response to gender-bind practices. However, the different training courses have also provided the 'testing ground' for the intellectual development of different analytical approaches.

Many training packages are now in practice, with a range of training experience undertaken with aid donors, Third World government practitioners and NGOs. Bergen Conference Norway, provided an important opportunity to evaluate a decade of gender-training experience. Some ninety conference participants reached consensus that of the diversity of experience represented it was useful to identify three general approaches. Although these have emerged as 'dominant', it does not mean to suggest that they comprehensively cover all methodologies.

Gender Analysis Training

The first, and by far the best-known and most extensively used, is gender analysis training. This originated in 1980 when the World Bank WID Adviser commissioned a team headed by James Austin, a well-known case-method trainer at Harvard, to conduct a series of workshops for World Bank staff. He brought in three women with WID experience—Catherine Overholt, Mary Anderson and Kathleen Could-who formed what is known as the 'Harvard Team'.

The basis of the Harvard approach is gender analysis. This is identified as a diagnostic tool. It consists of a sequential, threefold analytical framework to address the division of labour between men and women and their different access to and control of resources. Case studies are used as the 'pedagogical vehicle through which intellectual involvement is generated' (Overholt et al. 1984: xiii). These describe a set of events and provide the available relevant raw data but leave analysis and evaluation to participants. As Overholt has identified, in the real world the case situations do not have one correct answer.

The analytical framework developed for the analysis uses four interrelated components: *activity profile; access and control profile; analysis of factors influencing activities, access and control; and project-cycle analysis.* In the workshop format, participants use case studies in relation to the analytical framework. With this tool they identify gender-based divisions of labour and access to and control over resources. This enable them to highlight the often invisible nature of women's contribution as well as the differential impact of proposed project interventions on men and women. Repeating the process with different sets of data but guided by the same framework, the intention is to train participants to be able to use gender analysis as a toll in their own work. This shows them that the framework guiding gender analysis is applicable to all situations. Over the past ten years the Harvard Team has worked closely with, and had an impressive impact on, most North American donors. Institutions such as USAID, CIDA, UNDP and IDRC have adopted, and adapted as appropriate, gender analysists training. All have developed detailed tools based on the gender analysis approach for the training of aid donor personnel both at headquarters and in the field.

Gender Planning Training

A second approach is gender planning training, which is linked to Gender Planning. This began in 1984 with a course, 'Planning with Women for Development', initiated at the Development Planning Unit (DPU), University College, London, in collaboration with Caren Levy. This was a three-month short course specifically targeted at Third World planning practionners (Moser 1986).

Simultaneously, UK-based development NGOs expressed a need for short one-to-day course. Since then NGOs such as Christian Aid, Oxfam and VSO have used this short course extensively. In the past few years the same course format has been developed further for training courses varying between one and five days. Donors such as ODA, SIDA, NORAD and the Commonwealth Secretariat have used these, with trainers in each case developing contextual specific training strategies. One basic premise of this methodology is that it contains components for the training for trainers. Consequently, several Third World participants from both the DPU and LSE courses have developed their own training courses based on this methodology for use with governments and NGOs. One interesting example is that of the Mujery Planification del Desarolo Programme (Women and Development Planning) in Lima, Peru, that runs four different categories of training activities (Fort 1991). Caren Levy, in particular, has further developed gender planning procedures such as gender diagnosis and entire strategies. Finally, this has been used to advise such institutions as FAO, ILO, UNIFEM, CUSO and the Africa Technical Department of the World Bank on the development of their training strategies.

We have highlighted the most salient points of gender planning. The basis of this approach is planning, rather than analysis, and gender planning rather than planning for women in development. The purpose of the training is, therefore, to provide tools, not only for diagnosis, but also for translation into practice. These relate to the productive, reproductive and community managing roles of women, to decision-making within the household and to the nature of women's subordination. The purpose of simplification is to translate these concerns into specific interventions in planning practice. Tools such as the triple role, gender needs assessment, the WID/GAD matrix and gendered participatory planning procedures help planners to undertake gender diagnosis, define gender objectives and identify gender entry points. In addition, it assists them to recognise the constraints and opportunities in institutionalising and operationalising gender planning within their own organisations. These tools provide a common language that allows practitioners from different disciplines, of different persuasions and positions on WID/GAD issues, to communicate with each other non-threateningly. The simplification of complex realities has obvious dangers. However, it also has advantages in that these realities can be quickly grasped and translated for utilisation in planning practice.

Gender Dynamics: Training

Gender dynamics is a third and very different, training approach. It differs fundamentally from the first two in that it come mainly from the training experience of Third World grass-roots organisations, as against First World GAD researchers. In addition, its constituency is Third World practitioners, particularly women in NGOs, rather than government, or First world development personnel.

This approach has not been well documented. It comprises several indigenous, highly participatory, innovative and flexible methodologies designed to 'empower' women to recognise, analyse and address gender issues at the grass-roots level. Interpersonal skills, that engage 'not only the mind but the heart' (Aklilu 1991: 25), provide the basic training technique.

Gender dynamics is a consciousness-raising seminar that discusses questions relating to the nature, origin, extent, effects of, and alternatives to, gender bias...[to] identify gender bias at home, at work, and in society-at-large; interpret some experiences in the light of feminist values and principles; reconcile various points of view in the women's movement; correct sexist patterns of thinking, speaking and behaving; and integrate gender-fair values into one's personnel and professional plan of action.

As the term suggests, 'gender dynamics' is based primarily on 'interactive' lectures, role play and interpersonal dynamics. In some contexts, additional tools have included the use of popular theatre, such as the work of Sistern in Jamaica.

Components of a Training Strategy

Before undertaking gender training, a training strategy is required. This contains a number of components, which can be addressed in terms of a series of interrelated questions. The following discussion raises issues relevant to all three training approaches identified above. However, in the main it describes the most important components of a gender planning training strategy (drawing on experience in this field, particularly with donors and Northern NGOs).

Objectives of different training approaches

As Anderson (1991) has identified, training approaches and their effectveness are influenced by the social, economic and institutional context in which they occur. Nevertheless, the basic assumption on which all training rests is that this is a powerful transforming tool through which people learn new attitudes, knowledge or skills. Once acquired, this will make them become more effective at what they do (Anderson 1991). The results of a recent survey of gender training show a clear agreement that the long-term goal of training is to achieve a gender-equitable society, and is captured well in the goal statement made by the East and Central Africa Training Institute (ESAMI): To initiate change at the individual, organizational, social and policy levels which encourages gender responsive sustainable developments.

Training's purpose, however, may differ widely from a broad concern to create a gender awareness of gender issues to the specific need to impart skills and techniques. If training is undertaken because most staff are hostile to WID (in which case its purpose must be sensitization) then its objective is to made gender-blind staff aware of gender. Staudt (1990) argues, it is important not to forget that many agencies continue to identify the conventional gender ideologies of staff members, and a lack of acceptance of WID as a legitimate professional concern, as the strongest reasons for 'bureaucratic resistance'. Alternatively, if staff are interested and sympathetic but lack the necessary tools to integrate gender into their work, the purpose may be to provide them with the appropriate methodology. This does necessarily mean that staff will develop a 'feminist' orientation to the issue; their concern could be one of efficiency, not of equity. Of importance here is the WID/GAD policy matrix that can be used to inform staff of the rationale underlying different policy approaches. It is important, therefore, to clarify the objectives of training. These have direct implications both ror the development of a training strategy, and for the components of the training methodology. While many training courses combine a number of different objectives, it is useful, nevertheless, to state by distinguishing between four basic objectives.

There is training in sensitization or awareness-raising to the importance of women and development and gender and development issues. The objective of this type of training is to introduce participants, who can be identified as 'gender-blind', to both women and gender as variables in the development process. Most early gender-training courses were preoccupied with this objective. Although the situation has changed considerably, Cloud's (1991) review concludes that this remains the main domain of gender training courses, as the first of several stages in the training process.

Further, there is training in 'skill transfer in gender analysis and diagnosis. The objective is to impart the necessary skills to gender-aware participants to enable them to undertake gender analysis and diagnosis. While the specific tools may vary, their purpose it to enable participants to analyse a number of variables. These include the gender division of labour, access to and control over resources, gender needs assessment and the underlying policy approaches to WID. These tools can be used in gender diagnosis of concrete development contexts.

One more objective of training is the translation of skills into planning practice. This ensure that participants develop the capacity to translate their 'theoretical' apparatus into 'practice', through its implementation in ongoing work. It aims to achieve the integration of gender planning methodology into both the institutional structures and the operational procedures of the organisation in which participants work. By its very definition, gender planning training places greatest emphais on this objective.

Finally, there is training in motivational factors. Its objective is to motivate participants to 'do the job' the extent to which this necessarily varies. It depends on whether constraints in gender planning relate to personal attitudes or lack of professional skills. In addition, approaches to training vary, depending on the extent to which confrontation is considered appropriate. Gender dynamics training identifies motivation as the primary constraint and focuses on this objective.

Underlying the different training objectives are profound questions concerning the extent to which they address the issue of subordination. Associated with this question is that of the underlying policy approach to WID. Professionals differ widely in their perception, or recognition, that gender training is confrontational. The basic premise of feminists that the 'personal is political' presumes such issues to be highly contentious for those who do not agree that women are subordinated to men. Their assumption is that training on such an issue must be highly susceptible to confrontation. Obviously, training on planning for WID very neatly avoids this problem. Because it focuses on an efficiency approach, it provides the rationale to deal with women on their own, as a separate category. However, even for those who recognise the issue of subordination there are useful tools that can help in reducing confrontation. The highly aggressive challenges can so easily destroy the effectiveness of a training course, these are obviously important. In gender planning training courses, for instance, one successful way to diffuse tension is to distinguish at the outset between the 'professional', the 'personal' and the 'political', and to place particular emphasis on the fact that gender planning training concerns the 'professional.'

The logic is the following: if the 'personal' refers to the way in which individuals understand and analyses their personal relationships between men and women in their own society, the purpose of training is not to change such personal beliefs. Equally, if the 'political' refers to the feminists agenda in the individual's society, the training is not intended to challenge or change political stances on this issue. This allows participants to accept without hostility such tools as gender roles identification, gender needs assessment and the WID/GAD policy matrix. Ultimately, the distinction between practical and strategic gender needs is a critical tool that helps participants recognise the interrelationship between the political, professional and personal. Indeed, the diffusion of tension is an inherent part of the tools themselves. In demystifying the widespread belief that all interventions to assist women as 'feminist', it allows participants to 'put on the back burner's those interventions considered in appropriate. It also allows the beginnings of a re-examination of 'personal' as well as 'political' positions on the issue of women's subordination.

It is crucial to note that this mechanism to 'dilute' confrontation is appropriate for training those in the 'international community' working on Third World issues. One unrecognised complication in gender training is the important distinction between practionners working on development issues in their own environment, and those outside working in a donor capacity. For the latter, this training does not directly address gender concerns of their own society. Because it is, in a sense, one step removed from the reality of their personal lives, such training is easily identified as professional training. For professionals working in their own society this is not so this is the reason why training in gender dynamics is more widespread within Third World countries. Third World trainers consider it most appropriate to confront such issues directly than do those developing training methodologies for use in the international community.

> Women representative in countries with an expressed commitment to justice are in a position to press for greater equity in every area of national behaviour... it is very difficult for outsiders, particularly male outsiders, to suggest that the gender arrangements of another culture are unjust, especially those within the family. (Cloud 1991:4)

Target Group

If training is not designed specifically for the group to be trained there is no guarantee that it will work. The chosen objectives of a particular training course are, thus, closely interrelated to, an dependent upon, who is undergoing the training. This requires both an understanding of the structure of the organisation and its attitude to WID. So as to provide clear objectives that relate to work practices, it is necessary to understand how gender relations have a bearing on such practices in the organisation concerned. This requires a knowledge of the power and decision-making processes within the organisation and an understanding of the procedures most requiring change. The person responsible for the definition, development and implementation of the institution's policies, programmes and projects also have to be identified. So do the strategically important allies who can provide leverage in the acceptance of training.

Where does training start in an organisation? Three alternative scenarios can be identified, with important implications in terms of the entry point. Is the request for training from a 'top-down' mandate, a 'bottom up' movement from within the organisation or from a nervous organisation concerned that they are 'losing out'? Each has important implications in terms of the structure of support necessary not only to carry out training but also to ensure that it is taken seriously. The evidence shows that gender training is most effective not only when conducted on a sufficiently large scale but also when it occurs within a favourable policy environment. A clear directive from top management, the necessary resources, and appropriate systems of accountability provide such a context. Strong institutional commitment will only survive if senior management involve themselves in the training itself—to provide the sustained support necessary to institutionalise such training. For such reasons, training often begins with, or includes in the early stages, senior policy-making staff, followed by programme-level staff.

How much do staff need to know? This may depend on their level of seniority and work responsibility. While very senior managers often only need to be aware of the importance of the issues, it may be the middle-level staff who require the specific techniques. Therefore, within an organisation different objectives may be required for the various target groups. In most organisations, but especially those structured hierarchically, it is not appropriate to mix levels, given the sensitive nature of training. Senior staff do not want to be seen to be wrong in front of lower-level staff. The latter in turn are often intimidated, limiting their participation in the presence of more senior staff. However, different experiences can considerably enrich training courses. Senior staff may only be concerned with policy formulation, and can benefit from the contribution of those with operational experience. Ultimately, much depends on personal characteristics. Often very senior or junior staff are not hostile. It is those in the middle of their careers, for whom the defence of the *status quo* is most important. Once an organisation decides the most appropriate level to start training, and identifies the objectives for different groups, several further decisions have to be made relating to the composition of the staff trained. What are the common features, the criteria that bind them in training? Do they all work on the same sectorial concerns? Is it appropriate to mix staff from different sectors? Similar questions must be asked in relation to the sex of participants. Is it more appropriate to have both men and women together in training? Finally, what is the most appropriate size of group for training, and length of time for a course? While answers to all these questions are contextually specific and depend on the culture of the organisation, a number of general rules apply across the board.

The extent to which it is appropriate to mix professionals working on different sectors of development depends on the purpose of training and the methodology used. Because gender planning provides participants with tools that can be used cross-sectorally, the training is designed for mixed-sex groups. One of the biggest causes of tension in training groups with mixed groups is different levels of awareness. Where some participants are already aware of the issues and want training in gender planning, they can become impatient while waiting for colleagues to 'catch up'. In selecting target groups it is important, therefore, to ensure that participants have a similar 'level' of awareness of issues. Furthermore, it should be noted that mixed-sex groups often have different dynamics from single-sex groups. The training of women, whether in single-sex or mixed groups, brings home only too clearly the importance of not conflating the personal and the professional. For there is no a priori reason why women should be more sympathetic than men to the issues. Indeed, precisely because they are ofter professional women who have 'made it', they may be particularly hostile to gender training.

The size of the group also depends on the training methodology. The experience of gender planning training has shown that twelve to fifteen is the ideal number. Because of its highly participatory methodology, in larger groups there is less space for the participation of the whole group. This allows less interested participants to take a back seat. In smaller groups the lack of diversity of experience can make training less interesting. However, this question also relates to the length of training. Practice has not borne out the rule that the more senior professionals are, the busier they are, and therefore, the shorter the training period should be. Commitment to spending time on training depends on how seriously the organisation takes training, and who has asked participants to attend. Short gender training courses vary from an hour or two with the aim of sensitizing and creating awareness, to seven to ten days in order to provide detailed skills. It is certainly true that the more time allocated to training the greater the skilling that can be provided. However, it is important to be realistic about what is possible, and to be able to recognise that a critical mass can be reached in terms of conflicting commitments. While the average length of many gender training courses is one day, practice has shown the optimal length for senior staff to be three days.

Considering the training important depends on the institutional strategy in relation to WID. Those organisations with WID specialists and those that mainstream WID issues differ identifiably in their strategy towards training. Many organisations still prefer to see training as an outside job that they hire consultants to do in a 'top-down' one-off manner. However, as is well known, others have recognized the complex interrelationship between the different components of a training strategy. They have sought, therefore, to develop one interrelationship to their own policy, programme and project cycles, as part of a long-term overall institutional strategy. In deciding whether training is a priority, a clear relationship exists between the institutional strategy adopted and the extent to which training is considered important. Organisations that have separate institutional WID structures, which emphasise gender specialists, tend not to prioritize training. Since their strategy is to 'own' the issue, and they know it well enough themselves already, training is often very low in the order of priorities, if considered at all. In direct contrast are those institutions that priorities the integration and mainstreaming of gender planning. Here training is often the most important instrument to ensure that the institution increases the number of gender-aware generalists.

This distinction also has implications for the extent to which training is considered a product or a process. Organisations 'coerced' top-down, or through outside pressure, to adopt training without understanding its importance, are more likely to identify training as a product. Outside consultants control the entire operation, which is packaged and delivered with manuals. Organisations that consider training a high priority recognise that it is a slow, costly and time-consuming process. Training must be tailor-made for the needs of the particular organisation, and target groups. One-off manuals are less likely to be developed, with training tools developing as training itself gradually integrates into the institution.

While identifying training as a process, monitoring of both the content of the training and the identification of target groups is undertaken. Gender planning training at ODA, for example, began with one-day workshops with mid-level professional staff at headquarters in London. In the second stage it included regional development divisions in Africa, Asia and the Pacific, as well as the training, at their request, of more junior headquarters staff. In SIDa, the target group included headquarters staff, country DCs and WID officers, but in the second phase senior consultants participated. Training as a process can become a means to institutionalise gender policy. In both SIDa and ODA, for example, the introduction of a long-term training strategy has had important consequences in terms of changing planning procedures within the organisation. Training has been the vehicle for the introduction of new gender policy which integrates such tools as gender needs assessment and the WID/GAD policy matrix. Both organisations recognise that without the introduction of these tools in training sessions there would not have been sufficient consensus for their adoption.

Operationalising Training within an Institution

To undertake gender training requires very specific skills, which are often not recognised. Two issues are important. First, training is not teaching. Just as the distinction between academic research on gender issues and gender planning is important, so the difference between teaching and training is equally important. The same pedgagogic approaches are not necessarily appropriate. Training can be defined as the expansion or consolidation of technical skills to put knowledge into practice. It is not lecturing, with it emphasis on the transmission of theoretical knowledge and ideas. If teaching concerns the creating of an awareness, or consciousness, of the complexity of gender issues through an increased analytical capacity, training concerns developing the skill capacity to translate such awareness into very specific tools that can be used in practice. Training relies on a diversity of pedagogic techniques, such as exercises, small-group discussions, brainstorm sessions and so on. All are designed both to reinforce the skilling provided and to ensure that the participants themselves work thorough the issues so that they emerge confident to use them. In reality, training may require some teaching, but teaching can very successfully be done without training.

The second issue is that teachers are not necessarily trainers and gender planners are often neither. Frequently, in identifying professionals to undertake training in gender planning the assumption is that a gender planner, or an academic with a knowledge of gender issues, can train. As many problematic experiences have shown only too clearly, this is an incorrect assumption. Often trainers find it much easier to learn about gender planning, than gender planners or academics find it to learn how to train. The capacity of the trainer is one of the most crucial determinants of successful training. This therefore poses an important constraint that requires recognition at the outset in developing a training strategy.

In institutionalised gender planning training, the critical question concerns the extent to which outside consultants on the their own can successfully undertake training. This depends primarily on the purpose of the training. If the purpose is *sensitization or creating gender awareness*, an outside consultant can often be adequate. However, if the purpose of *training is to translate skills into the specific contexts in which trainees are working*, then senior cotrainers from within the institution are an essential prerequisite for success. In view of the time, expense and widespread reluctance of many institutions to accept this training principle, it is necessary to explain the reasons for its importance.

First, only those working within an organisation ultimately know how it works. This input is essential if gender planning is to be operationalised in the work practices of those involved in training. Secondly, institutionalising gender planning requires co-trainers who can articulate and identify the constraints and opportunities for this process, and provide the essential follow-up that results from successful training.

While outside trainers may feel confident, they lack the necessary status and position. They have little impact when they identify bureaucratic blockages or suggest intra-organizational alliances likely to push the agenda. Ultimately, trainers working side by side from within and outside the organisation develop a sophisticated understanding of the issues that are 'taboo' for each. There are some issues that it is more helpful for outsiders to raise, while there are other issues that only staff trainers from within the organisation can bring up. Hannan-Andersson (1991) for example, has identified that in the SIDA training strategy two different types of input—from the consultants and from SIDA's Gender Officer—were both complementary and essential. Consultants could provide a good background in gender analysis and gender planning. However, they could not help SIDa personnel and consultants in making the direct link to their own activities.

When training occurs without co-trainers, belligerent trainees often express aggressive hostility, or simply an off-hand dismissal of the WID institutional structure. Since it is difficult for the outside consultant to defend the WID office, this only serve to reduce the perceived lack of importance of gender planning. When co-trainers are present, the training enhances the importance of the WID staff and helps them in furthering their role as catalysts within the institution. Ultimately training will only be taken seriously within an organisation if they 'own' it. Nothing better helps the integration of training than the long-term visible participation of the senior WID/GAD staff as co-trainers. Much of the challenge to change existing practices occurs in the last part of the worship, when exited participants ask, 'What can we do?' The capacity to hand over to the WID personnel who then take the suggestions further reinforces the issue of training far beyond the classroom.

A third reason may be the status of training within the organisation. Many institutions identify training as a low-status, purely 'technical' activity, undertaken by junior staff with small budgets. This means that they view gender training in the same way. When senior staff become co-trainers, the status of training itself is 'upgraded'. Therefore many institutions when embarking on WID training do not initially involve the existing low-status training division. However, since the ideal training strategy is ultimately to hand over training to the organisation—whether they do it as one of several activities, or are hired full-time to train—the training becomes institutionalised into the ongoing mainstream training programme. While organisations such as USAID have a full-time training staff, others, such as SIDA and ODA, still prefer the strategy of using senior WID staff as co-trainers. In gender planning training two trainers work as a team, balancing active and passive roles in a highly structured manner. Not only is this type of training very stressful for trainers to cope with singly, but also the balance between the two provides an important dynamic. It can be helpful to have a male trainer. However, the capacity to train and the seniority of trainers are a trainers' most important assets, given the need to be treated with respect by senior staff.

Content of the Training

Obviously, the training methodology is the most critical determinant of the content of training. This then decides more specific details relating to such issues as the programming and format of the workshop, the structure of the content of each session and the materials required for each session. This general description of training strategies, therefore, concludes by highlighting the debate about the content of training. This concerns the extent to which it can be pre-packaged or whether it needs to be developed for specific contexts by trainers in collaboration with the organisation concerned. To a large extent the objectives of training decide the answer. If the concern is to create awareness or increase ability in gender analysis, then training packages can be formalised for widespread use. If the objective of training is the translation of skills into planning practice then the working procedures of the organisation must be understood.

Training must be designed to meet the needs of different organizational groups.

At a specific level, the debate over course materials, particularly case studies, illustrated this difference. Are pre-developed case studies appropriate, or is it necessary to develop specific materials to train participants how to operatonalise new procedures? Institutions training with the Harvard gender analysis approach base their training on pre-designed case studies. FAO, for example, have developed eleven case studies covering a range of countries and technical areas and have used these, with gender analysis framework tools, to train some 1,000 professional staff (Howard-Borjas et al. 1991.)

In contrast, given the particular focus of the gender planning methodology, it emphasizes the importance of using materials that a recurrently in use within organisations. It identifies this as critical since it makes the training central to the current work experience. Participants cannot, therefore, dismiss it as irrelevant to the institution concerned. It does, however, also mean that materials need to be more 'custom-built', and designed for specific training groups. SIDA, in its current training course, uses case studies based on SIDA documentation. These are not summaries of documents or versions especially written for training purposes. Case examples cover Asia and Africa, and review areas, such as water supply, road construction, hydro-power and health.

Evaluation Procedures of Training

There have been few systematic attempts to evaluate gender training quantitatively, other than questionnaires that assess the 'happiness quotient'. This is the level of satisfaction with training, but not the impact of training on work practices. Nevertheless, organisations dominate the impact of training in a number of ways. Gender planning training provides participants with several tools that allow practitioners from different disciplines, and of different persuasions and positions on WID/GAD issues, to communicate in a common language. This can be monitored in terms of the resulting cooperation and coordination in work practice between both departments and individuals. However, one problem, identified by Christian Aid, is the distinction between taking on the rhetorical 'spirit of the language' and implementing it in practice.

Anderson (1991) has outlined a potential evaluation approach to training through an input/output model that can reflect the variety of approaches taken to gender training. Inputs include the trainers, their materials, the content of training and the training method, the time, the place and the group who are trainees. In contrast, when the elements do not come together; participants can learn very little, despite well-prepared training and effective trainers. Those who have undertaken training know only too well how logistical problems of timing or space, beyond the trainer's control, can only too easily result in a disastrous workshop.

She provides a very useful threefold categorization of the outputs of training, as participant changes, institutional changes and external impact. She claims that the impact of training on participants can be identified interms of changed attitudes, increased skills and knowledge and changed behaviour. The latter are the most difficult to assess. Institutional changes are easier evaluate since they relate to changes in both institutional structures and operational procedures. These can result as much from 'bottom-up' pressure after training as from 'top-down directives'. Anderson does, however, caution that training may be only one of many initiatives to change practices. Then its purpose is to 'speed up' the restructuring.

The ultimate output, that of the external impact, is the most difficult to assess, because of its distance from the actual training. Different objectives of training and their underlying rationales, are obviously critical in the evaluation of trainng. Anderson distinguishes two external impacts of 'improved development' and 'increased equality. The former can be used to evaluate training based on what she calls the 'efficiency hypothesis'. If a major objective is to emphasise the importance of gender analysis as a tool for deciding how to use development resources more effectively to achieve goals in economic output. The latter can be used to evaluate approaches based on the 'equity hypothesis.' This focuses on gender in terms of its influence on the allocation of social and economic benefits from development, and thus, on equality between men and women. Obviously, any evaluation of the effectiveness of training ultimately depends on the approach taken.

Conclusion

Anderson's model of evaluation has yet to be tested. Nevertheless, from nearly a decade of experience the qualitative evidence clearly shows that institutionalised gender training within an organisation plays a deciding role in a slow process of change. The objectives of gender training are determined both by the underlying approach to gender issues—women's release from subordination or more efficient development - as well as by its skilling objectives, to provide analytical skills or the capacity to translate into planning practice. Over time the importance of gender planning training has shifted from changing attitudes to increasing skills and knowledge. Training has been particularly effective in providing sympathetic gender-aware planners with the necessary tools and techniques that they require. It also provides a common language allowing for non-threatening communication.

As participants themselves have confronted the ineffectiveness and inefficiency of palliative procedures and institutional structures designed merely to pay lip-service to WID issues, it may be useful to assess if 'bottom-up' demand for institutional and operational change is more successful than changes resulting from top-down directives. In some organisations gender training has proved to be not an end in itself but a means to change. It has provided the catalyst for changes in both institutional structures and operational procedures.

CHAPTER 3

Approaches to Gender Issues

Traditionally, Indian Census presents sex-wise data on different socio-economic, cultural, and demographic aspects on which information is collected during the census. The pronounced sex differentials in data sets of many variables have remained under constant focus and attention of data users and planners. The declining trends in sex ratio and invisibility of woman in economic pursuits in certain states had generated lot of anxiety among the scholars. In response to the interest generated about women's contribution to the informal economic pursuits, one of the central themes of the 1991 Census was to capture unpaid work of women. As such the wordings of the question on economic activity in the Individual Slip was expanded to include unpaid work on family farm of family enterprise.

The census organization has been constantly working on devising strategies for better capture of the census data for this segments of the population. One of the significant features of the Census of India, 2001 has been the continuation of its consistent and focused approach to the gender issues. To begin with, a special cell within the organization was established to oversee gender issues and sensitize the census functionaries at the different levels involved in supervision and conduct of Census of India, 2001. The approach to gender sensitization primarily focused on three aspects during the Census of India, 2001:

(1) Sensitizing the Directors of Census Operations and other senior functionaries of the directorates and the state government at every opportunity by an indepth discussion with them, on sex ratio, age, literacy and

female work participation of their own state, which enabled them in understanding and appreciating the problem in its proper perspective.

(2) To impart a thorough and appropriate training to all census functionaries with the help of special modules and data sets relating to gender issues.

(3) To undertake adequate steps to build up public awareness through widespread publicity campaign specially focusing on the contribution of women in various economic activities.

The major step taken in the direction of gender sensitization effort was to make significant improvements in the Instruction Manual for enumerators and also the Household Schedule. In the Instruction Manual, special efforts were made to draw the attention of the enumerators and supervisors about the basic count of population, especially with a view to net better the elderly, and the unmarried woman as also the girl child in the household. The instructions were also given for recording the name of members in a particular sequence so that no female members in the Household is missed even inadvertently. In order to properly capture the part-time and unpaid work of women, much emphasis was given in the Instruction Manual by way of providing instructions on probing methods and giving appropriate examples. A number of economic activities in which women are engaged as paid or unpaid work and are occasionally not reported as work, have been depicted through illustrative sketches. These pictures show women engaged in different activities pursued by them on formal or informal basis, within the precincts of the households or outside by lending helping hand to their male counterparts. The next step was to make the format of the Household Schedule more gender sensitive. For instance the questions on fertility, seeking information on number of children born were specially referred as daughters and sons to ensure that no female children are left out inadvertently.

The Office of the Registrar General, India had several consultative sessions with government departments and non-government agencies working on women issues to *address the gender issues in Census more pragmatically and systematically*. A special study was conducted to suggest specific methodology to be adopted for improving the recording of the female work participation at Census of India, 2001. A survey was conducted in villages of Punjab, Haryana, Uttar Pradesh and Bihar and some of the recommendations of this survey were adopted to improve the methodology for training of enumerators and other census functionaries in this regard.

In order to achieve the objective of complete and accurate coverage of women and their participation in economic activity, districts that showed very low sex ratio, female literacy and work participation rates at the 1991 Census were identified. There were 266 districts as per 1991 jurisdiction, which had either very low female work participation rate of less than 15 per cent or a deficiency of more than 50 females per 1000 males. These were treated as critical districts, which required additional efforts in terms of sensitization and training. With the support of several UN Agencies, special Census Advisors were engaged in almost all these districts for this purpose. Some Directorates held special thematic session where women officials were specially invited to undertake training on gender issues. Special efforts were made to engage as many as possible women enumerators and supervisors to undertake the field work. Wherever possible Anganwadi workers (local women officials involved in child and nutrition programme) were trained to work as census enumerator.

In addition to exhaustive illustrations and instructions in the Instruction Manual, audio cassettes eliciting probing questions on gender related issues were also made in different regional languages and used during training sessions. Special posters on female work were prepared and displayed for creating awareness among the general public about the importance of recording women's work. A number of audio and video spots appealing the women folk to come forward and report their economic activity were produced and relayed through radio and television networks.

CHAPTER 4

A Fresh Look at Sex Composition in India

Sex composition of the human population is one of the basic demographic characteristics, which is extremely vital for any meaningful demographic analysis. Demographic composition describes the population situation at a particular point of time and place and different variables affect the population dynamics. Fertility is a major component of population dynamics in affecting demographic structure. Indian Census has the tradition of bringing out desegregated information by sex on various aspects of population. The first and foremost is the simple count of males and females. Changes in sex composition largely reflects the underlying socio-economic and cultural patterns of a society in different ways. Sex ratio defined here as the number of females per 1000 males in the population, is an important social indicator to measure the extent of prevailing equity between males and females in a society at a given point of time. It is mainly the outcome of the interplay of sex differentials in mortality, sex selective migration, sex ratio at birth and at times the sex differential in population enumeration.

It is natural for an ordinary person to believe that males and females in the population exactly balance each other. Little do they know, how imbalanced the sexes are in different populations across the world. Around the year 2000, the world had 986 females against 1000 males. It is evident that except Indonesia and Japan, the other Asian countries show low sex ratios. The sheer weight of the population of these four Asian countries with low sex ratio appears to be largely responsible for the overall preponderance of males over females in the world.

Sl. No.	*Country*	*Sex Ratio (Females per 1,000 Males)*
	World	986
1	China	944
2	India	933
3	U.S.A.	1,029
4	Indonesia	1,004
5	Brazil	1,025
6	Pakistan	938
7	Russian Fed.	1,140
8	Bangladesh	953
9	Japan	1,041
10	Nigeria	1,016

Source: World Population Prospects (mid year estimates) 1998 revision, volume 2, Sex and Age, United Nations.

It is interesting to note that the sex ratio in U.S.A., Indonesia, Russian Federation and Japan has always remained above unity for the last half a century. The most dramatic decline of about 200 points in the sex ratio is seen in the Russian Federation. In U.S.A., it has shown as improvement from 1002 to 1029 in the last fifty years. Bangladesh has shown a continuous improvements in its sex ratio to reach from 880 in 1950 to 953 in 2000. Pakistan and China have also shown an improvement. Thus among the major nations of the world, India is the only exception.

According to the Census of India, 2001, the sex ratio stands at 933 for the country as a whole. This is a welcome improvement from the 1991 Census, which had recorded 927 females for every 1000 males. The sex ratio in the country has always remained unfavourable to females. Moreover, barring some hiccups, it has shown a long term declining trend. The sex ratio at the beginning of the twentieth century was 972 and thereafter showed continuous decline until 1941. In 1951 there was a marginal increase of one point, but thereafter it again dropped for two consecutive decades to reach 930 in 1971. In fact, between 1961-71, the country saw the sharpest decline of 11 points in the sex ratio. Thereafter, if has fluctuated marginally around 930 in successive censuses.

Census Year	*Sex ratio (Females per 1,000 males)*
1901	972
1911	964
1921	955
1931	950
1941	945
1951	946
1961	941
1971	930
1981	934
1991	927
2001	933

Note: 1. For 1991, the interpolated figures for Jammu and Kashmir have been used.

2. While working out the sex ratio for India for the year 2001, the estimated population of entire Kachichh district, Movie, Mallya-Miyana and Wankaner talukas of Rajkot district, Jodiya taluka of jamnagar district of Gujarat State and entire Kinnaur district of Himachal Pradesh have been used as the population enumeration of Census of India, 2001 could not be conducted in these areas due to natural calamities.

Except Kerala all other States and Union Territories have shown a downward slide. The major States that are largely responsible for the decline in the overall sex ratio in India are Uttar Pradesh, Bihar, Jharkand, Orissa, Chhatisgarh, Madhya Pradesh, Gujarat, Maharashtra and Tamil Nadu. Although the sex ratio in Punjab has been consistently low, it has shown a long-term upward trend and has now contributed to the overall deterioration in sex ratio of the country. In Rajasthan, the sex ratio kept fluctuation in a narrow band and always remained at a low level. Haryana, Andhra Pradesh and Karnataka are the States where the sex ratio has remained more or less stagnant. In West Bengal the sex ratio declined sharply from 1901 to 1941 and then made a gradual turnaround on an upward path to reach 934 in 2001.

The sex ratio in Indian population has always been of topical interest for the demographers, social scientists, women's groups, research scholars and various planners and policy makers. Why is it that India has such uneven composition of population as compared to most of the developed countries in the world? Several reasons are adduced to explain the consistently low levels of sex ratio and their further decline in the country. Some of the important reasons commonly put forward are listed below:

- Neglect of the girl child resulting in their higher mortality at younger ages
- High maternal mortality
- Sex selective female abortions
- Female infanticide
- Change in sex ratio at birth.

The imbalance in the number of males and females begins in the beginning. It is now a well-established law of nature that the males exceed females at the time of birth. It is believed that generally 943-952 female births take place for every 1000 male births, which in effect would mean that there is a deficiency of about 50 females per 1000 males in every birth cohort. Many demographers believe that left on its own, this is an unalterable constant.

Some likelihood of differential under registration of female births over time notwithstanding, the data on sex ratio at birth for the past many years as obtained from the SRS is indicative of a larger than usual shortfall in female births as compared to male births. The three years moving average sex ratio at birth worked out for India as a whole for the period 1982-98 leaves around 900. During the decade 1981-90 the SRS sex ratio at birth were above 900 whereas in the succeeding decade it has shown definite sign of a decline below 900. Thus for recent period there is some primary evidence that sex ratio at birth in the country as a whole is possibly lower than the generally accepted range of 943-952 but it needs to be corroborated by some more data.

The overall sex ratio of India is dependent on the sex ratios obtained in different States and Union Territories and their relative weights in terms of size of population.

The diversity in sex ratio among the States and Union Territories is phenomenal. At the Census of India, 2001, the sex ratio among the major States ranged from 861 in Haryana to 1058 in Kerala. In 1991 also, Haryana with a sex ratio of 865 was at the bottom with Kerala (1036) at the top. The changes in sex ratio over time, therefore, are dependent on the changes in the ratios of the individual States and Union Territories and their relative share in population.

State/ UT	*India/States/ Union Territories**	*Sex ratio (females per 1,000 males)* Total Population		Child population in the age group 0-6		Population aged 7 and above	
		1991	*2001*	*1991*	*2001*	*1991*	*2001*
1	*2*	*3*	*4*	*5*	*6*	*7*	*8*
	India	927	933	945	927	923	935
1	Jammu & Kashmir	N.A.	900	N.A	937	N.A	894
2	Himachal Pradesh	976	970	951	897	980	981
3	Punjab	882	974	875	793	883	886
4	Chandigarh	790	773	899	845	772	763
5	Uttaranchal	936	964	948	906	933	976

1	*2*	*3*	*4*	*5*	*6*	*7*	*8*
6	Haryana	865	861	879	820	862	869
7	Delhi*	827	821	915	865	810	813
8	Rajasthan	910	922	916	909	908	925
9	Uttar Pradesh	876	898	927	916	863	895
10.	Bihar	907	921	953	938	895	916
11.	Sikkim	87	875	965	986	860	858
12.	Arunachal Pradesh	859	901	982	961	829	888
13.	Nagaland	886	909	993	975	865	899
14.	Manipur	958	978	974	961	955	981
15.	Mizoram	921	938	969	971	911	932
16.	Tripura	945	950	967	975	940	947
17.	Meghalaya	955	975	986	975	947	974
18.	Assam	923	932	975	964	910	926
19.	West Bengal	917	934	967	963	907	929
20.	Jarkhand	922	941	979	966	908	036
21.	Orissa	971	972	967	950	972	976
22.	Chhatisgarh	985	990	984	975	986	992
23.	Madhya Pradesh	912	920	941	929	905	918
24.	Gujarat	934	921	928	878	936	927
25.	Daman & Diu*	969	709	958	925	971	682
26.	Dadra & Nagar Haveli*	952	811	1,013	973	937	779
27.	Maharashtra	934	922	946	917	931	923
28.	Andhra Pradesh	972	978	975	964	972	980
29.	Karnataka	960	964	960	949	960	966
30.	Goa	967	960	964	933	967	964
31.	Lakshadweep*	943	947	941	974	943	943
32.	Kerala	1,036	1,058	958	963	1,049	1,071
33.	Tamil Nadu	974	986	948	939	978	992
34.	Pondichery*	979	1,001	963	958	982	1,007
35.	Andaman & Nicobar Islands*	818	846	973	965	790	830

Notes: 1. While working out sex ratio of child population for 1991 Census in the age group 0-6 and population aged 7 and above for India, the population in the age group 0-6 and population aged 7 and above of areas of Gujarat and Himachal Pradesh affected by natural calamities have been excluded. The details of affected areas are given in the following Note numbers 2 and 3.

2. To make the data comparable with Census of India, 2001, the proportion of child population for 1991 census in the age group 0-6 and population aged 7 and above shown against Himachal Pradesh for 1991 excludes population in the age group 0-6 and population aged 7 and above of Kinnaur district where population numeration of Census of India, 2001, could not be conducted due to natural calamity.

3. To make the data comparable with Census of India, 2001, the proportion of child population for 1991 Census in the age group 0-6 and population aged 7 and above shown against Gujarat excludes the population data of entire Kachchh district, Morvi, Maliya-Miyana and Wankaner talukas of Rajkot district and Jodiya taluka of Jamnagar district of Gujarat state where population enumeration of Census of India, 2001, could not be conducted due to natural calamity.

It can be seen that the distributions of the number of States at 1991 and 2001 census have remained more or less similar.

Sex ratio	*1991*	*Percentage of population to total population, 1991*	*2001*	*Percentage of Population to total population, 2001*
880 & below	7	18.92	8	5.97
881-915	6	22.02	4	17.45
916-950	9	28.73	11	47.23
951-985	12	26.89	8	18.08
986 & above	1	3.44	4	11.27

Note: For working out the sex ratio of 1991, interpolated population of Jammu and Kashmir has been used. For 2001 the estimated population of the areas affected due to natural calamities in Gujarat and Himachal Pradesh have been used.

It would be interesting to note that although the number of States and Union Territories with the sex ratio less than 916 remains almost the the same, the percentage share of this population has declined from about forty one per cent to about twenty three per cent. Similarly the number of States and Union Territories falling within the range of 916-950 marginally alters but the share of this population increased from around twenty nine per cent to forty seven per cent. The contribution of these two groups of States/Union Territories appears to be the plausible reasons for the increase in overall sex ratio of India.

It may be noted that the number of States and Union Territories with sex ratio of below national average has increased from seventeen in 1991 to eighteen in 2001. In fact the proportion of population in the first category has increased from fifty four per cent to about sixty per cent. In spite of the increase in the number and relative weight in the first category, the overall sex ratio of the country has improved. What could be the possible reason for this? It can be observed that the highly populated States like Uttar Pradesh, Bihar, Rajasthan and Madhya Pradesh which together constituted about 34 per cent of India's population in 1991 and increased to 36 per cent in 2001, lie in the category of below national average. Therefore, the increase in the overall sex ratio is possibly due to the relative larger increase in the sex ratio of these four populous States.

Sex Ratio	*Number of States/UTs 1991*	*Percentage of population to total population 1991*	*Number of States/UTs 2001*	*Percentage of population to total population 2001*
Below national average	17	54.29	18	59.81
Above national average	18	45.71	17	40.19

The sex ratio of the total population have shown improvements in as many as twenty three States and Union Territories. However, during the corresponding period the sex ratio of the child population in the age group 0-6 has increased in only four States and one Union Territory.

Given in are the sex ratio of the total population and the child population in the age group 0-6 from 1961 to 2001.

Year	*Sex ratio in age Group 0-6*	*Over all sex ratio*
1961	976	941
1971	964	930
1981	962	934
1991	945	927
2001	927	933

It is clear that the sex ratio in the age group 0-6 has decreased at a much faster pace than the overall sex ratio of the country after 1981. The decreasing sex ratio in this child population perhaps has cascading effect on population overa period of time leading to diminishing sex ratio in the country. One thing is clear the imbalanced that has set in at this early age-group is difficult to be removed and would remain to haunt the pollution for a long time to come. To say the least, demographical the sex ratio of 927 of the population in the age groups is difficult to be removed and would remain to haunt the population for a long time to come. To say the least, demographically the sex ratio of 927 of the population in the age group 0-6 does not appear to augur well for the future of the country.

Percentage of Sex ratio	*Number of Number of states/UTs 1991*	*Percentage of population to total population 1991*	*States/ UTs 2001*	*Population to total population 2001*
880 and below	2	4.35	5	10.78
881-915	2	1.19	3	6.91
916-950	8	48.20	9	54.45
951-985	19	45.00	16	26.84
986 and above	3	0.37 1	0.05	

Note: Jammu and Kashmir and the affected areas of Gujarat and Himachal Pradesh are excluded from 1991 and 2001 for the sake of comparability.

The distribution of States and Union territories by ranges of sex ratio of child population in the age group 0-6 and their relative share in these ranges in terms of percentage of population to total population of the country for 1991 and 2001 is also given. It may be observed that the relative share of the States and Union Territories with sex ratio of child population in the age group 0-6, 951 and above has sharply declined from forty five per cent to twenty seven per cent. The number of States and Union Territories with sex ratio of child population below 915 has increased from four in 1991 to eight in 2001. Their share in this category has also increased from about four per cent to about seventeen per cent. Sharp declines have been reported in child sex ratios during 1991-2001, in Himachal Pradesh (951- 897), Punjab (875 to 793), Chandigarh (869 to 845), Uttaranchal (948 to 906), Haryana (879 to 820) Gujarat (928 to 878) and Maharashtra (946 to 917). Are the sharp declines in the child sex ratios indicative of an underlying trend of sex selective abortions in these areas? We may really have to wait for some more data before coming to any definite conclusions in this regard.

Percentage of Sex Ratio	*Number of states/UTs 1991*	*Number of population to total population 1991*	*States/ UTs 2001*	*Percentage of population to total population 2001*
880 and below	8	19.02	7	3.61
881 - 915	8	34.32	4	18.84
916-950	7	15.62	11	47.22
951-985	9	24.59	8	18.09
986 and above	2	5.52	4	11.27

Note: Jammu and Kashmir and the affected areas of Gujarat and Himachal Pradesh are excluded from 1991 and 2001 for the sake of comparability.

The distribution of States and Union Territories by the ranges of sex ratio of population in the age group of seven and above for the years 1991 and 2001 gives the percentage of population to the total population of the States and Union Territories in each of these categories. Although the number of States and Union Territories having sex ratio of seven plus population and their share of population have remained more or less same in 1991 and 2001, the number as well as share of the State and Union Territories in the range 916-950 has increased substantially. The number and share of States and Union Territories having sex ratio 915 and below has shown a significant decline. Keeping in view the dwindling sex-ratio, Govt. of India has recently issued an order to ban the pre-natal sex identification.

CHAPTER 5

Sex Ratio Imbalance

One significant feature noticed in recent census Reports in India is the dwindling sex-ratio. This is due to peculiar social attitude towards females. Besides this due to various social evils like dowry system etc., everybody wishes to have male children. The sex composition of India's population not only shows a shortage of females per 1,000 males, but this shortage has aggravated over time except in 1981. An eleven point decline in sex ratio between 1961 and 1971 was a matter of great concern during the 1970s.

Table 1

Sex Ratio in India

(Female Per 1000 Males) (1901-2001)

Census Year	*Sex ratio*
1901	972
1911	964
1921	955
1931	950
1941	945
1951	946
1961	941
1971	930
1981	934
1991	929
2001	933

Three questions arise in respect of the observed trend:

(1) Have the living conditions of females, particularly the access to medical facilities deteriorated during the 1980s as compared to the 1970s?

(2) Has the sex ratio at birth become more favourable to males in recent years?

(3) Has there been greater underenumeration of females in the 1991 census as compared to the 1981 census?

In most populations in the word the sex ratio tends to be favourable to females even though the males outnumber females at younger ages due to slightly more males being born than females (the sex ratio at birth varies between 102 to 107 males for every 100 females for biological reasons), but this advantage of males gets neutralied by about the age of 20 due to higher mortality among males than females as the latter have more resistance power to diseases than males. From this age onwards females outnumber the males. In India as well as a few other countries of South Asia, West Asia, and Africa, the situation is different due to neglect of females not only in the childhood but at almost all ages. It is noteworthy here that while sex ratio at birth is defined as the number of males per 100 females, the sex ratio of the total population in India ais defined as the number of females per 1,000 males.

Four possible reasons can be there for the decline in the sex ratio over time.

1. International Migration

Statistics on international migration for India are scarce. The volume of international migration in India, compared with the total population, has, however, always been insignificant. Further, there is no evidence at all of female selective emigration or male selective immigration of a magnitude which can affect sex ratio. Hence, this factor is ignored in further analysis.

2. Sex Ratio at Birth

In the absence of any hard accurate on sex ratio at birth (SRB) in India, we have been assuming 105 male births for every 100 female births for the past four decades, if not more. We have also assumed that the same has remained constant over time.

There is, however, a possibility that the SRB has changed over time. Biologically there are more male conceptions than female conceptions. But, at the same time, there are more male foetal losses (due to instantaneous and voluntary abortions) than those of females. This is established by the data available in this regard. Consequently, reduction in foetal losses are expected to raise the SRB. For example, the SRB in Sweden around 1780 was 104.3. By 1980, it increased to 107.2. In United Kingdom the SRB in 1861 was 103.5; it has increased to 107.8 in 1980. In Belguim, the SRB improved from 104.8 in 1900 to 105.8 in 1980, and in France it improved from 104.4 in 1851 to 105.2 in 1980.

In India, the mortality as well as foetal wastage at the beginning of this century was very high due to several factors. We have been able to bring down the death rate to just about 10-11 by the end of the 1980s, the infant mortality rate has also declined from almost 300 at the beginning of this century to 91 by 1989. The "Civil Registration System" meant for recording of each birth and death along with the sex of the child at birth has somehow not worked well in India and one cannot depend on those data. Further, the Sample Registration System (SRS) which has been in operation for almost a quarter of a century now has also not provided this vital information except for the first few years. The SRB in rural India during 1965-67 in the SRS was 107.5. There are some indirect indications that the SRB in India has been rising but it has not been feasible to provide hard data for this argument.

It is necessary to know the impact of rise in SRB on the overall sex ratio of India.

But there are more male foetal losses than those of females due to instantaneous or voluntary abortions. This is established by the data for certain other countries that are available in this regard.

Table 2
Trends in Sex Ratio with 1971 Age Composition and Different Life Tables

	Year Sex ratio at birth										
		108		*107*		*106*		*105*		*104*	
Year	*61-71*	*91-01*	*21-31*	*61-71*	*91-01*	*21-31*	*61-71*	*91-01*	*21-31*	*61-71*	*61-71*
1971	930	930	930	930	930	930	930	930	930	930	930
1976	925	934	928	926	935	930	928	936	931	929	930
1981	921	937	926	924	939	929	927	942	932	929	932
1986	919	940	922	922	943	925	926	947	929	930	934
1991	916	942	920	920	948	924	925	951	929	930	934
1996	913	943	919	919	949	924	924	954	930	930	935
2001	911	944	919	917	950	925	923	956	931	929	936
2006	910	945	917	916	951	924	923	958	931	930	936
2011	908	945	916	915	952	924	922	960	931	929	937
2016	907	945	916	914	953	923	922	961	931	929	937
2021	906	946	915	913	954	923	921	962	930	929	937
2026	905	946	915	913	954	923	921	963	931	929	937
2031	904	946	914	912	955	923	920	963	931	929	937
2036	903	947	914	912	955	923	920	964	931	929	937
2041	903	947	914	911	956	922	920	965	939	929	937
2046	903	947	914	911	956	922	920	965	931	929	938
2051	903	947	914	911	956	922	920	965	931	929	938
2056	903	947	913	911	956	922	920	965	931	929	938
2061	903	947	913	911	956	922	920	965	931	929	938
2066	903	947	913	911	956	922	920	965	931	929	938

Source: Ananthram, S. Doctoral Dissertation.

3. Differential Mortality

Biologically, right from birth onward, females have greater resistance to diseases than males. Consequently, in most societies the overall sex ratio is in favour of females. In India, and in certain other countries, situation is just the opposite due to the neglect of females not only in the childhood but at all ages.

Improved living conditions and the availability of medical facilities throughout the country over the past half a century or more has led to greater survival of both males and females and should have led to narrowing down the gap if not reversing the periling trend. Moreover, with certain social change leading to somewhat greater attention towards the girl child in recent years, one would expect a further narrowing down of male female differentials in mortality.

Table 3

Population of Males and Females and Estimated Decadal Male and Female Death Rates: India, 1901-91

	Population (thousands)		*(thousands)*	*EstimatedDeath rate for previous decade per 1,000*		
Year	*Males*	*Females*	*Males*	*Females*	*F*	*M*
1901	120,911	117,485	3,426	50.4	49.9	-0.5
1911	128,38	123,708	4,677	46.6	48.2	+1.6
1921	128,546	122,775	5,771	52.8	53.5	+0.5
1931	143,055	1135,922	7,133	35.2	37,7	+2.5
1941	163,825	154,835	6,990	27.2	29.4	+2.2
1951	185,528	175,560	9,968	28.8	30.2	+1.4
1961	226,293	212,942	13,351	20.5	23.4	+2.9
1971	283,937	264,013	19,924	17.3	18.6	+1.3
1981	353,324	330,005	23,319	15.0	15.2	+0.2
1991	437,598	406,333	31,265			
1975				15.5	16.3	+0.8
1980				12.4	12.4	0
1984				12.4	12.8	+.04
1988				11.0	11.0	0

The excess of males in India's population rose steadily and rapidly each census year from a difference of only 3.4 million in 1901 to 31.3 million in 1991. This widening gap has accelerated dramatically since 1951 except in 1981 when the pace of increase slightly slowed down.

The data on male and female decadal death rates from 1901-11 to 1971-81 and those for 1975, 1980, 1984 and 1988 indicate higher female mortality but there is no evidence of increasing male and female differential. In fact, there seem to be some narrowing down of the differentials after the 1951-61 decade.

Table 4

Male and Female age values for 1951-61, 1961-71, from the Census Life Tables, and for 1970-75, 1976-80, and 1980-85 from the SRS Life Tables, India

Year	*nqx*	*Male*	*Female*	*Ratio (F/M)*
1951	${}_1q_0$	0.15322	0.13826	0.902
	${}_4q_1$	0.08353	0.10023	1.200
	${}_5q_5$	0.03091	0.0788	1.225
1961-69	${}_1q_0$	0.13013	0.12837	0.986
	${}_4q_1$	0.06777	0.07557	1.115
	${}_5q_5$	0.03506	0.05066	1.445
1970-75	${}_1q_0$	0.12998	0.13505	1.039
	${}_4q_1$	0.07567	0.10301	1.361
	${}_5q_5$	0.02266	0.02613	1.153
1976-80	${}_1q_0$	0.12100	0.12720	1.051
	${}_4q_1$	0.06774	0.08992	1.327
	${}_5q_5$	0.01815	0.02266	1.248
1980-85	${}_1q_0$	0.10416	0.10415	1.000
	${}_4q_1$	0.05337	0.07290	1.366
	${}_5q_5$	0.01637	0.02026	1.238

Sources. Census of India, 1961 census, Life Tables. Office of the Registrar General, India.

We may also examine the pattern of Infant and childhood mortality over the past 2 to 30 years by comparing the qx values over time. The infant mortality rate (qo) has become unfavourable to females. For the other age groups, the pattern in not very clear.

4. Differential Undercutting of Females in the Census

Since censuses began in the last quarter of the nineteenth century, the deficit of females was, plausibly, attributed to incomplete enumeration in the first few census. This was particularly so in the northern and north-western regions of the country. In his 1881 report on the census in Punjab, the Superintendent of Census Operations, Denzil Ibbetson, wrote that a feeling went among the people that by recording sex and age, the British Raj "wanted soldiers for its Kabul campaign and young wives for its soldiers, in so much that in one place the people hurriedly wedded their marriageable girls to save them from impressment". Census officials believe that the tendency towards deferential female undercount because people not reporting about them was reduced substantially in later censuses, particularly after 1931 with the abandonment of the one-night enumeration. Data are not available that can put light on the extent of differential undercount in the various censuses prior to Independence. Estimates of percentage of undercount by sex derived for the post enumeration checks of 1951, 1971 and 1981 indicate that the differential between the male and female undercount has not widened. As the post melioration check of the 1961 did not tabulate the extent of undercount by sex, one can not say that there was no deterioration in female enumeration from 1961 to 1971, specially when there was deterioration in the total count from a net undercount of 0.8 per cent in 1961 to 1.7 per cent in 1971.

An examination of stateless sex ratio over the years indicates sudden fall in the sex ratio in Bihar (from 994 in 1961 to 954 in 1971), in Uttar Pradesh (from 909 in 1961 to 879 in 1971), in Tamil Nadu (from 992 in 1961 to 978 in 1971), and also in Madhya Pradesh and Orissa. If one assumes that the sex ratio in Bihar and Uttar Pradesh in 1971 were the same as in 1961, the country's sex ratio straight away improves to 935. It is, therefore, necessary to examine whether the decline in sex ratio between 1961 and 1971 was basically due to interconnecting of females or due to some other causes.

It appears male selective outmigration from eastern Uttar Pradesh and north Bihar to work in Punjab and Haryana made important impact on the sex ratio, but it should have led to an improvement in sex ratio and not to a sudden decline. There is also no evidence of any large scale epidemic during the 1960s in those areas which would have affected the female population differentially. It is, however, possible that with the availability of greater medical facilities more attention was paid to a boy and very little, if at all, to the girl child. Considering various possibilities, if there was no excessive udercount of females in 1971, the sex ratio in India in that year should have been around 937 instead of 930.

Table 5

Sex Ratio (Females per 1,000 Males): 1951-2001

India/State/ Union Territory	*1951*	*1961*	*1971*	*1981*	*1991*	*2001*
INDIA	**946**	**941**	**930**	**934**	**929**	**933**
States						
Andhra Pradesh	**986**	**981**	**977**	**975**	**972**	**978**
Arunachal Pradesh	*	**894**	**861**	**862**	**861**	**901**
Assam	**868**	**869**	**896**	**910**	**925**	**932**
Bihar	**990**	**994**	**954**	**946**	**912**	**921**
Goa	**1,128**	**1,066**	**981**	**975**	**969**	**960**
Gujarat	**952**	**940**	**934**	**942**	**936**	**921**
Haryana	**871**	**868**	**867**	**870**	**874**	**861**
Himachal Pradesh	**912**	**938**	**958**	**973**	**973**	**970**
Jammu & Kashmir	**873**	**878**	**878**	**892**	**923**	**900**

Karnataka	968	959	957	963	960	964
Kerala	1,028	1,022	1,016	1,032	1,040	1058
Madhya Pradesh	967	953	941	941	932	920
Maharashtra	941	936	930	937	936	922
Manipur	1,036	1,015	980	971	961	978
Meghalaya	949	937	942	954	947	975
Mizoram	1,041	1,009	948	9191	924	938
Nagaland	999	933	871	863	890	909
Orissa	1,022	1,001	988	981	972	972
Punjab	844	854	865	879	888	
Rajasthan	921	908	911	919	913	
Sikkim	907	904	863	835	880	
Tamil Nadu	1,007	992	978	977	972	
Tripura	904	932	943	946	946	
Uttar Pradesh	910	909	879	885	882	
West Bengal	865	878	891	911	917	
Union Territories						
A & N Island	625	617	644	760	820	
Chandigarh	781	652	749	769	793	
D & N Haveli	946	963	1,007	974	953	
Daman & Diu	1,125	1,169	1,099	1,062	972	
Delhi	768	785	801	808	830	
Lakshadweep	1,043	1,020	978	975	944	
Pondicherry	1,030	1,013	989	985	982	

* In Arunachal Pradesh the Census was conducted for the first time in 1961. Hence, sex ratio for the earlier censuses is not available.

The 1991 sex ratio for Jammu Kashmir is based on projected population.

Source: Census of India 1991, Series 1 - India, Provisional Population Totals, paper 1 of 1991. Registrar General and Census Commissioner, India.

In the 1991 census we observe a sudden fall in the sex ratio in Bihar from 946 in 1981 to 912 besides the decline of a smaller magnitude in several other states. If one assumes the same sex ratio in Bihar in 1991 as in 1981, country's sex ratio improves by 3 points to 932. The post-enumeration check, particularly in Bihar, would be able to throw more light on this sudden decline.

Return migrants of the Bihari males during the 1980s from other parts of the country could be one reason for a sharp decline in sex ratio of Bihar between 1981 and 1911. This could be checked when new data on migration become available.

It is noteworthy that the census growth rate in Bihar during 1971-81 as well as during 1981-91 was lower than the natural increase rate (birth rate minus death rate). For example, during 1971-81, the census growth rate was 2.17 per cent per annum while the natural increase rate based on Sample Registration System worked out to 2.64 per cent per annum. Similarly, during 1981-91, the census growth rate was 2.11 per cent while natural increase rate was 2.38 per cent. Consequently, there has been some outmigration of people from Bihar in both the decades. The return migration of males into Bihar from Punjab, Haryana, Assam, and Nepal should have led to higher growth rate in Bihar than the natural increase rate. The male and female census growth rates during 1981-91 are 2.28 and 1.92 per cent per annum respectively, both below the natural increase rate. The differential of 0.36 per cent in the male and female growth rate is another important pointer toward greater female undercount in Bihar in the 1991 census.

There is yet another factor which might explain at least a part of decline in sex ratio. This relates to the nature of commitment of the enumerators in an environment when people hardly bother about any accountability. When an enumerator goes to the household and collects information from the respondent, it is up the him/her whether he/she gives information about each and every member or not. In this situation, if there is female undercount, it is not fault of the enumerator who has made sincere effort. If, however, an enumerator is lax in doing his duty, he begin a local man, knows many details about the residents but more about the males; he may therefore file the information on the basis of his memory. Under such condition, there is every likelihood of missing many females in the census.

An important finding from the data on sex ratio over time is that it is considerably lower in the northern India, say, above the 22 x N latitude while it is substantially above the national average below this line. It possible that the proportion of the sexes at birth may be influenced to some extent by race and it will be noticed that fewer females are born in the north-west of India, where the Aryan element in the population predominates, than in the south and south-east, which is mainly Dravidian. Except in Chennai, where there is probably far less racial difference between the high and low castes than exists in Northern India, it is a matter of general observation that the higher castes, who claim larger infusion of Aryan blood than the lower castes of the same area, have also fewer females . . .". It may also be useful to examine whether there are other sociologically biological factors behind this phenomenon.

CHAPTER 6

Effects of Parental Divorce on Girl Child

Although granting a divorce decree is a legal event, the divorce process has begun with what has been called the 'uncoupling' of the spouses sometime before (Vaughan 1986), and the emotional, social and financial consequences of this uncoupling will affect the spouses, their children, their kin network, their relationships with friends, and their work performance for a considerable period afterwards. Divorce the event and divorce the process together form a turning point, leading to an altered path through life for those concerned for the rest of their lives and beyond through the experience of their children. The study of divorce has developed in depth and bread since the early work in which it was conceptualized as a rare and painful event. The aim of the social and psychological research on this topic 20 years ago was to develop preventive measures at best, or at worst, to improve ways of dealing with such a crisis. As the divorce epidemic of the 1960s and early 1970s gathered pace (the number of petitions granted rose from 25,000 in 1961 to 74,000 in 1971 and 160,000 in 1985), the academic debate broadened in perspective and it was accepted that there might be positive aspects of divorce (Riochards 1987). "Good divorce" was presented as preferable to 'bad marriage' which might involve conflict leading to violence within the home. Concern with individual freedom of action, viewing marriage as a relationship between two people rather than a social institution involving children and others, and the liberating aspects of divorce and single parenthood were emphasized (Itzing 1980).

The development of understanding of the full impact of divorce has been impeded by lack of knowledge of the functioning of continuing married families. For example, we are only just beginning to study the relationship between family and work careers (Martin and Roberts 1984) the allocation of resources between the members of intact families, and those now living in separate households.

The consequences of divorce for children are now being studied over a longer period. These studies cover both the short term and medium term consequences for children of parental divorce and are beginning to differentiate between those children who react relatively well and relatively less well to the experience of parental divorce. Both Wallerstein and Kelly and Guidobaldi et al., for example, found particular difficulties for adolescent boys, who perhaps (given that nine-tenths of children live with their mothers) felt that the absence of a parent of the same sex was a problem; boys also find it more difficult that girls to share and take through their experiences with their peers.

It is also clear that divorce brings serious economic problems, particularly for the mother-headed family. Income falls with only one earner whose earnings are likely to be low, while commitments remain very similar to the level in the intact family. Seventy per cent of single parents in the UK live on welfare income. In France, Bastard ad Vonceche (1988) have studied the attitudes of custodial mothers towards seeking income from various sources, and found an interesting variation between the women who believe society owes theme a living and those who welcome the opportunity to manage their household budget independently, even if the total income is at a lower level than during the marriage. But economic uncertainty faced all the custodial mother families studied in Britain (Eekelaar and Maclean), France (Bastard), USA (Weitzman), Australia (MacDonald), South

Africa (Burman), Belgium (van Houtte), West Germany (Willenbacher), Japan (Minamakata), Poland (Krczewski), and Hungary.

This chapter reviews earlier analyses of the impact of divorce on children in adult life, and then report data about women's experience of parental divorce in a thirty-six year birth cohort study. First, we describe the data from UK cross-sectional and US longitudinal studies. UK data (Eekelaar and Maclean 1986) show clearly a move into poverty for female-headed families after divorce for a small but nationally representative sample of households who had experienced divorce within the decade before interview in 1981. In this small study, only one of the families had been on welfare income at marriage, compared with 11 per cent at separation and 29 per cent at interview. Among female-headed families where the mother remained alone, 56 per cent were on welfare at interview and 15 per cent where she had remarried. We found also a marked disparity in income levels in the one parent families (only 20 per cent were above our poverty line of 140 per cent of supplementary benefit entitlement) compared with 63 per cent of remarried parents and 60 per cent of non-custodial parents. Maintenance or child support payments played only a very small part in the family income of mother-child support payments played only a very small part in the family income of mother-child families and could only benefit the families when the mother herself worked more than part-time, since if she received supplementary benefit (now income support), any child support payments were automatically deducted from the welfare payment.

British Longitudinal Data

Meanwhile, we can make a reliable estimate of the extent of the problems, if any, amongst children of divorcing parents by using data from the MRC National Survey of Health and Development, a study of 5,000 people born in the first week of March 1946. They comprise a social class stratified sample of one-third of all births in that week. Information on a wide range of medical, psychological, social and educational topics has been collected at least every two years in childhood and slightly less frequently in adult life, by health visitors, school nurses and doctors, teachers and youth employment officers, and professional interviewers. The most recent data were collected in 1982 at the age of 36 years when the response rate was 85 per cent.

Findings from this birth cohort echo other work in finding significant excess of emotional disruption among the children of divorcing parents in the short term and the long term as measured by the prevalence of bedwetting at 15 years, which was twice that of those bereaved or in continuing marriages, and of delinquency at 21 years, which was twice as high. Two sets of factors may have been involved. First, the emotional vulnerability of young children at the time of the separation may affect the development of emotional coping processes, and, at the time when this sample were children, such a process may have been reinforced by the adverse expectations about the future of children whose parents had divorced (Wadsworth 1984). Second, the material disruption involved for many children at divorce, e.g. moving house and moving school, may also contribute to the difficulties experienced (McLanahan 1985).

At 26 years the educational attainment of boys and girls from manual and non-manual workers' families was adversely affected by parental divorce before the age of 15, and this effect was greater for those losing a parent through divorce than through death. Perhaps a parent who dies remains an emotional presence in the family in a positive sense—the loss is seen as involuntary, and discussion of the lost parent is likely to be emotionally positive, and to draw the extended family network together. In the case of divorce, the child may be presented with negative images of the absent parent, and lose touch with him or her and with that side of the family. But, in particular, the reason stated for loss is not well understood by the child, and often not discussed with the child who may even, at a young age, fee blame for the event.

This educational underachievement was associated with lower economic activity rates and lower earnings at the age of 36 for men. For example, men aged 36 with divorced parents were more than twice as likely to be unemployed than men from intact homes, and twice as likely to be in the lowest income group (Maclean and Wadsworth 1988). We linked these associations to educational underachievement and lack of feelings of self-esteem among the men.

We hesitated to include women in this analysis as women's careers in the labour market are likely to be more intermittent and complex than men's as a result of marrying and having children.

Educational Attainment

The level of educational qualifications achieved by members of the 1946 birth cohort by 26 years, according to the experience of parental divorce and death and their father's social class at birth. The educational disadvantages for men were clear both for those non-manual and manual families of origin, and this may be one of the important links in the chain that results in economic disadvantages in later life for men whose parents were divorced when they were children. For women from non-manual origins, those from divorced families were over twice as likely to have no educational qualifications than those from intact families. Although this pattern of educational underachievement was also present within the manual group for women from divorced families of origin, the association with parental divorce and death was weaker than for the other groups. This may have been because barriers to educational achievement for the majority of women from manual backgrounds were so substantial that parental divorce was simple one amongst many problems with which to cope. The level of educational qualifications achieved by women was significantly higher for those from both non-manufal and manufal families of origin if their mothers had gone to secondary school themselves, but women from divorced families still had a significantly higher risk of leaving school with no educational qualifications even when the effects of mothers' education and fathers' social class, at the time of the child's birth, were taken into account ($\chi^2 = 5.85$, $p = .01$ with 1 d.f.). Educational underachievement in women from non-manual divorced families may be due to downward social mobility after parental divorce, as well as to the emotional trauma. In contrast, the effect of parental bereavement carried little excess risk of educational underachievement.

Work History

For the men, educational underachievement led to lower earnings and lower labour force participation. We might expect to find a similar effect, perhaps modified by having children, for the women after parental divorce.

Various hypotheses may be offered to suggest that women from disrupted families have a different chance of returning to the labour market after childbirth compared with women who experienced no parental loss. For example, as for the men, their chances may be reduced because of their lower level of educational attainment. On the other hand, these women have been found to marry and start childbearing at an earlier age (Kiernan 1986) and they are on average one year younger at the birth of their youngest child (by 36 years) than those mothers who did not come from disrupted families. This would increase the chances of having returned to paid work by age 36 years. Finally, if women from disrupted families are less likely to be married to men with middle-class occupations, this could also increase their chances of being employed.

The occupations of the women at 36 years, according to the experience of parental death or divorce before 15 years. As there were no significant differences in reasons for not being in paid work, housewives and those describing themselves as unemployed were grouped together. The majority of men who experienced parental divorce and who were not working nor seeking work in their mid-thirties had some history of illness or handicap. It is not possible to distinguish an equivalent group from the large number of women aged 36 years who were not in paid employment. In the 1946 birth cohort there was a tendency for the women from divorced families, and to a lesser extent from bereaved families, to be employed in part-time jobs rather than to remain at home, while the proportions in full-time jobs rather than to remain at home, while the proportions in full-time jobs rather than to remain at home, while the proportions in full-time jobs rather than to remain at home, while the proportions in full-time work were almost identical.

But is experience of parental divorce related to lower occupational status for the women who do work? The proportion of women whose parents divorced and who had achieved occupations in social classes I or II was only two-thirds that of those from intact or bereaved families, and a greater proportion of them were in manual occupations.

Table 1
Work status of partners when survey members were 36 years, and its association with childhood experience of parents divorce or death (0-15 years)

Work Status	*No loss (1)*	*Parents divorced or separated (2)*	*Parental death (3)*
In paid work	95.1	89.0	94.2
Looking for paid work	4.1	5.5	4.9
Not looking for paid work	0.8	5.5	1.0
Total (= 100%)	(1274)	(91)	103
Unknown	(10)	(1)	(-)
Not living with partner	(170)	(9)	(11)

Comparing cols 1 and 2: (x2 = 17.88 with 2 d.f., p<.001)
Comparing cols 1 and 3: (x2 = .19 with 2 d.f., not significant)

This association between the woman's own social class and her experience of parental divorce was still significant even after taking account of two other early life influences, the father's social class and the mother's education (χ^2 = 3.83 with 1 d.f. p = 5.0). Some, but not all, of this associations was due to the different rates of part-time work (which we found earlier to be more common for women at 36 years from disrupted families). But most of the difference in social status was explained by earlier educational underachievement.

Women's own social class provides only a partial picture of their economic and social circumstances and can only be used for women who are at work. We therefore looked also at their husband's socio-economic status. Participation of the current spouse in the labour market did show a significant association with family disruption; men married to women from divorced families were more likely not to be in paid work. As the number were very small, individual case histories were examined. The majority of the men who were not looking for paid work suffered from ill-health which raised the question of whether women from divorced families of origin were more likely to marry more vulnerable men. The small numbers and the limited information available on spouses did not allow us to test this hypothesis.

Family History

For women even more than for men, educational and occupational achievements are interrelated with marriage and fertility patterns and it is not satisfactory to consider one without the other when looking at the consequences of family disruption. The influence of family disruption on this cohort in terms of a lower age at first marriage and starting childbearing, and a higher risk of own marital breakdown for those who married as teenagers has already been found. By 36 years, the excess risk of divorce was not as strong among women from divorced families as it was among men, and was similar to the influence of parental death, whereas men who experienced parental death were no more likely than men from intact families to be divorced by 36 years. For the majority, parental loss through death was the loss of their father, and the different divorce patterns between the sexes may reflect the different meanings attached to that loss by boys and girls. But given the sex and social class differences in age at first marriage, this pattern perceived at 36 years may yet change. We may speculate about a role model effect for men whose fathers left home. Women whose fathers died may try to replace their fathers by marriage, which in turn, may lead to greater marital instability in later years when their husbands fail to match up to the idealised father image.

Table 2

Men's own marital history at 36 years according to experience of parental divorce or death in childhood (men)

Marital history	*No loss (1)*	*Parents divorced or (2)*	*Parentaldeath separated (3)*
(a) Never married	10.4	11.5	7.2
In first marriage	76.3	60.4	76.3
First marriage broken by divorce or separation	13.0	28.1	16.5
First marriage broken by death	0.3	-	-
Total (= 100%)	(1457)		(96) (97)
	Unknown	(3)	(-) (-)
(b) Never married		10.4	11.5 7.1
Married once	81.8	71.9	86.7
Married twice or more	7.8	16.7	6.1
Total (= 100%)	(1461)	(96)	(98)

Women from divorced non-manual families were significantly more likely than their peers from intact families to experience marital breakdown by the age of 36 years.

To explore further these marital, educational and social class differences between women from intact families and those from divorced families, data on emotional difficulties at 36 years were examined.

Table 3

Women's own marital history at 36 years according to experience of parental divorce or death in childhood (women)

Marital history	*No loss (1)*	*Parents divorced or separated (2)*	*Parenal death (3)*
(a) Never married	6.0	4. 0	2.6
In first marriage	76.5	72.0	71.1
First marriage broken by divorce or separation	16.3	23.0	23.7
First marriage broken by death	1.2	1.0	2.6
Total (= 100%)	(1454)	(100)	(114)
Unknown	(-)	(1)	(-)
(b) Never married	6.0	4.0	2.6
Married once	84.9	79.2	82.5
Married twice or more	9.1	16.8	14.9
Total (= 100%)	(1454)	(101)	(114)

The Present State Examination (PSE) was administered to cohort members at 36 years by trained research nurses. This is a measure of current emotional state and the score reflects the number of symptoms that are present across a variety of disorders including anxiety and depression. The maximum score for women at 36 years in the 1946 cohort was 38, although 40 per cent of women have no symptoms, and hence no score.

The mean score for the group of women who had experienced parental divorce was 4.2, significantly higher than the mean score of women from intact families (3.0) [F = 6.68 with 1 d.f p<.01]. This relationship was not changed when taking account of fathers' social class, which was not strongly related to the PSE score. The relationship between parental divorce and emotional state at 36 years remained significant even after taking account of many other early life experiences, such as parents' mental and physical health (Rodgers 1990). Rodgers also found that the PSE score was higher the greater the number of negative life events reported in the previous year, but more negative life events were not reported by women from divorced families of origin and did not account for the association between the PSE score and parental divorce. In contrast, there was no association between parental death in childhood and the PSE score.

For some people, alcohol intake and smoking may increase as a response to stressful life events and we therefore looked at these aspects of behaviour in our sample of women.

At 36 years, cohort members were asked to keep a diet diary for a week. The mean daily intake of alcohol among women who drank that week was 9.46g. similar to the average intake recorded by there national surveys. For women from divorced families, mean daily intake was significantly higher than for women from intact families. The significance of this 'association' was not accounted for the the early life factors of social class and mothers' education. The difference in average intake was highest for women with better educated mothers; in this group, women from divorced families had two and a half times the intake of those from intact families. In contrast, alcohol intake was not associated with parental death in childhood.

Patterns of smoking were also investigated as smoking has also been suggested as a response to stress and because of the social class gradient in smoking. Those who experienced parental divorce or separation were indeed more likely to be smokers at 36 years (45 per cent compared to 32 per cent of those from intact families of origin and 39 per cent from those who had experienced parental death) x2 = 8.38 with

2 d.f. p = .01)

Summing Up

Data on the quality of parental relationships among families where separation did not take place might well have revealed similar level of emotional problems and reduced educational and socio-ecoomic attainment amongst those whose parents had poor relationships. Such a comparison would be particularly useful and would exclude the social and financial impact of divorce. However, the MRC survey does not include such data. It is also possible that these data may now be of only historical interest, rather than useful for current policy formation, as divorce now is more prevalent and less stigmatizing for spouses and their families. However, it is unlikely that the emotional circumstances leading to separation have lessened in their impact on children—and the change in economic circumstances remains as great as ever. In this study, parental divorce had an impact not only in childhood but also in adult life, but the effects were diferent for men and women, and different among women according to their social class of origin.

Women from divorced families seemed as likely as other women to work full-time, but they were more likely to work part-time than to remain in the home. This may be due to economic insecurity in childhood reinforcing a desire for economic independence, strengthened by having seen how mothers can work. It may also be related to their husbands' earning ability, in that these women appeared to marry more often unemployed men, and therefore perhaps needs to work.

The family histories of women from divorced families showed less disruption that for the men - perhaps because life with one parent of the same sex leads more easily to satisfactory family formation than life with on parent of the opposite sex.

Parental divorce leads to more long term emotional and socio-economic disadvantage than parental death confirms earlier suggestions at this is due to the more negative emotional impact of such an event as well as to the greater likelihood of downward social mobility in the remnant family after divorce.

The overall picture is of measurable impact, with different levels of magnitude according to the woman's socio-economic class of origin. The girls from non-manual homes showed a sharper loss in educational and occupational attainment and marital stability as well as increased addiction to alcohol and tobacco.

CHAPTER 7

Abortion Issue and Feminism: A Case of Poland

One issue in particular has produced wide divisions in society and led to highly emotional debates. Here the divisions are largely independent of politics, however attempts have been made to use them for political purposes; it has been suggested that the debate was intended to distract attention from other problems. The event that gave rise to these divisions and discussions was a draft act' on legal protection of the unborn child', proposing the introduction of a complete ban on abortion in Poland and of penalties for both having and performing an abortion.

The draft was submitted to the Seym by deputies of the former administration before the recent democratic elections to the Seym and Senate in June 1989. It provoked not only discussion and controversy, press articles and TV debates, but also street marches and demonstrations. Moreover, it gave rise to the opportunity for increased awareness of the situation and rights of women in Poland, and for some tentative attempts to organize movements in defense of those rights. While discussing the problems related to abortion in Poland, i.e. its legal regulation,the extent of the phenomenon, options about it, the new draft and the ideologies and attitudes of both the pro-abortionists and their opponents, it is essential to bear in mind the situation of women in Poland. This, however, is a very difficult task, not only because of the dimensions and complexity of the problem, but also because of the lack of reliable studies of Polish women's situation. The need for such studies could not even be discussed until recently. One of the many paradoxes resulting from the Communist system of government is that women ostensibly have equal rights combined with their actual exploitation. Under the banner of equal rights for women, the system burdened women with additional duties but failed to grant them any actual rights: this discredited the very slogan used and for some time has deprived the ideology of quality and the struggle for women's rights of its potency.

Situation of Women in Poland: An Overview

Many foreigners coming to Poland have the impression that women in Poland are truly free and enjoy equal rights. Indeed, one could believe this after a superficial examination of the Polish situation. Polish women receive education equal to that of men. There are now some statistics which suggest that they are even better educated than men. In 1987, 30 per cent of the adult population had secondary and higher education; amongst men the proportion was 27 per cent while amongst women it was 33 per cent (*Statistical Yearbook, 1988*). Women's employment is also a mass phenomenon. In 1987, 75 per cent of women aged 25-29 were employed. In practice, however, this does not mean that all the employed women work from choice or want to satisfy their own ambitions or achieve self-realisation through professional work. For many women, employment is simply an economic necessity. Their husbands' low wages are not enough to support their families and the women must take on paid work. The fact remains, however, that the vast majority of women are now employed in Poland, and the percentage of those in education is now greater than that of men. Women also have full electoral rights, and equal rights are protected under the constitution. The question arises, however, of how those equal rights came about and what opinions about them are today.

What was peculiar to the women's movement in Poland

at its very beginning in the nineteenth century, was its connection with the struggle for independence. At the time, that struggle was of prime impotance in Poland, and no group, including the women's movement, could avoid expressing an opinion on it. The first organised group whose aim was the improvement of women's status and education was that of the so-called 'enthusiasts', the best known of whom was the writer Narcyza Zmichowska. The group operated in Warsaw in the years 1840-50. The enthusiasts were engaged in the underground struggle for independence and for that reason suffered political oppression. Most of the activities were imprisoned and exiled by the Russian authorities, thus putting a stop to the group's operation.

In contemporary courses, information can be found about the rather specific role of women in nineteenth-century Poland. In the Russian sector for instance, successive generations of men took part in insurretions for which they were imprisoned and exiled to Russia. The women who were left behind had to take over the responsibility of providing for themselves and their families. Such conditions did not favour the organisation of women's rights movements. But despite the division into male and female roles, the struggle for independence was a common national experience. In those days, women were already taking part in the struggle, joining underground movements and receiving their share of the persecution and repression suffered by those who struggled against the authorities. The division into countrymen and enemies mattered much more than that into men and women.

And yet the first signs of progress towards equal rights for women could be seen in the latter part of the nineteenth century. The first technical school for women was set up in the 1880s and women were granted the right to study at Polish universities in Cracow and Lvov in 1897. The Polish Society for Equal Rights for Women was established in 1907 and, amongst other things, it struggled for the right of women to vote. Women were finally granted that right in 1918 when Poland regained independence; in the first elections to the Polish parliament they not only voted but also ran for and were elected to seats.

Over eighty different women's orgnisations were established in Poland between the First and Second World Wars; there were a variety of types, from professional groups to religious organisations. Women's journals and books intended for female readers were published. Women had their own parliamentary Society, there were women's funds and scholarships and women's club such as the Peasant Women's Clubs organised by the Farmer's Society. At the same time, in the Polish tradition, there was little separation of the sexes. This is illustrated by the absence of clubs from which women were excluded. It is something of a paradox that clubs refusion to admit women have only recently been imported to Poland through the influence of western clubs, even though such clubs are aline to the Polish tradition.

The situation changed radically after the World War II. The 'grassroots' movements were replaced with institutions imposed from without. *'Equal rights for women'* was one of the slogans of the new socio-political system, and its promotion was at times somewhat strange. Fair-haired female tractor drivers smiled down from posters as the symbol of the new equal rights of women who had access to formerly male jobs. A single mass women's organisation, the Women's League, was set up in 1945. Its aims included the promotion of women's professional work, the organisation of assistance in everyday life and educational activities. But the League was an organisation established by a superior authority as the only women's union and it came into being without the involvement of the women themselves. Like many other organisations set up in those days by the new authorities, it was treated as part of the imposed rule, failing to promote the interests of the group it was originally supposed to represent. Such an organisation could hope for no social backing whatsoever.

Various activities at this time were really only window dressing, for example, one or two people with no party affiliation were co-opted to the administration to show that the Party was not the only ruler of Poland; the same was true of token women serving as evidence of women's equality. Such steps only served to discredit movements which used women's rights as their slogans. All activities carried out under that banner were seen as window-dressing, controlled from above and not genuine. The main effect was that women were burdened with much heavier duties. Women were exploited as a cheap labour force taking practically no part in decision-making and government (Limanowska 1989). There were persistent efforts to compromise women's culture, showing it as worse, less ambitious and less progressive than that of men; with time this led to the suppression of such culture. The discrediting of women's right movements resulted in a lack of support and popularity for such movements. Women declared themselves in support of the struggle for the rights of all people, both men and women.

Therefore it is not surprising that foreigners who at first consider Polish women enjoy a lot of freedom need only spend more time in Poland in order to change their opinion altogether, and to see the women as slaves who sacrifice themselves for their families. Women in Poland have jobs, look after the house and raise children and they have no access to organised help: there is a permanent shortage of places in day nurseries and kinder-gardens. Women's multiple duties have been particularly burdensome during Poland's present crisis. The effects on women were discussed at the UN expert consultation Women in Development in May 1989, in Warsaw. It is the women who pay for the crisis: stricen by poverty, the households have to give up various services and women must take over the tasks. They struggle to achieve the least possible reduction of their families' living standards, which, in practice, leads to proliferation of their chores such as queuing for hours, sewing and other additional duties. This extremely difficult situation is not accompanied by any more towards its transformation, but by a passive conviction that nothing can be done, and dignified efforts to cope with the growing burden.

Some achievements of the struggle for women's rights have had rather unexpected consequences. The superficial character and artificial nature of various activities supposedly undertaken in the interests of women has of tender proved them of women's support. But in just one area, the post-war changes seem to accord with the demands of women. That area is the regulations, in force since 1956, concerning the admissibility of abortion. Today those regulations are accused of being too liberal, and struggle is going on to change them.

Admissibility of Abortion in Poland

In Poland, as in many other countries, debates about abortion and the conditions of its admissibility developed during the 1920s. New codes were then prepared to replace the legislation of the partitioning states, still in force in Poland during the first years of independence. At first there were plans to preserve the ban on abortion in the penal code, together with the penalties it provided. When the new draft penal code was submitted for discussion, those who supported the decriminalisation of abortion were very active. Various arguments were used. Some concerned the inefficiency of punishment, the provision in question being 'dead' and seldom applied as most abortions remained secret forever. Others consumed its harmfulness, as abortions were being performed by amatcurs which threatened the women's health, or even their lives. Furthermore, the price of abortion increased due to its illicit nature. Other arguments concerned the lack of effective care during pregnancy and assistance to mothers. It was argued that the birth of a child gives rise to its parents' duty to provide for it; but if they were to be unable to maintain the child, or if that child's birth would result in serious hardship for children already living, e.g. if the mother is employed and maintains the family but would have to quit her job to have another child, abortion should be admissible.

The Codification Commission included the draft code a

provision according to which an abortion performed by a physician to protect the mother's health, the family's welfare or an important matter of public interest, would remain unpunished.

The draft did not please everybody. Some found it to liberal, while others criticized what was, in their opinion, undue limitation of women's freedom. Eventually, the penal code passed in 1932 included a provision stating that an abortion should not be treated as an offence if it was performed by physician to protect the woman's health or if the pregnancy occurred as a result of a criminal act such as rape, incest or underage sex.

The discussion about conditions for abortion was resumed almost immediately after the World War II. The voice of anti-abortionists prevailed. Their arguments were mainly Demographical. The country had suffered great loss of population which now had to be made up. For that reason, some were demanding a total ban on abortion, including abortions performed for medical reasons. According to the chief ideologist of the anti-abortion camp, a physician A.B. Henke MD, the sense of duty to become mothers should be instilled in women even if they have to pay for it with their lives: 'a mother, a pregnant woman, finds herself in the forefront of the fighting line just like soldiers, policemen, doctors and nurses, and should be prepared to lay down her life for the child if necessary (Scientific Session of the Poznan Medical Society 1948). This natalist policy also led to a ban on advertisements which might hider an increase in the population and even to the removal from bookshops and libraries of books dealing with birth control and abortions.

On the other hand, the various arguments in favour of abortion indicate that they spring from broader ideologies and value systems. In the case of opposition to abortion, the ideology have priority to social as opposed to individual interests. In a country exhausted by wars and occupation, the need to increase the population was considered the overriding interests to which the individuals—i.e. women-had to conform even if they were to die in doing so. A similar starting point can be found for the reasoning of other anti-abortionists, including those whose interests were the exact opposite of those of Poland: similar 'social interests' determined bans on abortion in Hitler's Germany and Stalin's Russia. We should stress that such argument are not found in the present Polish discussions, during the present period of high birth rate levels.

The discussions which developed during the political "thaw' which followed the death of Stalin in the mid-1950, a commission was created by the Ministry of Health to examine the implementation of the abortion provisions and to submit its own opinion on that issue. The Commission favoured liberalization of the provisions and extension of the right to abortion. It was argued that preserving the old provisions simply helped to cover up the fact that many people could not afford a large family. It was therefore contrary to the public interest to force women of limited means to have their abortions performed by amateurs at great risk to their life and health. According to the commission, the provisions had proved ineffective and were commonly infringed. The introduction of new regulations was proposed and the new act, passed in 1956, is still in force in Poland today.

The aim of this act is clearly stated in the preamble: i.e. to protect women's health against the effects of abortions performed in unsuitable conditions by persons who are to trained physicians. The act provides a broad description of the conditions in which abortion is permitted. These areas follows: if there are medical reasons: if the pregnant woman lives in difficult conditions; or if there is a suspicion that the pregnancy results from an offence. The act does not, however, provide for the women's rights to make the decision. But in the current discussions, it is stressed that, in practice, the decision depends on the woman alone. This results from broad interpretation of the 'difficult living conditions' clause. Physicians base their decision on the woman's statement.

After hearing it, they decide whether the conditions are sufficiently difficult or not. The enforcement of the act has, in effect, been handed over to the physician who chooses whether to perform an abortion. It should also be stressed that the implementation of the act was liberalized till late 1950s. At first, physicians who decided that an abortion was admissible could not perform it themselves and abortions could not be performed in private surgeries. These restrictions were relaxed in 1959; the doctor who finds abortion admissible is now allowed to perform it and private surgeries can be used. As large number of abortions performed in private surgeries are not registered, this change has resulted in considerable difficulties in counting the number of abortions.

The only indication of probable time limits is a general statement that abortion is prohibited in the case of medical contra-indications. The first document to deal specifically with this subject was a 1981 instruction which mentions a pregnancy of over twelve weeks as an example of a contra-indication.

The 1956 Act was constantly and fiercely criticised in catholic circles. It was argued that human life is sacrosanct and should be protected from the moment of conception. At the same time, fears were expressed about the wider impact on sexual morality. The act, it was argued, lead to demoralization, lax morals, a cynical attitude to love and even to the physical and moral degradation of the nation.

In 1958 the PAX Catholic Association made an appeal to the Seym for the act to be annulled, and to the faithful, physicians and medical staff in particular, for its sabotage.

Discussions intensified again in the years 1980-81. Catholic groups made another appeal for the act to be abolished. Most active in this field were movements connected with the Catholic Church using characteristic names such as Care for Life, Gaudum Vitae or Pro Familiar. They pronounced in favour of the protection of unborn children, explained the harmfulness of abortions and engaged in various activities to support women who were still hesitating over whether to have an abortion or not, such as providing telephone guidance and homes for unmarried mothers.

Criticism of the act at this time did have an effect. In September 1981, ministers' instructions were issued concerning the conditions for abortion. Physicians were required to provide a more detailed justification when allowing abortion on the grounds of difficult living conditions. The basic requirements, however, were not changed. The physician still makes the decision based on the woman's statement. However, the physician was instructed to try to persuade the woman not to have an abortion. The physician must now inform the patient about the harmfulness of abortions and the possibilities of receiving help if she were to decide to have the baby. Those who criticize the act stress the fact that these instructions lack the force of a statute and only affect doctors employed in the public health service. Since most abortions are performed in private surgeries, their range is very limited.

In 1989, the *Anti-abortionists* produced a draft for a new abortion act. The draft Act gave rise to discussions in which highly emotional arguments were used. One of the arguments used against the present act is that it is a Stalinist regulation imposed from without and actually aline to Polish society. It is difficult to tell whether the act was really imposed from without, but its supposed Stalinist nature can easily be examined. We will therefore briefly discuss the Soviet abortion regulations.

Abortion was decriminalized in the USSR in 1920. This was motivated by the wish to protect the life and health of women and the need to protect them from 'greedy extortioners'. The performance of abortions free of charge, by physicians in hospitals, was permitted. Abortions performance of abortions free of charge, by physicians in hospitals, was permitted. Abortions performed by amateurs for profit were prohibited, leading eventually to a complete ban on abortions performed in private surgeries.

In 1936, during the rapid development of Stalinism, abortion was again banned. Only abortions performed for eugenic or health reasons were permitted. Penalties for abortion were included in the penal code.

It was not until after the death of Stalin that these provisions were changed. In 1955, the 1936 Act that banned abortion was annulled. The new preamble justifying abortion mentioned the protection of women's health against the effects of illegal abortions and the failure of the struggle against abortion through offering social assistant and information. Furthermore, the act also emphasized the need to create conditions for the woman's independent decision about motherhood. Thus stress was put on protecting women's right, including the right to make decisions about pregnancy.

It is difficult to say whether other countries in Central and Eastern Europe were influenced by the Russian legislation when liberalizing their own regulations, or whether that liberalization was imposed on them. As we have seen in Poland and elsewhere, between the wars, the trend towards liberalization took place without Society influence. Most countries, namely Bulgaria, Czechoslovakia, Romania, Hungary and Poland, did liberalise their regulation of abortion in the years 1956-57. The subsequent fate of those regulations varies greatly from one country to another. For example, in the German Democratic Republic, the woman's right to make the decision about abortion was held to be one of the conditions of their equality: the woman was to decide about the timing and number of births. Such decisions were treated as one of her chief rights alongside the right to education and professional training and the freedom to made decisions about marriage and the family (1972). In some other countries, such as Czecholsovakia, Hungary and Bulgaria, the admissibility of abortion was limited. The restrictions were justified on pro-natal grounds. The population increase was very low in those countries and the availability of abortions was limited in order to increase the birth rate.

The suggestion that the liberalized abortion act was an

element of Stalinist legislation cannot therefore be confirmed. The question also remains unanswered as to what degree such processes were independent of or were influenced by Soviets liberalization in 1956. Today, however, this question has lost much of its importance.

After discussing the development of the legal regulations now in force in Poland and their rationales, some data concerning the practice will now be presented. Is abortion a frequent phenomenon? What are society's opinions about it? Why do women have abortions?

Abortion in Poland

It is difficult to say how many abortions are performed in Poland each year as many of them are probably never disclosed and registered. It is thought that a number of abortions performed in private surgeries are kept secret by physicians in order to avoid taxes. Such abortions are legal but are not registered and the available statistics only refer to registered abortions.

In the 1980s, about 130,000-140,000 abortions a year were registered in Poland, that is 13.2 per 1,000 women aged 15-49, and 18.2 per 100 live births (still births excluded) (Zielinska 1986).

It is very difficult to estimate the number of abortions which are unregistered, and the data quoted by different sources vary greatly. Some estimate that there are between 55,000-85,000 per year (Klonowizc 1974). The pamphlets published by opponents of the knew draft abortion act estimate the number of women who would be liable to punishment-that is, who have had an abortion—at 300,000 per year. Church groups quote the higher figure, estimating the number of abortions at 600,000 or even a million per year (Primate of Poland in Defence of Life 1982). As can be judged from the data on registered abortions, we are dealing with a steady trend: after the legalization of abortion, the number of cases registered went up rapidly but then became stable after 1970 and has plateaued year after year. Despite the high prices, the number of abortions performed in private and cooperative surgeries keeps increasing. According to the patient, such surgeries offer better treatment, greater secrecy and prompt admission. As reported by a Seym Commission which examined the functioning of the abortion act in 1973, the most obvious impact was on the number of deaths and complications resulting from abortions. After the act was introduced, the number fell drastically, from 255 to 12 deaths per years.

What is the attitude of society towards the legalization of abortion? Studies carried out in the 1970s on various samples show that the number of those who opposed abortion never exceeded one-third of the sample. Those who support the ban are predominantly peasant women, lower educated persons and the elderly. Despite the fact that only a small proportion of women, 0.6 per cent, consider abortion to be morally right, over one-third, 37 per cent, said they would rather have an abortion than an unwanted child. The reason for this is that those who declare themselves opposed to abortion do not think the ban should be unconditional. Their attitude depends on the motives for the abortion. When asking about abortion as a method of birth control, the proportion opposing abortion is high. But the disapproval decreases, or even disappears, if the reasons given for abortion are poverty, a threat to the mother's life, the mother's mental illness or a large family.

The studies of abortion were small scale only. But there are certain common findings. A study of 200 women who had had legal abortion showed the most frequent cause to be difficulties with finances and housing. One should bear in mind that the term 'difficult housing conditions' in Poland may mean that the family lives in a single room or with in-laws, having no hope whatsoever of getting a flat of their own.

The results of a study of 300 illegal abortions which resulted in court cases are more interesting still. The women had illegal abortions for the following reasons: ignorance of the possibility of a legal operation; instigation by another person, often the unborn child's father; and being afraid to consult a doctor. Women may also choose an illegal abortion if the doctor has refused to perform a legal one. These women may be refused for various reasons: the pregnancy may be too advanced; or they may be seriously ill; or they may have had many abortions before; or it may be only a short time since a previous abortion. If a legal abortion is unavailable, women will resort to illegal means. These findings confirm the suggestion of pro-abortionists who argue that women who are intent on having an abortion are sure to find an illegal operation, no matter how dangerous this might be to their life or health.

Attitudes towards abortion have also been reported from a study of professional medical ethics. One of the questions concerned the respondent's attitude towards doctors who refuse to perform abortions because of their beliefs, despite the fact that they realise the danger of pregnancy to the woman's life and health. It should be mentioned here that there is no 'conscience clause' in Polish law enabling a doctor to refuse to operate for ethical or religious reasons. However, in a Catholic society where the church has repeatedly apealed to physicians to boycott the abortion act and the performance of abortion is generally perceived as a sin, one might abortion for reasons of conscience. It appears, however, that this is not the case. A clear majority o respondents, over 70 per cent of a national random sample, considered suc refusal to be wrong, improper or even inhuman. In the late 1960s over 25 per cent of respondents accepted the doctor's refusal. Contrary to our expectations, these opinions were to related to the respondents' age, but rather to their level of education. The higher the levels of education, the greater the proportion of people condemning the doctor's decision. Similar findings were obtained when that same question was put again, in the 1980s, to a different sample of unmarried women aged 17-30.

What is the general opinion about abortion? Does Polish

society believe that the woman has the right to decide whether to have an abortion or not? In a 1988 study of a national random sample, the respondents were asked to express their opinion about a woman who had an abortion because she did not want to become a mother. Most respondents thought the woman was wrong, 70 per cent, as opposed to 23 per cent who believed her to be right. Most of them thought that a woman has no right to make such a decision, 54 per cent, as opposed to 37 per cent who stated that she does have that right. Seventy-five per cent were aware of the fact that the law does not prohibit abortion in such cases; and 90 per cent believed that abortion is a sin.

An attempt was made by the Centre for Public Opinion Surveys, attached to the Committee for Radio and TV, to find out about society's backing for the new draft act which proposes a ban on abortion. Forty-six per cent of respondents supported the new regulation and 44 per cent were against it; 10 per cent stated that they had not formed an opinion. The findings are interpreted as further proof of society's almost equal division into advocates and opponents of the new draft. However, it must be remembered that it was very difficult to get information about the draft. First, there was a delay in publication; and then the only journal to publish it was *Polityka,* a weekly which is rather hard to obtain. The general public may be presumed to have heard about the basic assumptions of the draft, including the prospect of imprisonment for women who have an abortion. It seems doubtful, however, whether it is widely known that the draft provides for no exceptions whatsoever, that abortion is banned even when the woman's life and health are endangered or a grave injury of the foetus has been diagnosed. It may be supposed that, had the respondents been aware of this, they might have answered differently. This is possibly indicated by other findings of the study of a national random sample carried out by the Centre for Public Opinion Surveys; namely that a majority, 59 per cent, of respondents supported abortion in the case of an AIDS infected woman, while only

16 per cent thought that she should have the child. It may therefore be said that Polish society's opinions depend largely on the reasons for the abortion. The draft act, however, submitted to the Seym in recent months, fails to take this differentiation into account.

The Draft Abortion Act

The new draft abortion act, submitted to the Seym by a group of deputies, is entitled 'the act for the protection of the unborn child. Its advocates stress that penal provisions and bans are not its essential part but only consequence of its underlying assumptions. These assumptions include the inviolability of human life, and the distinct nature of the individual from the very moment of conception. Thus, the draft actually grants legal capacity to the foetus from the moment of conception. Once born, the child may demand compensation for injury it suffered as a foetus; but neither the possible kinds of such harm nor their potential perpetrators have been specified. It may also be judged that, with a regulation as broad as this, the child is also entitled to compensation from its mother for any behaviour or conduct that could have negative effects on the foetus. The draft act imposes on the child's parents the duty to care for its whether they enjoy parental authority or not. Parental authority concerns the period from the moment of conception to the child's majority. The duty to render certain services has also been imposed on the child's father if he is not married to the mother: this extends duties he has already under existing regulations. Thus, the draft permits neither the establishment nor the denial of paternity before the child's actual birth. In those cases, the moment of birth still remains the date from which an action can be instituted.

The draft starts with a proclamation of the extensive assistance and care a pregnant woman is to receive. This takes the form of medical care, a pregnancy allowance, the institution of a family advisory service, and a place in a home for unmarried mothers if necessary. The Council of

Ministers of the Polish People's Republic is to be charged with putting this into effect. As stressed, however, by opponents of the draft, these are only declarations, which will be impossible to implement in the present economic situation.

It is the provisions to be introduced into the penal code which have given rise to the greatest concern. The include the following provision, which is unconditional and provides for no exceptions whatsoever. 'Whoever causes the death of an unborn child shall be subject to the penalty of deprivation of liberty for up to three years.' The penalty may be aggravated if threats or deceit were used against the mother; or the court may renounce the infliction of punishment if this can be justified. The penalties for causing damage to the body or impairing the health of the unborn child, and for violating its genetic endowment are rather less severe.

The draft also proposes the introduction of a ban on all experiments and medical interventions in relation to an unborn child, other than those which serve the protection of its life and health.

Ideological and Philosophical Justifications

An individual's attitude towards the admissibility of abortion is usually part of his or her philosophy of life and moral attitude, which will concern a broad range of problems and cannot be discussed separately from a broader philosophy. We will therefore now present the justifications given by anti- and pro-abortionists, in the context of their underlying philosophies.

Opposition to Legal Abortion

In repeated discussions on the admissibility of abortion, the Catholic Church has taken up a position. That standpoint is particularly important in Poland due to the large proportion, over 90 per cent, of believers in the population; the large proportion of the population who attend church, listening to sermons and the Church's precepts, and the attendance of children and young persons at religious instruction. The

Polish Catholic Church has joined the opposition to legal abortion; moreover, during the session of the Seym Commissions that examined the discussed draft, the experts' Team of the Episcopate's Commission for Family Matters pronounced in favour of its introduction.

In recent years, the Catholic Church has constantly attached the legality of abortion. This standpoint was justified in the 'Declaration on Abortion' of 1974, approved for publication by Pope Paul VI. The standpoint expressed in it is derived from natural law. It has been proclaimed in the Declaration that the right to life can be suspended neither by society nor by public authorities: such a right does not result from its recognition by any person or institution but precedes such recognition. Life should be protected and favoured. Admittedly, there are interests which may be more valuable than life: but life is the condition and basis for all the remaining values. The right to live cannot be subjected to any conditions which depend on the length of life.

The Declaration defines some grounds for abortion as 'not always wicked', quoting such grounds as a danger to the mother's life or health, the possibility of giving birth to an abnormal child or a loss of honour or a disgrace. To states, however, 'Never may any of these grounds result in a person's objective right to decide about another person's life, even if that other person has only just been conceived.' The law may renounce a punishment: but it ceases being law if it clashes with what is righteous and just.

The guiding principles of the authors and advocates of the draft act on 'legal protection of the unborn child' are very much the same. As stated somewhat imperiously in the justification of the draft, it is a fact beyond dispute that: 'a human being is a separate individual from the very beginning of his (sic) development, and is autonomous, from the person of his (sic) mother in particular. Life is the supreme value and the carrier of human dignity, irrespective of the stage of development in which the human being finds himself (sic).'It is therefore proposed that 'any act that results in the death of the conceived child' should be treated as an offence. Life should be protected whether it develops in the mother's womb or *in vitro*. According to the authors, the entire contents of the draft follow from the recognition of the foetus as a separate human being from the moment of conception. As maintained, however, by opponents of the draft, the proposed regulation is inconsistent here. For practical reasons such as the inability to acquire proof, it does not permit the establishment or denial of paternity before the child's birth. Also the fact that separate penalties have been provided for abortion is criticized as inconsistent: if life were treated as one and the same value before and after birth, penal provisions that deal with murder should also deal with abortion. But the provisions that deal with murder should also deal with abortion. But in providing for different penalties, the authors are themselves admitting that they treat an individual differently according to whether or not he or she has been born.

The broader ideology underlining the Church's attitude towards abortions quite apparent in the above mentioned 'Declaration on Abortion' among other documents, and in the encyclicals of Pope Paul VI. They deal not only with abortion but also with contraceptives and the freedom of sexual behaviour, as well as the aims of intercourse. As stated in the Declaration, sexual freedom 'is by no means human' if the person believes he or she may enjoy that freedom 'ignoring both the law and the essential orientation of sexual relation on giving birth to life. The Church accepts only a limited range of options for planning the size of one's family using natural methods of contraception only, and excluding not only abortion, but also contraceptives and all methods of artificial birth control. That standpoint can be found in, amongst other things, the encyclicals Homeowner Vitae proclaimed by Paul VI.

The natural methods of birth control only recently officially accepted by the Catholic Church are presented as effective and the only ones which are admissible. The Rev. J. Buxakowski who reported on the Church's standpoint during the Seym Commission, stated that the natural methods of birth control 'are decidedly the safest and most reliable ones, and that artificial contraceptives cannot be compared with them in this respect'. No evidence has been quoted to subtantiate that statement. The reliability of contraception is an essential issue in Poland. The authors of the abortion draft treat a large number of contraceptives as early-abortive and propose that they should be prohibited s such. Besides, the Church's view on this question is widely propagated, during religious instruction and at special course preparing the young for life in the family. The propagation of belief in the exceptional reliability of natural methods of birth control may have far-reaching consequences.

The new draft is closely related to the Catholic philosophy of life and Catholic morals. According to the philosophy, sexual relations should take place between spouses only, and should be aimed at reproduction. Giving birth to children is 'the supreme mission of the woman' and she should be prepared to risk her life or health to fulfill that mission. A very limited range of birth control is permitted based on natural methods only. From the viewpoint of Catholic philosophy, those methods have two virtues: first, they do not interfere with nature and, second, they lead to a periodical sexual temperance which is valued in this moral system as it encourages moderation and control over one's urges. The natural methods are thus presented as highly reliable, but no evidence is given to support this view.

Supporters of Legalized Abortion

During all discussions, the opponents of the draft act 'on legal protection of the conceived child' also pronounce against abortion. It might be supposed therefore that the pro- and anti-abortionists differ not in their respective attitudes towards abortion, but regarding the acceptable limits to be placed on availability. But a close look at the two standpoints demonstrates the more fundamental nature of their differences.

First of all, the draft is blamed by opponents for lacking a positive programme. The mother is to receive support: but in the Polish socio-economic situation, this is not practicable. The draft provides for no educational programme; no activities for the propagation of contraception and no practical measures to help the woman. The only provisions capable of being implemented are the penal ones.

Another reason for opposition is the fact that the draft provides for no exceptions: even the performance of abortions to save the woman's life or health is prohibited. When asked about this question, the advocates of the draft failed to answer explicictly. But in the light of cannon law, abortion is criminal, and the act's criminal nature remains unchanged, no matter how lofty the aim that leads to its perpetration..such as an effort to save the mother's life' (the Canon Code—a commentary, Lublin 1987). If, therefore, the draft reflects the Church's attitude towards this issue, aboritons in such cases would be prohibited. Hence, the opponents of the draft argue that those introducing it are imposing the Catholic philosophy on the nation, irrespective of individual religious beliefs. The ban on abortion to save the mother's life is held to be contradictory to the authors' assumptions. They seek to defend life 'irrespective of the stage of development of the individual in question', as they put it elsewhere, but propose to sacrifice a more developed individual, the mother, in favour of a less developed one, the child, even if the latter might not even be viable.

A further argument concerns the effects of a ban on abortion. It is clear that a legal ban of this kind does not produce the intended effects, i.e. the end of abortion, but has other effects, both unintended and unwanted by the legislator, i.e. the deaths resulting from abortions performed in bad conditions, particularly for women without substantial financial resources.

Yet another argument points to the inadequacy of these legal measures. Even the advocates of the draft, when asked whether they really thought that woman, including those who already have children, should be imprisoned on a large scale, stated that the sentences should not usually be carried out. According to the opponents of the draft, the attempted introduction of the ban reflects the Church's failure in this respect. Despite having widely propagated its view and informed the faithful that abortion is a mortal sin, the Church had failed to achieve its intended results and so now it tries to resort to legal measure which are, however, quit in-applicable to this issue.

Above all, the opponents of the draft demand the creation of a positive programme to prevent abortion. They demand straightforward sexual education for the young, and the accessibility of contraceptives. In Poland, where practically everything is in short supply today, there is also a shortage of contraceptives. According to some statements made during the recent discussions, abortion is practically the only method of birth control which is fully accessible to all Polish women. the women who decide to have abortions are victims of a situation where deficiencies in education and a shortage of contraceptives make abortion the only possible solution. These women, already victims of the system, would then suffer an extra punishment.

Finally, yet another argument appeared, though it has bene used hesiantly: namely, that the woman has the right to make decisions about her own body and about the pregnancy developing in her womb. Some call the ban on abortion a compulsion to have children and a violation of civil liberties. The draft activated various women's groups which started coming out in defence of their own interests. Here the cause of defending women's rights forms a framework within which opponents of the draft operate. But before we consider the still tentative attempts to express that ideology and to create a movement to struggle for its implementation, a certain contradiction must be explained. We being with a question: how is it that in a Catholic country where the faithful constitute over 90 per cent of the population, opinions and action concerning abortion clash so strongly with the Church's doctrine?

Our attempted explanation of this contradiction must begin with the answer to another question: what is the implication of the fact that over 90 per cent of Polish society are believers and define themselves that way? Are they acquainted with all the elements of the faith and doctrine of the Catholic Church, and do they accept the whole of that faith and doctrine? Obviously it is most difficult to find an answer to these questions; but we can try, using research findings. In the 1988 study of a national random sample questions were asked concerning the respondents' belief in god, heaven, hell and the after-life, the last judgment, Satan and sin. Further questions concerned their attitude towards religion. As few as 3 per cent of the sample called themselves agnostics, and 1 per cent failed to gave a decided answer. The remaining 96 per cent stated that they were believers; just 8 per cent were religious but never went to church. Thus, an overwhelming majority in society are practicing believers who therefore also listen to sermons and have the opportunity to learn about the Church's attitude towards various issues. Does it mean, however, that these people necessarily accept all the separate elements of their religion? It appears that the greatest proportion believe in God. 93 per cent, and a large proportion also believe in the existence of sin, 86 per cent. Fewer believe in hell and Satan, 62 per cent and 63 per cent respectively. But 76 per cent believe in the last judgment, 71 per cent in heaven and 68 per cent in the after-life. It appears, therefore, that the fact that a person defines himself as religious is not actually enough to justify the conclusion that such a person believes in all the elements of the Catholic philosophy of life.

Answers to another question asked in the above survey seem more interesting still. The respondents were asked about the observance of religious dictates in the practice of everyday life. The most commonly expressed opinion was that the dictates which one finds wrong should not be observed at all (44 per cent). Some thought that one should ostensibly observe wrong dictates, but that, in practice, they should be circumvented (13 per cent). Thus, over half of the sample, 57 per cent, were of the opinion that the individual should not observe dictates that he thinks are wrong. Less than one-third maintained that such dictates should always be observed, even if one disagrees with them. Compared with the proportion of believers, the latter group is strikingly small.

Polish Catholicism should not be regarded simple. The fact that majority of Polis society believe in God, consider themselves believing Christians and go to church, is by no means tantamount to a readiness to submit meekly to all dictates of religion and the church. Nor is it tantamount to all the faithful having a universal and equally strong belief in all elements of their faith. If one's opinion clashes with a dictate of religion, most state that the dictate should not then be observed. The above findings may at least partly explain the contradiction between Polish Catholicism and the increase in abortion. This does not mean, however, that women who have abortions generally approve of them, or are unaware that they are a sin.

Sometimes these contradictions are explained at the individual level, and the woman's decision to terminate the pregnancy is treated as autonomous and free. In practice, according to the woman's statements, the choice she make is very seldom truly autonomous. Pressure is brought to bear on the woman by two conflicting sets of expectations. One is the Catholic system of values, which not only bans abortion but also prohibits contraceptives, demands a sexual temperance, and the fulfillment of 'the women's mission' that is maternity. The other set of expectations includes sexual values and needs which the Catholic system either ignores or treats very specifically. Such value and needs matter not only to the woman herself, but also to her partners. Faced with an unwanted pregnancy, the woman's environment and partner may influence her decision to have an abortion. Even if he does not demand abortion in so many words, her partner may abandon responsibility, treating the pregnancy and the decision about abortion as the woman's problem only. In this situation, the woman submits to the pressures of life and not of faith. However, this may result in the woman feeling frustrated and being burdened with a bad conscience.

Preparation of the Drafts

The draft act 'on legal protection of the unborn child was submitted to the Seym by deputies. It was signed by seventy-four deputies, of which only eight were women. It gave rise to much discussion and both proposers and opponents tried various ways of expressing their opinions. The draft was also discussed that a joint session of two parliamentary commissions: Social Policy and Health, and the Legislative Commission. The session took place in an atmosphere seldom found in Poland: a group of opponents of the draft picketed the Sey, building, using the slogan' 'Contraception - yes, imprisonment - no'. The session was interrupted to enable representatives of the Commission to listen to the Picket's arguments. The emotional tone of the debates spread to those participating in the session. Apart from members of the two Commissions, the participants included a group of representatives of the Episcopate of Poland.

The two parties used the same arguments to support entirely different standpoints. When the Church party argued that the present act violates women's dignity, opponents of the draft made an identical accusation contending that it is the draft which violates that dignity, treating the woman as nothing but a 'container for the conceived child'. Emotions prevailed over reasonable arguments. Finally, a motion to submit the draft for general consultation in society as a whole was passed. Afterwards, the chairman of the Episcopate's Expects Team, Jerzy Buxakowski, took the floor once again and stated that *'the laws of nature cannot be submitted to any plebiscites whatever...Both abortion and contraception are against the laws of nature, that is of the human body.'* Buxakowski expressed his opinion that the consultations should be carried out in selected circles only, scientific, ethical and the like, and found any other forms of consultation, such as a plebiscite or referendum, to be dangerous as this 'might set people at variance, disintegrated and antagonize society rather than unite it.'

Highly emotional discussions also took place on TV and radio, as well as in newspapers. Representatives of both camps came to the 'open studio' on TV to voice their opinion and the debates dragged on late into the night. The editors of newspapers received hundreds of letters from their readers: they now stress that those in favour of abortion prevailed. In various circles. signatures were gathered in protests against the draft. The writers of such letters were not only female students or intellectuals, but also various groups of workmen. In addition, the Seym, the Spokesman of Civic Rights, the Ministry of Health and other institutions received letters from the public. In letters of another kind, groups of female parishioners protested against young girls' statements on TV which called the draft a reversion to the Middle Ages and an attempted introduction of the inquisition. Both parties to the discussion insulted each other, advocates of the draft calling its opponents murderers and Stalinists, and the opponents arguing that the advocates were trying to impose the Catholic church's attitude upon the whole of society and that they were proposing a return to the Middle Ages and the Inquisition.

The timing of these discussions is important. The commissions examined the draft on 10 May, that is, about three weeks before the elections to the Seym and Senate. The elections were to be the first party free elections in Poland since the World War II, and the debates concerning the draft could be used in a variety of way during the electoral campaign. Indeed, the draft both interested and divided society so much that it could not be left out of the campaign. At many pre-election meetings with the voters, candidates to the Seym and Senate were asked not only about their opinions of the draft, but also the way they would vote in the Seym and Senate if they were elected and the draft put to the vote. Those who asked such questions were not satisfied with evasive replies and insisted on explicit statements. Whatever the actual reply, it always met with a hostile reaction from a part of the audience.

The discussions on the fate of the draft were 'suspended', for the days of the elections, but afterwards the issue returned to the headlines.

The divisions caused by the draft can also be seen in Catholic circles. Such circles are admittedly consistent in their opposition to abortion; but some groups within them also oppose the draft. They believe it should be possible to appeal to the people's consciences, and to the Decalogue in the case of the faithful, but not to penal sanctions, when propagating the appropriate attitude to abortion (Standpoint of the Club of Catholic Intellectuals in Poznan Concerning the Legal Admissibility of Termination of Life Conceived 1989).

It must be noted that not all opponents of abortion share the Catholic Church's opinions about other issues, and their opposition is not always based on the Church's arguments. Nevertheless, the strongest supporters of the draft are found in precisely such Church circles. In the Church, the faithful are taught that abortion is a murder and a sin, and are asked to sign the draft without being fully informed of its contents.

Attempt must be made to answer the question about the broader value system underlying the draft, and the moral approach it represents. Elements of that approach were expressed during the discussion and the introduction to the session of the parliamentary commission. It was held that no action which involves an intervention in the natural order of things can be acceptable. Any such interventions, like abortion or the use of contraceptives, is wrong and sinful. The woman is granted only limited influence over the number of her pregnancies. She may either abstain from intercourse and give up sexual relations, or use natural methods of birth control based on the menstrual cycle. From the moment of conception, the new human being is an autonomous individual and should not be destroyed, even if his further developments bound to result in the death of his mother in whose womb he is developing.

As a result of holding abortion and contraception to be equally wrong, the Church has lost the support of those who advocate a ban on abortion and believe the best way forward to be the development of contraception.

It is also noteworthy that opponents of the draft state during all public discussions that abortion is an evil that should be eliminated from our lives. But they propose entirely different methods for that elimination: sexual education and contraception. It should also be stressed that nowadays contraceptives are very difficult to obtain in Poland. Hence the opinion that if contraceptives were readily available, the need for abortions would disappear or at least be greatly reduced.

The most interesting effect of the submission of the draft to the Seym has been the activation of women's groups needs and even the establishment of women's organisations. This trend is interesting because it is initiated 'from below' instead of being imposed upon the women. Many of the protests against the draft were spontaneous and poorly organised. These included street demonstrations, the signing of petitions and the sending of letters. Some of these actions gave rise to more permanent movements aiming to represent women's interests for example, pamphlets distributed during a demonstration in Warsaw were signed by a 'Movement for Women's Self-Defence' from Bydgoszcz. Apart from information about the draft and the negative effects expected to follow a legal ban on abortion, the pamphlets contained an appeal for active steps to be taken, and a description of the situation of women in Poland: 'We are overcharged and overworked but we never rebel—and that is why we are not respected.' The pamphlets exhort women to take part in demonstrations and to protest by any means possible. The draft is defined as a violation of women's dignity and humanity, and a precedent which could lead the way for further violations of privacy in the future. Another movement which has recently applied for registration is the Polish feminist association. For this group, the draft and events associated with it provided the impulse to become better organised.

Thus, there is evidence that the draft encouraged women to establish movements top provide education, to formulate their problems and to campaign for their rights. The opponents of the draft stress women's rights, particularly the right to make decisions about their bodies. Since a human foetus cannot grow entirely outside the woman's body it can not be considered an absolutely autonomous and independent being, in whose favour the woman should resign her right to make decisions about her own body and even endanger her life for health. Naturally, she may well decide to take the risk—but nobody should have the right to force such a decision upon her, and she herself should never be punished for deciding against it. According to this standpoint, abortion is either the woman's right, or at least a 'lesser evil', lesser than the woman's death, the birth of a disabled or sick child, one infected with AIDS for example, or the birth of a child whom nobody loves and nobody wants to raise from the moment of its birth.

The conflict between these two points of view still cannot be resolved. A woman who decides to have an abortion today makes two different decisions: one concerning the removal of the foetus from there womb and the other concerning the destruction of that foetus. A separation of those two decisions will soon be technically possible the woman's decision concerning her own body, a removal of the foetus, will not be tantamount to destroying that foetus and will not necessarily involve its death (Tushnet 1984). But for the time being, it is still impossible to separate those two rights: that of the woman to make decisions about her own body, and that of the new human being to live. Today if a woman wants to terminate a pregnancy, only one of those rights can be observed: there is no way of settling the conflict between them. Law has to choose one of the two options, compromise is impossible.

It is doubtful, however, whether the conflict we are now facing will be solved after the two rights in question are separated: the women's right to make decisions about her body. Hopes to this effect seem rather illusory, as do the hopes that the accessibility of contraceptives might solve the problem of abortions in Poland; they have already proved false in the USA where contraceptives are easy to obtain. However, it may be supposed that the accessibility of contraceptives might at least reduce the number of abortions.

But can the problem of women's rights be separated from that of the child's rights at all, even if such a separation becomes imaginable in the biological sense? The answer seems to be: no, or at least such a separation will not be possible in Poland in the foreseeable future. Admittedly feminist in public. However, the traditional model of a 'woman's role' in Polish society has changed very little. According to this model, women are expected to sacrifice themselves for their families, and this become particularly important in these days of economic crisis. This model still influences young people. Earlier students of secondary schools aged 16-18 were asked about their conception of a modern man and a modern woman. Admittedly the sample was rather small, only thirty-three persons, but the findings are significant. It appears that a modern man is simply an ideal man. Instead a modern woman is an independent professional who develops her interests, is the man's equal and is smartly dressed and well groomed. But nearly all respondents—girls as well as boys—state that the ideal women should not be all that modern, at least in the current difficult conditions. The respondents stressed the multiplicity of the woman's duties, her specific role in the family and her dilemma resulting from the impossibility of reconciling work with family roles. Hence the belief that a modern woman should be single. When asked about a conflict between the two groups of roles, all girls gave priority to the home and the family rather than to professional ambitions. It is rather striking that the young generation can think of no way of solving that conflict and perceive the woman's renouncement of their extra-familial aspirations as a necessity, and her role within the family as the paramount one. It seems that the feminist movement in Poland still has a great deal of work to do.

CHAPTER 8

Social Policy and Feminist Research

In social policy, however, the feminist intervention has been focused almost exclusively upon redefining the content of the discipline, and making issues of gender more central to it, but has paid rather little attention to issues of method. Although feminists have achieved some considerable success in these endeavours we believe that it is important to consider whether our impact upon the study of social policy might be advanced further by paying more attention to issues of method in feminist research. The central question which needs to be posed in this: Are there some ways of doing research in social policy which are more conducive than others to making visible (i) women's needs and interests and (ii) the importance of gender relations in welfare provision?

This discussion is structured around three main themes which are prominent in the literature on methods in feminist research:

(1) What methods make gender issues most visible?

(2) Who is research 'for'?

(3) The relationship between the researcher and the researched.

Whilst all three are inter related, it is useful to consider them separately in the first instance. They do not exhaust the range of issues about feminist research practice, but they offer a good basis for exploring the potential for transplanting these debates into research on social policy.

Visible Methods of Gender Issues

One of the main themes of the feminist debate on research method shows concerned the relative merits of quantitative and qualitative research, with a major emphasis being upon the value of small-scale, qualitative methods for research which seeks to make visible the needs and experiences of women.

Strong and influential arguments in favour of qualitative research can be found in a variety of places. The case depends not only upon the utility of qualitative methods, but also on a critique of more conventional approaches, especially the large-scale survey. The case against survey methods, in particular, rests partly upon technical and partly upon epistemological grounds. The technical arguments are concerned with the artificial nature of the way in which questions are asked in surveys, and with the meaning of the data collected by these means. These technical arguments are not really specifically feminist ones, although one of the most influential statements of this position is to be found in Oakley's (1981) work where she does cast this in the context of feminists debates. She argues that the survey researcher's belief that people can be interviewed in a totally 'objective' way, with no interventions on the part of the interviewed and keeping the data bias-free, just does not stand up to the reality of interviewing in practice. Similar points have been made by other writers on methodology who were not taking a feminist standpoint.

However, when it comes matters of epistemology, questions raised by feminists are distinctive. One of the most cogent statements is to be found in Hilary Graham's (1983) article on women and the survey methods, which is given a title which neatly encapsulates her position: 'Do her answers fit his questions?' the argument here is that the knowledge base of social science disciplines has male bias built into it in a strong sense—it reflects the way in which men see the world, how they view their own and women's place in it, what they assume to be normal and abnormal ways of living. The feminist critique of the content of social science disciplines begins from this position; the argument of writers like Graham is that we should be considering how far this male bias has infected the process of generating data and the methods by which this is done. A particular target of feminist criticism has been the survey method. Since it is also a method used commonly in social policy research, it is important to be clear about the nature of such criticisms. Again it is useful to distinguish between the technical and epistemological levels, although the two are, of course, linked.

More technically, the case against the survey is sometimes made by feminists on the grounds that surveys typically study either households or individuals. If the household is the unit of study, this emphasises the divisions between households rather than within them—a serious problem in any work which is about household resources, because it requires the researchers to make the assumption that all members of the household benefit equally from resources coming into it. Where individuals are the unit of study, the web of relationships in which women are involved, and which are so central to the organization of many women's lives, are obscured. In either case, the significance of gender relations in social life is rendered invisible. Though a significant criticism against any survey which does obscure gender in this way, in a sense this point is more technical than fundamental. It does not call into question the basic concept of a survey and it is possible to take it on board in the process of survey design. In this context, it is helpful that major national surveys such as the General Household Survey and the Family Expenditure Survey—both of which are used extensively in social policy research—collect data in a form which enabled it to be analysed either in household or in individual units.

A more fundamental criticism against surveys is epistemological rather than technical in nature. The argument here is that surveys try to find out about people's lives in ways which reflect women's experiences very inadequately.

The survey method assumes that social life can be studied through measurement, and that the principal means of gaining measurable data is through putting experiences into words: 'What can't be put into words in an interview or on a questionnaire can't be recorded and can't be studied'. From a feminist perspective, it can be argued that women's experiences typically cannot be easily verbalized in this ultra-rational and objectified way and that social scientists who wish genuinely to under and women's experiences need to listen to women in a different kind of way.

The argument that quantitative methods in general, and surveys in particular, represent a distortion of women's experience has been very influential among feminists. However, it is by no means accepted universally that this should lead to a complete rejection of survey methods. Some feminists have made a strong case that quantitative research has positive value for feminists in certain contexts. There is no doubt that this is true. Clearly, a piece of research like the Women and Employment Survey does ask questions informed by an undertanding of women's lives and gives authoritative data about their distinctive and inferior place in the structure of employment. In that sense, it is extremely useful in making visible certain aspects of gender relations. It has been influential in writing on social policy, as elsewhere.

However, it is equally clear that such work does not exhaust the range of questions which feminists would wish to ask about women's experience of employment. A good illustration of how different methods can open out our understanding of gender issues can be found in Sheila Cunnison's (1986) study of the work of sheltered housing wardens—a topic which is highly relevant within social policy, since women working for low wages in effect sustain whole sectors of welfare provision. Her work arose out of an interest in trade unionism, and she was concerned to undertand how it could happen that women working as wardens accepted terms and conditions which would have been out of the questions in another setting such as a factory.

They were one call twenty-four hours a day, received no extra pay if they were called out during the night and were expected to carry on their normal duties whatever else had happened. Not only did they accept these expectations, but they frequently went well beyond them, performing domestic and nursing tasks for residents which fell outside their job descriptions.

Cunison poses the question 'Why do women consent to this apparent exploitation?' In answering that question, she contrasts two different concepts of the motivation for work, one industrially based (you only do what you are paid for) and the other based upon women's work in the family (you respond to other people's needs without consideration of gain). Sheltered housing wardens, she argues, experience their work in the latter rather than the former way, partly because it is literally based 'at home' (since most live on the job) and easily become an extension of their domestic role. She arrives at this conclusion via research which depended upon a range of methods, mostly qualitative: semi-structured interviews; further meeting with wardens and unstructured interviews; regular visits to housing schemes; and observation of various kinds, including following wardens around for a whole day.

Cunnison's work affords a good example of how systematic, detailed study of a qualitative kind is capable of making visible women's experiences, and of understanding what meaning those experiences have, in a way which cannot be addressed in a survey. Large-scale surveys are extremely useful for demonstrating that women's exploment is concentrated in certain sectors—including low-paid sectors of welfare provision—but it you wish to understand how and why it is possible for our society to go on relying upon the exploitation of women's labour to sustain whole sectors of welfare provision, you really are asking a different kind of question and need different methods of investigation to answer it.

This example is just one of the many which we have

chosen to illustrate why feminists who work in the field of social policy might pay more attention to questions of method. We should spouse a single 'correct feminist method'. But I do believe that it is important to consider the potential of the variety of techniques available for illuminating the kind of questions which we wish to ask, and to think more systematically about how they can be deployed.

In particular, we trust that there is space for a more sustained development of feminist work which focuses upon issues of experience and meaning in the context of social policy. Of course there are some precedents for this. In the inter-war period, feminists who were concerned about the living conditions of working-class women produced some very interesting work based upon informal interviews, diaries and letters—the very stuff of qualitative research. Clare Ungerson's (1987) study explicitly tries to use qualitative methods to illuminate policy issues. However, such examples are relatively rare and authors tend to feel the need to justify their approach to a social policy audience. In addressing more explicitly questions of method, feminists could put this kind of research on a more secure footing.

Who is Research for?

The concept of feminist research implies renouncing any claim that social research can be and political activity. The political commitments of the researcher are intrinsically woven into the activity of research. The literature on feminist research uses as a key criterion of good work that the research should be 'for' women, in a strong sense.

This positon is set out well by Harding (1987), in the introduction to her collection of articles on feminist methodology. The case starts from the recognition that all social science knowledge has tended to have a built-in male bias, and, consequently, our very under-standing of the social world comes through men's eyes. The argument for counteracting this amounts to much more than an exercise in which women are 'added in', but the overall picture is left essentially unchanged. It is important that the whole picture should be redrawn so that social knowledge, especially of a kind which could be influential in shaping social policies and changing social institutions, should reflect the interests of women. Harding (1987:7) puts it:

> Women should have an equal say in the design and administration of the institutions where social knowledge is produced and distributed for reasons of social justice: it is not fair to exclude women from gaining the benefits of participating in these enterprises that men get.

Equally with these arguments about epistemology, there are overtly political issues about the role of the feminist researcher and the commitments of sisterhood. At a minimum, all feminists would agree that women are discriminated against, excluded and oppressed in our society. Anyone claiming the feminist label would be committed at a personal level to bringing about some change in that situation. But how far should such commitments enter into the professional business of conducting research?

Clearly, there are different possible views on this, and many feminist social scientists would reject a stance in which research becomes simply an extension of other political activities. On the other hand, few would feel comfortable about producing a price of research which was actually going to damage the interests of other women. Presumably, somewhere between those positions is where most feminists would want to locate themselves, but working that out is not easy. Even meeting the minimum criterion of not damaging other women's interests can be more difficult than it seems.

Again, these debates are not exclusive to feminist writing but they are given a particular slant and importance in this context. They clearly ar every pertinent to work on social policy, where research often is oriented towards some kind of policy change, and where therefore the possibility of damaging women's interests is a real one. More generally, the fact that it is more often women than men who are on the receiving end of social policy means that the idea that feminist research should be research 'for' women has particular resonance.

A good example of a piece of research which is specifically 'for' women is the community study of male violence conducted by Hanmer and Saunders and their colleagues (1984). The researchers set out to uncover the extent of women's experiences of violence both inside and outside the home, and their work is geared to practical action and policy proposals. They chose the method of intensive study of seven streets in inner-city Leeds and, through patient exploration with sympathetic interviewers, documented just how widespread is women's experience of violence and the threat of violence. Their work had an interesting impact upon debates in criminology, since the levels which they documented were very much higher than those found in the British Crime Survey, which was being conducted at the same time.

This piece of work is very clearly 'for' women in a variety of ways. Not only does it make visible women's own experiences, in an aspect of their lives which normally is quite literally concealed, but also the researchers are committed housing their research to help women change their own situation. Their book thus contains simple, clear instructions to community groups on how women can conduct a similar survey in their own area and what they might do with the findings.

This approach to research to research may well feel comfortable from a feminist perspective, but, of course, researchers who take this route often find themselves subjected to criticism from colleagues who believe that research should be political and value-free. These arguments about the nature of research are not specifically feminist ones, although feminist researchers need to be on top of them, and to know that the grounds on which we operate can be defended intellectually.

Relationship between the Researcher and the Researched

The idea that feminist research should be 'for' women leads naturally to a reconsideration of the relationship between the researcher and the people who are the subjects of the research. The key themes here are: personal identification, lack of exploitation, eroding the hierarchical relationship.

One of the most well-known feminist statements of this position is to be found is Ann Oakley's (1981) discussion of her research on motherhood, in which she argues that the idea that a researcher can maintain an objective distance from her subjects is not only unrealistic, but also—from a feminist perspective—politically unacceptable when women are the subjects of the research. Oakley rejects the conventional idea that a researcher should maintain social distance, should not be prepared to enter into informal discussion with subjects, and should retain complete control over the interview process. She argues that this creates a hierarchical relationship in which the researcher invests none of herself but expects other women to lay open their own experiences. A feminist should not be in the business of 'objectifying her sisters.

Moving even further away from the idea that research should be an entirely objective activity, in which the process is not contaminated by interventions from the researchers, Liz Sternly and Sue Wise (1983) present a strongly argued case that feminists should use their own experiences as a key research resource. The case for so doing depends partly on recognizing that not only is all social knowledge necessarily constructed out of personal experience (men's as well as women's), but that women are in a distinctive position in having to construct new perspectives upon the social world, to counteract the orthodox views which reflect the life experiences of men. Sue Wise (1985) has provided an interesting example of using her own experience as a research resource in her discussion of becoming a feminist social worker. Another important exponent of a similar position is the Canadian feminist Dorothy Smith, who argues that the experience of being a social scientist is necessarily different for women and men, in a fundamental way, and therefore that women social scientists have to draw upon their own experiences and understandings of their world in order to be able to reshape social knowledge.

The personal identification of women with the subjects of their research, and the use of their own experience as a legitimate way of pursuing it, are theses which have just begun to creep into the feminist literature on social policy. In Clare Ungerson's (1987) study of informal careers, an explicit attempt is made to link the researcher and the researched. In her introduction to this work, Ungerson writes of her experiences of informal care within her family, of her concerns about her own responsibilities in this matter, and about how this influenced her both to undertaken research in this area, and to conduct it in ways which would make people's experience visible.

Ungerson's approach is notable because it is still rather unusual in the literature on social policy research. For the most part, these issues are not discussed, although one suspects that this type of research may be more widely practiced than it appears. The importance of confronting these issues in the context of social policy research is obvious, however. The arguments for not objectifying your sister have particular relevance when research is being conducted on women who are in the weakest and most vulnerable positions—which is frequently the case in social policy research. At the same time, this alternative model of the relationship between the researcher and the researched does depart quite significantly from conventional notions of the research process and raises questions of politics and methods in their sharpest form. If this model is to become the orthodoxy in feminist work in social policy, it is important to be very clear about the intellectual, political and ethical grounds upon which research is being conducted.

Feminist Research as a Discipline Social Policy

The aim in raising these questions is to promote more debate among feminists working in the field of social policy about issues of method. It is quite properly a matter of debate among feminists as to whether we should be largely favoring qualitative methods, practicing research which is 'for' women, and developing less hierarchical models of research practice in which our own experience is a prominent feature. These are all issues on which it is perfectly legitimate for feminists to take different positions. My main point is that they should be debated by feminists working in the field of social policy, rather more than they have been hitherto.

To conclude with the observation that one of the main reasons why this has not happened so far is, we suspect, that social policy as a discipline—or area of study, for readers who prefer this formulation—in general has paid much less attention to methodological issues than have the social science disciplines upon which it draws. Although it has a strong empirical tradition, for the most part issues of method have been tested as technical questions rather than matters for intellectual debate. As a consequence, certain ideas about what constitutes 'proper research', and what should be its relationship to social policy, have held sway in a rather unexamined way. These ideas do not accommodate very easily the kind of feminist perspectives upon methods which we have been discussing. In raising issues of method to a higher profile within the discipline, feminists would be making a contribution to its advance on a broad front.

CHAPTER 9

Gender Policies and Programmes Functions

Successful gender planning depends not only on an appropriate problem analysis, and policy formulation but also on an adequate methodology to implment the policy. Over the past decade professionals working on WID issues have clearly articulated the constraints and opportunities in institutionalising gender planning within existing organizational structures.

To utter dismay, far less attention has focused on the operatonalisation of gender into current planning practices. Traditionally, operational procedures in the planning process have been identified as the 'technical' domain of planning, in which the major problem identified has been a lack of adequate procedures. The response by those involved in WID issues over the past five years has been to ensure that WID policies, programmes and projects have been developed, along with associated planning tools such as guidelines, manuals and checklists.

It is only recently that gender planners have realised that the problem no longer relates principally to a lack of gender policy, or to partially formulated gender policy. The rigour of current gender diagnosis and analysis has helped to ensure that 'technically' such policy is becoming increasing sophisticated. The most important problem now is the inability to translate gender policy into practice. Why does this so frequently fail to occur? Why does the content of WID/ GAD programmes and projects of soften change during the implementation process? These are the questions that need to be addressed.

Policy

Since colonial and post-colonial governments first identified the problems of Third World, 'low-income' women as a policy concern, many types of interventions have been designed to help them. However, until recently there has been very little systematic classification of these various policy initiatives. It categorised five WID policy approaches—on a continuum from welfare, through equity, anti-poverty, and efficiency to empowerment—and evaluated each in terms of the roles recognized and gender needs met.

The operational procedures and levels of intervention associated with each policy approach are not necessarily similar. For example, the early welfare approach did not articulate itself as WID policy as such. Ministries of welfare or charitable groups made interventions at programme or project level. They targeted 'vulnerable' groups that included women, rather than specifically targeting interventions to women. The first defined WID policy, at donor level, was the 1973 Percy Amendment to the US Foreign Assistance Act. So was its particular focus on top-down statutory intervention at policy level to improve the position of women through legislation.

Despite the apparent limitation of equity as policy approach, its importance lies in the fact that it was the first approach to highlight the need for the identification of policy direction through a formulated WID policy. This is the first stage in an gender planning process. It is now broadly recognized that a clear, precise and unambiguous policy-level statement of the importance of WID provides the starting point for operatonalising WID concerns. At the same time it is important to realise that the particular policy approach to WID adopted, and consequently the content of such policy, may differ widely.

Experience of the UN System

Following on the formulation of WID policy has been the development of plans of actions and sets of guiding principles. The purpose of these has been to define more specific goals, priorities and strategies for the inergration of WID issues into particular policies, programmes and projects. Several planning initiatives by the United Nations, linked to both the 1975 International Women's Year, and then the 1976-85 UN Decade for Women, illustrate these changes. They reflect not only increasing levels of professionalism, but also changes in planning methodology.

The UN World Plan of Action for the Implementation of the Objectives of the International Women's Year (UN 1976a) was an early initiative intended to provide guidelines to national governments for action over the ten-year period up to 1985. It was the General Assembly that proclaimed this the Decade for Women, with its objectives equality, development and peace. Produced at a time of widespread legitimacy of national plans, it is a classic example of the blueprint 'survey-analysis-planning' plan to introduce women's issues into the political agenda. The methodology comprised three clear stages: of survey collection of data on women, its analysis, and the provision of recommended solutions. The Plan of Action outlined proposals for general national policy, as well as identifying nine key areas for action, with recommendations addressed primarily to government. For example, in the education sector the survey revealed that 'in many countries women and girls are at a marked disadvantage'. The analysis showed that 'this constitutes a serious initial handicap for them as individuals and for their future position in society. The action proposal included the provision of 'equal opportunities for both sexes at all levels of education and training according to national needs and international standards'.

In each sector the Action Proposals provided an electric checklists of measures without setting gender objectives or indicating the entry strategy for their implementation. Some measures advocated were for such practical gender needs as adequate training or child-care facilities.. Others, intended to reach controversial strategic gender needs such as equality of opportunities in education and equal pay rights, were unlikely to be implemented in practice.

The UN Plan of Action imported a model for many governments to develop their own national policy statements and plans of action. Jamaica, for example, was one of a number of Caribbean countries that extended its national policy statements to include not only general principles but also immediate goals and proposed measured. In each case it identified the responsible agency. Thus, in the Jamaican Bureau of Women's Affairs *National Plan of Action*, goal number 5 states:

> recognizing that the evidence of physical and sexual abuse within families and societies is increasing—the government will pursue means of providing adequate protection and means of redress to women and children who are victims of family violence, incest, rape and sexual harassment. (Government of Jamica 1987:17)

It then identified several important constrains to achieving this goal, including the fact that social attitudes condone physical abuse within the family. The proposed measures included the implementation of an act for the prevention of abuse to women and children to be administered in the family court. The Ministry of Labour was identified as the agency responsible for this measure (Government of Jamica 1987). However, further stages in the implementation process were not outlined, which raises the question whether these measures were seen simply as procedural in nature.

Such policy initiatives have been important in practice it has provide very difficult to implment many recommendations. One negative outcome has been that this has often serviced simply to reinforce the prevailing cynicism as to the relevance of gender issues to main team national planning. This manifests itself in hostility of the opposition, and the despair of women's organizations, who have lobbied long and hard to get such issues on to the agenda. To what extent is the planning methodology responsible for this problem?

In their revaluation of the Women's Decade, Tinker and Jaquette commented that it not only 'promoted and legitimised the international women's movement'; it also 'required attendance by governments at the three world conferences elevated women's issues to the level of international diplomacy' (1987: 419). A third very important effect was its influence at the international level on planning procedures to operationalise gender concerns. The 1985 Nairobi Conference recognized the limited impact of the Plan of Action during the decade in terms of its goals of equality, development and peace. Consequently the Forward Looking Strategies (FLS), adopted by 157 nations at the conclusion of the Nairobi conference, provided a far more specific set of guidelines and recommended strategies for adoption by UN member states. It was produced as result of comprehensive surveys and questionnaire completed by all member states on progress and obstacles to women's development. It outlines concrete proposals and actions followed between 1985 and 2000 and makes impressive reading, containing as it does a substantial agenda relating not only to practical, but also to strategic gender needs. The FLS alludes to the essentially political nature of the planning process.

However, as a UN document it is limited in its ability to set specific goals and targets, or to define entry strategies. it therefore, confines itself to putting into place a few internatioal structures to monitor progress, and thereby indirectly exerting pressure on national governments. The focus for WID in the UN system is based at the Division for the Advancement of Women in Vienna. It monitors the implementation of the FLS to the year 2000 by preparing annual reports on WID progress for the Economic and Social Council of the UN (UNCSDHA 1989).

Finally, at the UN level it is necessary to mention the 'Convention on the Elimination of all forms of Discrimination

Against Women'. This is the most comprehensive international legal instrument dealing with the rights of women, now ratified by some ninety member states. Unlike other items agreed by consensus at the UN assembly, ratifying this document means that a country has a legally binding commitment to work for the elimination of discrimination against women (Commonwealth Secretariat 1988b). The Convention requires that governments set up national legislation banning discrimination. Some thirty articles outline the international principles to implement equality in areas relating to political rights, pubic life, education, and pay, maternity rights, social services and child-care provision. The Committee for the Elimination of Discrimination against Women (CEDAW) supervises the implementation of the Convention. This is undertaking through monitoring and reporting procedures, requiring ratifying nations to provide reports at stated intervals.

The reporting procedures of both the FLS and the Convention have resulted in sophisticated gender diagnosis on a wide range of issues relating to the status of women. This may be their greatest achievement. Diagnosis is under taken on a four-year cycle and, consequently, has the potential for integration into national planning cycles. Since national women's bureaus have responsibility for the data collection, this provides the opportunity for close liaison and collaboration with other ministries.

Despite such measures, however, few countries have integrated gender into national development policy or planning procedures. In both the FLS and the Convention, government's participation in monitoring procedures is voluntary. The evidence to date shows that many fail to respond promptly, if at all, while many countries have yet to ratify the Convention. As INSTRAW (1988) has commented, it is only when women's organizations and others begin to monitor the work of CEADAW that the Convention will become a powerful tool for eliminating discrimination. Even in countries working to achieve absolute equality in the law, there is a wide gap between *de jure* equality and the actual state of affairs (UNCSDHA 1989).

From WID Mandates to Project-cycle Handbooks

The UN experience illustrates chances in planning procedures at the policy level, particularly during the 1975-85 period. This is applicable to an international institution with a mandate to monitor progress globally. Complementary to this is the experience of the donor community, discussed here in relation to the OECD countries. Particularly during the 1980-90 period, these countries had an impressive record in the development of complex planning procedures, and detailed tools to ensure that different stages in the planning process operationalise gender concerns.

The first critical stage in the formulation of WID policy is when organistions recognise the limitations of their gender-blind procedures and establish a *WID-Mandate or Policy.* All nineteen members of the OECD's Development Assistance Committee (DAC) comply with the requirement that WID policies should be explicitly based on specific mandates. All therefore have such a document. This is a legally binding policy document, adopted at a high level, to show political commitment. Within its general guidelines, different options follow. These range from parliamentary law (Italy and the United States), to ministerial directives, to internal guidelines emanating from the ministry or agency responsible for development cooperation (adopted by all other OECD countries). The scope of mandates varies considerably. Canada, for example, has one of the more complex mandates. An extensive policy framework defines the scope of the WID mission assigned to CIDA, as well as the orientation, operational objectives and strategy.

Within such mandates different approaches to WID reflect complex internal political processes undertaken to ensure that such a mandate is adopted. It also reflects the fact that policies themselves often are redefined over time. Within the OECD countries the full spectrum of WID approaches exists. While most countries now have adopted a combined welfare/efficiency approach, others have what is termed a 'gendered efficiency' approach. Occasionally, when women are identified as a central target of development assistance, empowerment is more explicitly articulated. For example, USAID, in a 1982 policy paper, clearly reflected an efficiency approach when stating that 'the key issue underlying the women in development concept is inadequate planning and designing of projects, results in diminished returns on investment'.

In contrast, a recent policy definition of the Netherlands Ministry of Foreign Affairs (1989:2) combines an emancipatory/efficinecy approach:

> The advancement of women is a necessary component of development cooperation. It is required both by a fair approach to the female half of the target group, which has long been overlooked, and by an expedient approach to their substantial contribution, which has too long been under-estimated. Thus while the improvement of the position and status of women is full valid as an emancipatory end in itself, the utilization of women's potential is a the same time an efficient means to improve the quality of development as a whole.

Recognising that a WID mandate is not enough, OCEAD countries have sought to operationalise it through several different types of interventions. While mandates provide general guidelines, the next important procedure is a *Plan of Action.* Its purpose is to provide operational strategies to implement the WID policies outlined in the mandate. The plan identifies objectives and responsibilities over the full range of the agency's area of operations, and provides specific guidelines for the implementation of different departments and divisions. By 1990 all but two of the DAC members had adopted such Action Plans.

A further procedure is that of *WID specific sector guidelines.* These provide more stringent measures to ensure that WID is operationalised at the sector level. To date, most specific guidelines have been elaborated in areas where women's roles are identified as critical. These include agriculture, health, weather and the environment. The guidelines highlight substantive issues at the sectorial level, also providing summarized checklists to help staff in drawing up terms of reference. Sometimes general action programmes or WID manuals include sector-specific details. An alternative procedure has been to *integrate WID criteria intogeneral sector guidelines*. This procedure obviously involves greater collaboration and negotiation between WID and other sector experts. Again it is more likely to be undertaken in sectors where women are visible, and not in those sectors, such as urban, energy or industry, where the role of women is less obvious.

Some donors given less priority to sectorial interventions, and emphasise more the importance of procedures for *country-level WID guidelines*. Here WID or gender issues are integrated into the country programme/frame documentation included in negotiation procedures between the donor and the recipient countries. These are the major decision-making processes for selecting sector, programme and project priorities. The procedures can include either country-specific WID profiles and plans, or the integration of WID into national plans of action. Finally, there are *WID project guidelines* that provide detailed instructions as checklists to ensure that the project planning cycle integrates gender.

Ultimately, commitment to the integration of WID into the planning process has to be measured. The purpose of *monitoring procedures* is therefore, to gauge the extent to which each of these six procedures has been implemented. To date, monitoring procedures have focused on the implementation of Plans of Action through such measures as progress reports and 'built-in' monitoring procedures. But progress has been very slow, with the most important problem being the lack of adequate or appropriate indicators. Here is also important not to conflate the need for two different sets of indicator: first, indicators that assess the implementation of procedures; and secondly, indicators that assess or measures the impact of interventions on the situation of women in developing countries. In the latter case a well-known problem is the lack of desegregated baseline data against which to measure impact.

In monitoring changes in operational procedures one problem is the difficulty of developing adequate quantitative measurements of process. The DAC evaluation, for instance, comments that although all OECD members have adopted action plans, very few have integrated monitoring procedures to review the process of WID integration in their agencies. Measures, both quantitative and qualitative, are needed to decide benchmarks for WID integration activities. These do not necessarily have to be onerous to develop or cumbersome to use. Measurements such as the numbers of times aid officials raise WID issues in donor exchanges, or the inclusion of WID in the terms of reference, provide simple but innovative indicators. USAID is one of the few agencies to undertake a rigorous evaluation of the implementation of its WID policy. Undertaken in 1987, its conclusions were both depressing and salutary. This is particularly the case, given the political mandate and impressive budget invested both in increasing institutional capacity and in the development of detailed planning procedures. The evauation cońcluded that WID was operating against a range of constraints. These included the attitude of USAID staff, which was one of tolerant indifference. Although lip-service was given to the importance of WID, this was seen as a reaction to special-interest politics rather than a serious concern for development. A lack of regularized systems and procedures revealed that it was the initiative and enthusiasm of individuals that had been the most significant variable influencing the degree to which USAID programmes and projects in corporate WID cocerns.

Constraints in Operational Procedures

USAID's response to the question as to what has gone wrong with operational procedures desired to translate policy into practice was to develop a new, more complex set of guideines for incorporating gender into its activities. This was called the Gender Information Framework (GIF), in which both the language and the concern have changed from women in development to gender and development. While it is still too early to see if this set of new tools has changed USAID's practice, the importance of this initiative lies in what it reveals about the agency's perception as to the constraints in the implementation of policy. These were identified as being of a technical nature emanating from inappropriate or inadequate planning procedure. The solution was to develop 'better' or more appropriate procedures. But is this apparent *failure* due to technical constraints, or are there also fundamental political constraints operating? The fact that donor agencies have developed so many different procedures makes it important to identify the opportunities and constraints in the implementation of policy.

It is useful to start by asking whether the problem is that, from its formulation, the policy concerned is essentially 'symbolic'? One reason why policy so often is not carried out relates to the fact that it can easily be formulated without the intention to carry it out at all. It has been argued that effective implementation requires 'unambiguous policy directives' (Sabatier and Mazmanian 1979). 'Perfect' implementation then requires 'complete understanding of and agreement upon, the objectives to be achieved' (Gunn 1978: 173). In introducting the concept of 'policy message', to embrace both the substance of policy and the way it is communicated, Hambleton (1986) argues that there are limits to the degree of clarity that can be expected in the policy message. He identifies a number of sound reasons for policy ambiguity.

Although it may be easy to specify policy standards and objectives, usually it is extremely difficult to show clear performance indicators or targets. This is particularly true where policy is complex or extensive in its goals Policies to improve the status of women present a classic example of this case, with globally relevant indicators of status so difficult to identify. Ambiguities may result from uncertainty, which occurs when understanding is of, when policy-makers have little control over those carrying it out. In such cases the temptation is to leave police vague. Again policy objectives to 'bring women into development' provide a widely experienced example of this phenomenon. And of greatest relevance to gender policy, ambiguity may be fostered deliberately by policy-makers. Their intention is to conceal conflicts of objectives between the different actors involved, thus leaving room for manoeuvres, negotiation and renegotiation.

Some policy messages are inended to be heard but not acted on. These policies are not intended to achieve real change but simply to provide 'symbolic ressurance' that something is being done. Symbolic policy is one of the biggest problems faced by those working with a WID agenda. This can be the consequence of policy formulated under outside pressure placed on countries by donor agencies to integrate WID into their development programme. It can also be the consequence of policy formulated without realistic objectives by those unwilling or unable to recognise that policy implementation always involves some kind of compromise.

Procedures to operationalise WID concerns can focus on WID-specific interventions at policy, programme or project level. Or they can emphasise 'integration' or 'mainstreaming' of gender into existing policies, programmes and projects. This raises the question as to which are the more appropriate planning procedures. Anderson and Chen (1988) argue that 'programming approaches' to WID can be classified in the same way as institutional structures. Targeted interventions are obviously those specifically directed at women. This means that their express objectives are to meet practical or strategic gender needs with their budgets allocated entirely for this purpose. This approach has been justified as necessary to overcome the gender-blindness that has excluded women from the benefits of development. In contrast to this is the 'integration' or mainstream approach in which women as much as men are taken into account in all stages of the planning cycle. The rationale for this approach, is that every project activity affects all segments of economy and society. Consequently, development efforts should take account of those effects on women. From their review of the relationship between different programming and institutional arrangements, they conclude that there is no internal logic that dictates the connection between one structural arrangement and its programmatic thrust. Both institutional and programmatic approaches have been successful sometimes and have failed completely at other times.

Despite this conclusion, there is never an interesting relationship between different policy approaches to WID and different emphases in programming. Changing positions in this debate have coincided with developments in policy approaches to WID, which appear to have determined to only the type but also the level of intervention. While the welfare approach targeted 'vulnerable' groups that happened to include women with interventions at programme and project level, the equity approach focused on integrating women into development with interventions primarily at policy level. The anti-poverty approach that quickly replaced it represented not only a toned-down version of equity but also an important shift to a different level of intervention. These were the women's projects, so summarily described by Buvincic (1986) as small-scale, situation specific, and using limited financial and technical resources. Women, many of them volunteers with little technical expertise, carried out such projects intended to benefit only women. The golden era of women's projects was the 1970s and early 1980s, associated with the global networking of the WID concept. However, the anti-poverty approach and women's projects have not disappeared.

For various agencies, the shift to mains mainsteaming has been a direct reaction to the manner in which separate women's projects appear to have further marginalised women. A common problem identified in government planning procedures has been for important ministries, such as agriculture, to cease allocating resources to women-specific projects. This was done on the basis that the Women's Bureau had their own budget. Equally, as Buvinci (1986) has argued, resources for poor women are often accessible only if there is not a cut-back in investment for poor men. This has resulted in a marked preference for cheaper, non-threatening welfare projects that do not have the potential to redistribute resources from men to women.

For some agencies, mainstreaming has also marked an apparent epistemological, if not ideological, shift from women and development to gender and development. Again this has also been accompanied by a semantic shift in emphasis from 'integrating' to 'mainstreaming'.

Above all, the shift from targeting to main streaming must be associated with the increased popularity of the efficiency approach. This identifies women as the most incorporate for more effective and efficient development. Reflecting the World Bank's position on the efficiency approach to WID is its Operational Issues Paper on the Forestry Sector, in which Molner and Schreiber explicitly state:

> Women are key actors in the forestry sector throughout the developing world. Ensuring their direct involvement in foresry projects, both as beneficiaries and participants, can: a) ensure that projects achieve their immediate purposes and broad socio-economic goals, and b) maximize returns on investment in this sector. (1989:i)

The relationship between policy and programming approaches to WID and GAD differs. Separate projects are associated with a welfare or anti-poverty approach, and integrated projects with an efficiency approach. In reality, however, successful implementation relates more to recognition, with adequate budget and staffing, that to whether it adopts a separate or integrated approach. A women's projects can be identified as a mainstream project if decision-makers give it priority and an adequate budget (Levy 1989).

Simultaneously, the fact that it is a mainstream policy or project does not a priority mean that there cannot be special components for women within it. For instance, a project targeted at both men and women may require specific women's 'components' to ensure that women participate equally with men. Often agencies do not clearly distinguish between a women's project and a component for women in a mainstream project.

The World Food Programme (WFP) (1987), in their General Guidelines state that a 'women-only' project or a 'women's component' can be normally justified only as bridging strategy to bring women to a threshold level from which they can enter mainline activities equally with men. One problem here is the failure to recognise women's need to balance their triple role. This means that unless men also take on reproductive activities, no amount of 'bridging' can bring them up to men's threshold. The most obvious women's components in mainstream projects is child care. In reality, this is a family need but is identified as a practical gender need of women because of their reproductive responsibilities.

Since the mid-1980s most donor agencies have adopted the policy of integrating women into mainstream programmes and projects. They use both WID-specific procedures (such as WID-specific sector guidelines) and mainstream procedures (such as integrating WID criteria in sector guidelines). SIDA, for example, has what it terms a 'gendered efficiency' approach. This emphasizes that integration of women in to existing development cooperation programmes, rather than establishing separate women's projects. The reason for this approach is twofold. First, women already participate in most sectors, and effects are needed to facilitate a more effective role for them. Secondly, neglect of women in development cooperation programmes results in a negative impact on women themselves, and on development in general. Efforts to involve women more equitably invariably result therefore in better development cooperation (SIDA 1989:2).

The empowerment approach to WID seeks to intrvene at all three levels of policy, programmes and projects, and combines both mainstreaming and targeted approaches. It recognizes that both types of programming are important. Women-focused projects remain critical, especially at the level of small-scale NGOs, because so man poor women can never be reached in mainstream projects. In addition, mainstreaming, unless meticulously monitored, can in effect mean men. There is a very real danger that widespread proliferation of gender, rather than women and development may ironically result in women losing out again.

Problem as Analytical Tool

The fact that the introduction of gender into existing planning procedures has not fundamentally changed the situation suggests that on its own this cannot confront the real problem. However meticulous the procedures developed to integrate gender into the project planning cycle, it is necessary to assess whether they fall into the trap of being what Thomas (1979) identifies as 'contentless' and contextless'. One important criticism of rational comprehensive planning is that in assuming 'consensus' it fails to recognie conflict, or to provide the operational procedures to confront it. In 'grafting' gender onto an existing planning methodology, the procedures in the planning cycle have not changed. They do not incorporate new stages that include the negotiation of conflict, or participatory debate. Because it assumes that the problem is a technical one, the introduction of additional interventions within the existing framework of procedures is identified as solving the problem. Therefore, another constraint may be the analytical tools themselves.

One tool that has received special attention is *gender diagnosis and analysis*, and the extent to which it recognises subordination. The Harvard approach was designed to create awareness. Its tools are intended to ensure the meticulous documentation of differences between men and women in divisions of labour, as well as in the ownership and control over resources. Its assumes that feeding this information into the project cycle, based on rational comprehensive procedures, is sufficient to change practices. It careful avoidance of identifying the cases of the inequality between men and women means that it does not seek to provide tools to confront conflict in the implementation process. This is not surprising, since it is based on a consensus, rather than conflict, planning model. Anderson (1990), one of those responsible for developing the Harvard approach, identified a gap between gender analysis and incorporating this analysis in some effective way into actual programme design and implementation.

The Harvard approach is closely linked to the efficiency approach to WID with its economically deterministic underlying assumption that there is a direct relationship between increased access to resources and employment and increased status for Third World women." [The] Gender analysis approach..avoided the ideological tone that worried critics...the approach demonstrated that the issue of women was an issue of economic efficiency, rather than an issue "only" of equality. Gender analysis, therefore, provides tools for policy interventions to help women to participate more efficiently in the labour market, through ameliorating measures such as child-care provision, or transport. It does not provide the tools for policy intervention to help women to 'empower' themselves to organise and challenge existing relations. Policy which equates increased efficiency with equity focuses almost entirely on practical gender needs on the assumption that increased access to employment will make women equal or more equal, with men.

However, women face additional and more intractable barriers to access than do men, because of their mothering role (multiple pregnancies and child care) and *because of cultural traditions*, some times reflected in law or policy, that tend to keep women more home-bound than men and more restricted in their work choices and social interactions. These barriers are worse in conditions of poverty, but they persist evening industrialised countries. They restrict women's access to the information and resources required to respond to economic opportunities. Is the current reticence of agencies in recognising subordination a widespread collusion with the idea that better education, health and employment opportunities will make women equal with men? Or is it a sensitivity towards addressing an issue that in reality is so threatening? Gender needs assessment, as a contextually specific planning tool, provides agencies with the capacity to confront this issue more directly. The distinction then between different gender objectives is clear: meeting practical gender needs through development projects assists women either to perform more effectively and efficiently the activities they are already undertaking, or to take on new activities in their existing roles; meeting strategic gender needs through development projects assists women to achieve greater equality, and therefore changes existing roles, which, as ODA has argued, may be considered appropriate in those contexts where 'the status and opportunities of women are inferior to those of men'.

Most governments are committed to policies of equity ad equal opportunities, as endorsed in the UN Forward Looking Strategies. However, along with many donor agencies and NGOs, they remain unable or unwilling to articulate the problem of women's positon as one of subordination.

Experiences with Project Planning

Given the impressive number of planning procedures developed to operationalise gender concerns, it is important to identify how far meticulous gender planning tools can ensure the implementation of gender to the planning process. One important opportunity for gendering planning procedures is project planning. Many donors still consider this the most important planning procedure for developing countries. Consequently, some of the most innovative initiatives to integrate gender have been developed in relation to project planning. The remainder of this chapter will focus, therefore, on the factors influencing the integration of gender concerns into the project planing cycle.

Donors have both adapted and adopted the generalized project cycle, to suit their own particular agenda. Governments, NGOs and donors alike now use the logical framework approach, with different modifications. The extent to which the different phases, or stages, of the cycle are clearly identified, however, varies depending not only on the level of professional planning expertise and financial accountability, but also on ideological position of the procedures, often relying on 'common good sense.'

In addition, several new planning tools have been introduced to integrate gender into the project cycle. Although variations exist, it is useful to divide them into three broad categories:

(a) Checklists and guidelines are intended to be integrated into all stages of the cycle, although their relevance at different stages of th cycle is unspecified. Guidelines, checklists and impact statements are often used interchangeably to both measures and monitor the extent of women's integration in development programmes. Antrobus provides a useful distinction between guidelines as 'indicators for translating policy mandates on women and development into action at the programme and project level'; checklists, which 'are more specific and aim to provide a more detailed memory aid, giving conceptual clarification and practical suggestions'; and impact statements, which are intended to 'get people thinking about the consequences of their interventions'.

(b) General project-cycle tools comprise detailed procedures identified for each stage of the cycle, sometimes in manual form, and are intended for projects despite sectoral concerns.

(c) Sector-specific project guidelines are detailed procedures laid out for each stage of the project cycle, and for designated sector.

This methodology for gendering the project cycle assumes

that at each stage of the project cycle an iterative process occurs which includes gender diagnosis, gender consultation and participation, the identification of gender objectives and an entry strategy, followed by monitoring and the inclusion of appropriate institutional structures and traingin procedures. In theory this is fine; in practive it is more complex. Therefore the following description of their gendering of the project cycles identifies the problems encountered in attempts to incorporate gender, as well as emphasizing the particularly important interventions at different stages of the cycle. It draws on the comparative experience of a number of institutions that have tackled this planning problem. Although stages are discussed separately, they are of course highly interrelated.

Project Identification—Policy Direction

The introduction of the issue of gender into project identification, the first stage in the cycle, determines from the outset the project's orientation. This stage is concerned with relating development goals and resulting sectoral priorities to appropriate projects. These not only have to fit into, and support, a coherent development strategy, and meet sectoral objectives, but they also have to be considered suitable by both the implementing agency and the donor.

The issue of gender is important in two ways in project identification. First, at a general level, gender, along with class, can be identified as an important determinant of development goals in terms of broad sectoral resource priorities. For example, donors often given priority to large-scale infrastructure projects such as dams, hydro-power or electricity, on the basis that their impact will 'trickle down to reach the poor.' Yet the low-income population may not be able to pay for the water or electricity. So such projects, although generally assisting the country's 'development', more specifically meet the needs of factory-owners or upper-income households. Since it is women in the low-income households who take primary responsibility for water and fuel collection, such projects are unlikely to meet their needs. The fact that project identification can predetermine women's participation in projects has been widely recognized. CIDA, for instance, in their 1986 Project Identification Memorandum (PIM) state

> The project identification stage involves the selection of projects that are compatible with CIDA's aid framework (including the WID Policy Framework) and contribute to sectoral and country strategy. Certain projects have greater potential to influence the lives of women. Provided they are compatible with other CIDA objectives and these of the recipient, such projects should receive preference. (1968a:6)

At a specific level, gender is important in terms of the type of project selected. An important distinction exists between women's projects and mainstream or integrated projects, as discussed in the previous section. In reality, the debate between mainstreaming or targeting is critical throughout the project cycle. It affects choices on issues such as staff selection, training procedures and institutional structures Therefore, a priori, gender must be recognised as a policy priority. As a generalization, projects targeted at those sectors—basic needs provision, small-scale production and farming and traditional food production—have greater potential to reach low-income households.

Project Preparation

The recognition of gender in project identification does not ensure that the project is gendered. It is in the project preparation stage, when target groups are defined, project objectives identified and the project designed, that most has been achieved in integration gender.

It is now acknowledged that gender must be integrated into target group definitions. SIDA (1989), for instance, has argued that the use of collective terms within development cooperation, such as 'families', 'the poor', 'farmers', 'slum dwellers', 'target groups', 'rural population' and 'small-scale entrepreneurs', has negative impact for the integration of women. It is therefore necessary to break down these terms by gender. In practice, however, gender is still not usually included at the design stage—above all, because most planners still lack a gender planning methodology. Particular problems often occur when planners, overnight, as it were, are informed that 'women must be included'. If, because of 'political' pressure for endorsement purposes at the appraisal stage, the project is required to 'include' women, the document is often simply amended with the phrase 'and women' added to each appropriate stage in the cycle. This happens when an agency funds a project designed by another, or when gender-blind projects are sent for appraisal to WID or social advisers. The fact that there is no logical rationale behind such changes means that usually the project does not in practice become 'gendered. The most baltant example of this practice occurs when existing project documents add the phrase 'and women' in a different type-face.

Yet an even more common confusion is the illogical identification of gendered and non-gendered categories in the same target group. For instanece, 'farmers, land-lease labourers and women'; 'women and resource poor-farmers'; 'farmers, including farm women and agricultural labourers'. Are all such unspecified project target groups in reality men? When monitoring procedures require agencies to 'count' how many projects include or 'reach' women, lack of accurate gender desegregated data can result in the under-recording of resource allocations to women. FAO, in a recent analysis of three departments regular programme activities concluded that '68 per cent of projects were not explicitly directed at women to any degree' (FAO 1987: 1). Because this figure only included projects in which the word 'woman' appeared, it presumably missed projects in which 'resource-poor farmers' or 'landless' happened to include women.

Despite constraints such as these, gendered target group identification now has elaborate procedures. However, other methodology has been variously termed 'gender analysis' (USAID), 'gender investigation' (World Bank) or a 'gender perspective' (SIDA). One detailed procedure is that of USAID.

It comprises four different techniques: the desegregation of data by gender; gender distinctions in terminology; the inclusion of explicit strategies to involve women; and the use of gender-isaggregated bench marks in monitoring and evaluation. To ensure its adoption, USAID has developed the Gender Information Framework (GIF).

Based on the Harvard case-study methodology, the gender analysis guide outlines a two-step gender analysis process. First, it identifies where gender might intervene in social and economic production systems (in terms of allocation of labour, sources of income, financial responsibilities, and access and control of resources). Secondly, it analyses the implications of gender differences for project design. These are identified in terms of key differences between men and women's constraints and opportunities in development activities (relating to labour, time, access to credit, education and training, skills and knowledge).

SIDA's (1989) gender perspective identifies two analytical tools. First, *gender-specific target group analysis.* As factors for consideration, this identifies household composition, the division of labour in terms of the different trowels of men and women at household and community level, and the responsibility, access and final control over resources at household and community level. Second is *gender-specific impact analysis.* In projects where women may not be considered the 'target group;, such as a hydropower project,there can still be both negative and positive impacts for women, which a gender-specific impact analysis can identify. USAID's GIF and SIDA's target grup/impact analysis both provide examples of specific tools intended to ensure the provision of gender-desegregated data in all stages in the project cycle. The USAID Document Review Guide explains the importance in project/programme design and evaluation, to disaggregate data by gender whenever possible, to incorporate gender considerations and to include decision points in project implemntaion to allow project adaptation as new data become available.

It is important that gender diagnosis is what it says it is; the diagnosis of both men and women, and the relationship between them. Projects can fail equally if they ignore men in target group identification. SIDA cites the example of health projects, where inputs in child care, nutrition family planning and care of pregnant women had limited impact if directed solely at women. Men have ultimate authority with the family. Consequently, eve if the women are well informed, they often cannot make changes to family eating habits unless their spouses have sufficient information to agree. For instance, to grow different crops requires that male farmers have the necessary information to make the recommended changes.

Gender Needs Assessment and Gender Objectives

The integration of gender into project objectives requires detailed specification of the changes which the project needs to achieve for both men and women. The basis issue here relates to the assessment of gender need, and the extent to which the methodology distinguishes between practical and strategic needs. CIDA, for instance, in their PIM document provide a guide of eleven issues to ensure that their objectives address key aspects of WID. They state that projects should be examined in terms of whether they lead to jobs, skills, training, improved markets, more public services, housing, food production or other gains that directly benefit lowest income groups, in which women frequently are found in the largest percentages; facilitate access to and control over resources by poor women, including women heads of household.

One constraint of a checklist such as this is that it does not priorities needs into a 'cause and effect' hierarchy, or state the likelihood of their being achieved. Thus it identifies practical gender needs relating to jobs and skill training alongside strategic gender needs related to controlling resources. As ODA points out, project objectives need to identify whether they recognise the distinction between different types of needs. Christian Aid recognises that objectives to reach practical gender needs automatically do not reach strategic gender needs. These often require specific, often highly sensitives, interventions in their own right. In its Gender Guidelines, it shows its priorities in terms of gender needs:

> Our task is not simply to support the involvement of more women or to fund more women's projects, but to equip women with the means to challenge and overcome their constraints. We should address ourselves to both the practical and strategic needs of women. We should support projects that enable women and men to understand the structural inequalities which adversely affect the participation and development of women, and that include action to address those inequalities. (Christian Aid 1989: 1)

Project Design and Gender Consultation and Participation

Project design includes questions relating not only to what is designed, but also who designs, and how it is designed, all of which involve issues relating to gender. The procedures discussed under project design, which late to personnel and feasibility studies, also relate to later stages in the project cycle.

One difficulty in planning relates to the division of labour at different stages in the project cycle. Staff identifying project objectives may not design the project. Unless both are gender-aware, project objectives may not be taken into account in the design phase. Agencies commonly separate out the design of 'technical', 'ecoomic' and 'social' components of projects to different experts. This encourages 'technical' experts to leave the social development issues to the socio-economists, or anthropologists. In order to solve he problem of gender-blind personnel, most donor agencies have integrated training.

Training provides no guarantees that staff will be sensitive to issues in practice has resulted in the operationalisation of a further critical planning tool. This is the development of clearly gendered terms of reference of all project staff. This identifies the gendered information and analysis required to ensure gendered interventions at each relevant stage of the project cycle.

Socio-economic Feasibility Study

The timing of feasibility studies is ofter critical to project success, with severe difficulties experienced in making changes later in the project cycle. The socio-economic feasibility study can provide the first critical entry point for gender issues in the project cycle. To ensure they include gender, many agencies have redefined their project formulation stage to include social studies.

At the project design stage it is the gender-specific potential inputs and outputs that the feasibility study needs to identify. Molner and Schreiber (1989) identify four specific issues: pre-project benefit likely to be forgone by women and there households (with special attention to households headed by women); work-load implications for women; probable gains for women; and differences and potential conflict between probable gains and loses for women and those anticipate for men, households in general or for the community as a whole. CIDA (1986a) identifies the project feasibility study as a synthesis of separate studies that deal with four essential aspects of the project, which they identify as technical, managerial socio-economic and financial. CIDA states that the feasibility study should identify the institutional and other; changes needed to facilitate, increase, accelerate and retain the access and control over resources of the sector by women. Information on the degree to which women have control over resources can be used to assess the extent to which they are likely to retain control over benefits of the project. It also assists in identifying potential conflicts that may occur if project design challenges existing roles, benefiting women and disadvantaging men.

Like USAID, with its socio-economic studies, CIDA uses

the Harvard case-study approach. However, it also stipulates that information should be obtained from local people (men and women) and local academics, leaders, women's organistions and NGOs. Equal consultation with and participation of local women and men is essential, although it is difficult to achieve in practice. Gender diagnosis also has important implications for project design. Information on women's reproductive role can be used to assess whether the project will have implications for their need to balance their triple role. Buvincic identifies a critical design fault in income-generating projects as the underestimation of the difficulty of stereotypical female tasks, and the overestimation of their transferability.

Since many issues relating to the feasibility studies are equally important at the appraisal stage, they are discussed below.

Appraisal

Project appraisal is intended to provide a comprehensive review of all aspects of the project and lays the foundation for implementing the project and evaluating it when completed (Baum 1982). Traditionally, appraisal covered technical, institutional, economic and financial aspects of the project, with social and environmental appraisal being a more recent 'add-on'. From a gender perspective, this is a critical stage in the project cycle. For donors it is often the first state when they formally participate in the project. Therefore, it may be the only opportunity to make any fundamental changes in the framework already developed.

Donors have increasingly realised the need not only to ensure that all terms of reference for appraisal missions are gender-aware, but also to get gender specialists on the appraisal team. Does the team need a gender specialist if all members are gender-aware? This debate is similar to the mainstream-target debate continued above. In addition, one specific problem that occurs is the assumption that women professionals will automatically monitor the gender aspects of a project.

The greatest resistance to mains treaming often comes from women professionals. They argue that it undervalues their professional expertise. By default, they become a 'women's' expert, as against a technical expert.

Both NORAD and SIDA identify as an important priority the appointment of a WID specialist on the appraisal team for both projects and country-sector mission reviews. The task of the specialist is to act as a catalyst. The resident in-country WID officer cannot be expected to take on this responsibility. Their status may not be high enough, and as part of the residential mission the are likely to experience problems integrating into a visiting team. However, specialists are considered to be a short-term strategy; in the longer terms SIDA expect to mainsteam the issue. A recent example of terms of reference for a SIDA appraisal mission—for continued support to the road sector in a developing country-required it to give attention to increasing the participation of both women and men in the sector support. To facilitate this it required a gender assessment of roles, responsibilities, access to resources, an the resulting needs and problems of both women and men.

Integration of Gender into Technical, Financial and Economic Appraisal Reports

Where gender is recognised at the appraisal stage, it usually consists of a statement about women, added to the social appraisal. This is the standard response to a checklist question about the way in which the project 'affects' women. However, it results in a twofold problem. Not only is the social appraisal rarely authentically gendered. None of the other 'technically' focused appraisals contains any social dimensions. Yet there are critical gender issues in all the different appraisals undertaken. Although many are sector-specific, analysis of the anticipated project impact in terms of women's triple role provides the basis for identifying effects on them at the local level.

Economic appraisal reports are considered the most

important, with cost-benefit analysis utilized to identify alternative project designs, from which the one that contributes most to the development objectives is selected. One important issue in cost-benefit analysis is the extent to which the invisible work women do in their reproductive and community managing work has an economic value. This has been a particular problem in recent structural adjustment policies where projects to shift production from non-tradable to tradable goods have failed to value women's time as peasant workers. It is not simply that such interventions can harm women; gendered cost-benefit analysis shows that economic returns are not reduced in projects that specifically ensure benefits to women. The direct involvement of women can improve the probability of projects meeting their essential objective. In spite such conclusions, the assumption still common among economists is that 'involving women as direct beneficiaries or participants and devoting special resources to achieve this is peripheral, if not determinental, to the attainment of central project returns. Once those responsible for the technical appraisal recognise gender as a planning issue, specific components relating to project layout and design, location and scale and type of equipent can be identified. Among the most widely cited are: that project location can deferentially affect the participation of men and women; that unless the project specifically itemizes women as beneficiaries, land for 'landless' and legalized plots for 'squarters' in both cases reaches men; and that unless the project consults women, prioritization in delivery of basic services is usually those that benefit men.

A particular training problem in the technical appraisal is the *selection procedure for personnel*. Generally this is based only on technical expertise and not on gender-awareness. When the project includes training components, women do not always get equal access to such training, nor do the location, hours and length of training help them to participate. Again it raises the problematic issue of mainstreaming or targeting.

Project Ratification of Negotiations

In his description of the project cycle (1982) identifies negotiation as the stage at which the donor and the borrower endeavour to agree on the measures necessary to ensure the success of the project. Such agreements are then converted into legal obligations, set out in the loan document.

This stage is often identified as one of formal ratification. However, the extent to which 'political space' exists for real negotiation around differences of opinion between either donor and recipient, or from different groups within the recipient country, will determine its importance in the project cycle. For some agencies it may be the stage for document ratification, such as CIDA's Project Approval Memorandum (PAM). For others, such as SIDA, there is a negotiation period between appraisal and agreement, which can be lengthy. This stage is then an important gender entry point for shifting the agenda. Since senior staff generally control this stage, the extent to which those negotiating represent women's interest depends on the gender-awareness of participants in the negotiation process.

Implementation

Implementation is the period of construction and subsequent operation of the project. Baum has argued that although supervision is the least glamorous part of the project work, it is the most important. For no matter how will a project has been identified, prepared and appraised, its development benefits can only be realised if it is properly executed. Given the widespread failure of gender policy in a implementation phase, it is particularly important for gender planning. Several gender-related issues here require specific identification and close monitoring. Many are similar to those raised in earlier stages in the project cycle. At this stage it is important to ensure that gender objectives are carried out in practice. Those most affected, therefore, are the implementing agency and the target group itself. So often when the project is one of infrastructure provision the implementing agency does not include social scientists among its personnel. Staff composition is critical not only in terms of sensitivity in understanding the project, but also because of its implications when the target group participates in the project. Too often professionals, both consultants and nationals, bring their own stereotypical assumptions about the role of local women in society.

CIDA (1986b) argues that an important issue concerns how managers or administrators are motivated, trained and/ or persuaded to consider women's contribution. This raises the issue whether it is better to use existing organizational structures or create new ones for the implementation stage. Widespread concern at the way highly over-bureaucratized male-dominated institutional fail to reach women has resulted in an increasing focus on local women's and NGO groups at the grass-roots level. With women's groups, the problem, however, is not so much the groups themselves, but their resources and stiffen. The widespread use of women as volunteers not only means that 'staff' often have inadequate training. As Buvincic (1986) has argued, it leads to the perpetuation of women's lower status among those implementing projects. Buvinic claims that the use of women volunteers is based on the 'cultural prescription' that work with low-income women shouldbe done by women. She claims that the validity of this belief his gone largely unterested in the Third world. Lack of expertise is often a hindrance to project success, while the cultural need to have women staff members interact with women beneficiaries will vary according to the poverty of the group and the task required. It is important, however, not to conflate the problems of untrained volunteers who are also women, with trained, paid woman project staff.

Finally, it is important to recruit women professionals into management positions. However, this will help local women only if the former are gender aware. Where the project involves extension or community workers in implementation, the terms of reference must include women in this activity. However, 'women's components' such as creche facilities, or extra training may be necessary to ensure that women gain access to employment on equal terms with men.

Role of the Target Group in Implementation

When implementation or maintenance involves the target population, women's participation varies with project type. Projects with labour components increasingly use women to provide free or cheap labour. These projects can range from the provision of infrastructure and housing to those allocating handouts such as food, or providing services such as health. Recognition of the triple role is obviously essential, if the participatory component is not simply to extend the working load of low-income women, who participate to get services. As discussed, community management does not mean that women participate in community-level political processes. The failure of implementation agencies to ensure that women participate in decision-making processes has resulted in the creation of separate women's community-level organisations. These ensure that women can express their own choices and make their own decisions.

Whether projects have the institutional capability to support and project women's interests and, if not, how this can be developed. It raises critical issues concerning an agenc's capacity to ensure that it effectively sustains those support structures, created to help women in potentially conflictive situations. Where the project is simply reinforcing gender roles this may not be problematic. However, where objectives have included strategic gender needs of women,or where women themselves have identified these during participation, the project often cannot sustain itself unless an adequate support structure exists. Finally, it is important to recognise that women in the target population are not a homogenous group. For instance, women who are better off and do not need to work for a living self-select themselves for project participation. In contrast, those who head households, and who often are the poorest with the severest time contrainsts, exclude themselves form projects that require time for group discussion, participation and voluntary labour.

Monitoring and Evaluation

Although monitoring is sometimes identified as a separate stage in the project cycle, increasingly it is identified as an ongoing activity accompanying the implementation process. Ideally, a project should establish an on going data-collection system for monitoring purposes. However, this is only realistic for large-scale or prototype projects, but is too ambitious for most projects. Here mid-project missions or on-ground monitors can provide essential feedback during project implementation at a reasonable cost. However, unless the project already has undertaken gender diagnosis and integrated gender, it is unlikely to include it at this stage. Yet monitoring of women's participation can be ensured if all the data found during the project implementation is collected and analysed on a gender-disaggregated basis. In addition, special studies and surveys may be required, for which adequate financial provision should be made. Molner and Schreiber (1989), for instance, identify the collection of data on women's own perceptions of the project's impact; on conflicts between men and women's interests in project outputs; on the extent and distribution of project 'costs' and project-induced 'losses' among various users and beneficiaries; and on the needs, demands and constraints of different users over time.

Evaluation is the final stage in the project cycle, providing an insight into factors that contribute to project success or failure. As with monitoring, it is essential to ensure that the indicators developed are adequate and relevant to the evaluation of gender. Another constraint may be the lack of adequate resources. For example, CIDA only evaluates a few projects, because of resource constraints. It has recommended, therefore, that priority should be given to projects that address WID concerns.

The first important step is establishing the reasons for

evaluation. Projects are evaluated against their original objectives, so, if these were not gender aware, neither is the evaluation likely to be. However, the evaluation of gender in the project can ensure that the second phase includes gender. SIDA tries to emphasise socio-economic aspects within evolutions. To ensure objectivity and independence, evaluations are not generally undertaken by the operational agency but by outside consultants or separate departments set up for this purpose. This makes issues such as the terms of reference, and consultant selection procedures, discussed earlier, of particular importance. Again it is important that the evaluation team includes a gender specialist, an accepted professional, not the in-country WID officer. Another argument, made by CIDA, is the need to involve host nationals in the research process. Not only does this help the evaluation process, but it also ensures a transfer of research techniques and expertise to the recipient. Both with consultant sand nationals it is preferable to have female interviewers interview females, while in certain countries it is imperative.

Political Agenda of Gender Planning

The previous description of the range of analytical and planning tools developed by various agencies for use in the project cycle illustrates two important issues. First, there are very real difference between the tools and techniques developed to date. At one end of the spectrum are brief, generalized checklists, at the other end are complex, detailed procedures integrated into each state of the cycle. Second, despite the gender approach adopted, there is a broad consensus concerning specific tools, such as gendered terms of reference, staff training and gendered selection procedures. Both these issues have important implications. They illustrate exactly how complex, time-consuming and expensive it can be to gender the project cycle. Each stage requires detailed scrutiny to identify the techniques required, and continual monitoring of their effectiveness concern introduced. This, if nothing else, serves to illustrate precisely how difficult it is to operationalise gender planning.

Has the extensive introduction of new procedures changed the situation? Lack of comparative data means it is not possible to assess the process of differed agencies about their planning tools. Nevertheless, it cannot be assumed, a priori, that the greater the sophistication of existing tools the more effectively gender is integrated into the planning cycle. Agencies are reticent about evaluating their own experience, preferring to view whatever changes and shifts that have occurred in the most positive manner possible. However, there is a consensus that there is still a long, uphill struggle before changes in procedures have any substantial impact, both in terms of changing attitudes within their agencies, as well as in fundamentally improving the situation of women in developing countries.

A recent evaluation of UNIFEM's work mainstreaming gender documented the continuing indifference, ambivalence and active resistance that efforts to mainstream women into development policy and programming still encounter. It concluded that 'resistance, born out of prejudice or protective self-interest is a fundamental fact'. Even those professionals sympathetic to WID seriously underestimate the effort involved. However, after more than five years this has still not been accomplished. The question can then be based whether the 'lack of regularized systems and planning procedures' is the essential problem in operatonalising WID. Recognition of these problems in operationalising gender has resulted in the development of several strategies to challenge the blotches in planning procedures.

Operationalising Gender Planning

A number of important shifts are identified. These have occurred not only in the focus but also in the level of intervention. This includes changes from women in development to gender and development, from project to programme and policy level, and above all from 'targeting' and 'integrating' to 'mainstreaming'. Mainsreaming as much as targeting or integrating willful unless the planning methodology provides procedures to confront blockages. This requires the complex but necessary identification of the fact that planning methodology is both technical and political in nature.

From the experience to date, some important conclusions can be made. *First*, like many donors, SIDA has recognised the importance of a combined strategy. Its gender policy approach is modified efficiency combined with empowerment. The former is integrated into sector programmes through sector action plans, while the latter relates to specific actions for women through the direct support programme and other special funds for democracy, human rights, the environment and other specific areas such as population and culture.

Secondly, SIDA has recognised that their biggest constraint his been the *lack of an adequate planning methodology*. SIDA, therefore, his simplified and standardised the tender planning methodology to ensure its incoporation in to all interention. Highly complicated procedures, while impressive are time-consuming and more open to misunderstanding, and on both counts are less likely to be carried to SIDA, therefore, identify three simple procedures for all planned interventions: the integration of gender into mainstream programmes as opposed to separate projects/components: the identification of responsibilities and roles with SIDA; and the incorporation of gender planning methodology into all normal planning routines.

Thirdly, SIDA recognises the impossibility of acting effectively on a fronts at the same time and, therefore, prioritizes within its gender strategy. *Fourthly*, it identifies the preparation stage as the most important stage in the planning cycle. It recognises that the critical criteria for the selection of entry points through which gender is introduced are 'political', and related to the points in SIDA's planning cycle where there is greatest political space for negogiation. As a result, three stages of SIDA's programme cycle have been selected as entry points.

CHAPTER 10

Gender Roles in Family and the Household

The development of gender planning as a planning tradition in its own right is the consequence of the inappropriateness of current planning stereo-types. These relate to the structure of low-income households, to divisions of labour within them, and to power and control over resource allocations between different members in such households. Despite common rhetoric of *'planning for people'*, in much of current policy and practice, based on Western planning theory, there is an almost universal tendency to make three broad, generalized assumptions, despite the empirical reality of the particular planning context:

1. that the household consists of a nuclear family of husband, wife and two or three children.

2. that the household functions as a socio-economic unit within which there is equal control over resources and power of decision-making between all adult members in matters influencing the household's livelihood.

3. that within the household there is a clear division of labour based on gender. The man of the family, as the 'breadwinner', is primarily involved in productive work outside the home, while the woman as the housewife and 'homemaker' takes overall responsibility for the reproductive and domestic work involved in the organization of the household.

In many societies these Western planning stereotypes of household structure and the gender division of labour within it are seen to reflect the 'natural' order. Consequently, the state and family ideologically reinforce them through the legal and educational system, the media and family-planning programmes, without recognition that within the family the woman's position is subordinate to that of the man. Such an abstract stereotype model of society has severe limitations when applied to most Third World contexts.

Heterogeneous Household Structures

The first assumption is that the predominant household structure consists of a nuclear family of husband, wife and two or three children. In reality this is no more than an idealized traditional planning stereotype even of Western industrial society today. Yet the failure to recognize that low-income households are not homogeneous in terms of family structure is still widespread. Although nuclear families may be the dominant type in some contexts, other structures exist. This is the case not only in industrialised countries but also in the developing world. Planners trained in European and North American planning schools have successfully exported such assumptions.

Linked to the model of the nuclear family as the basis unit of society is the concept of hardship. The idea that a 'head', normally assumed to be a man, represents and manages the household, Rogers argues, is a 'figment of the statistician's imagination'. In his definition as 'head of household', the man as the bread winner is perceived to be the financial supporter, with all other members defined as 'dependants'. This is the case in both rural ad urban contexts, when the woman is the primary income-earner, and it is the man who more accurately should be defined as a dependent. Frequently women are only counted as heads when it becomes impossible to list the oldest male present, be it the grandfather or grandson, because there is no likely candidate. In her detailed description of the treatment of women in quantitative statistics,

Regers (1980) provides chilling, if salutary, examples of the manner in which the data-collection categories indifferent agricultural projects, by making women's agricultural participation invisible, effectively excluded them from land, credit, extension and other services. The designation of hardship in national household surveys has been questioned. However, it continues to be widely practised with the assumption that attitudes and motivations of all members of the household are identical with those expressed by the male household read.

More recently, several non-nuclear family structures have reached the attention of policy-makers. It is now accepted that the extended family does not necessarily disappear with 'modernization' or 'urbanisation'. where it remains vital follow-income survival strategies, as happens in countries experiencing stringent adjustment conditions, extended families of widely different and complex structures may not only survive but increase in numbers. However, the most important non-nuclear family household structure still 'invisible' in many planning contexts is the female-headed household. This was first noted by researchers in the Caribbean, but now is recognized as a global phenomenon. Among the over wide range of househouse, two main types have been identified. First, *de jure* female-headed households, in which the male partner is permanently absent due to separation or death, and the women is legally single, divorced or widowed. This is common in situations of urban poverty. Second, de facto women-headed households in which the male partner is 'temporarily' absent. Here the woman is not the legal household head. She is often received as a dependent although she may, for most of her adult life, have primary if not total responsibility for the financial as well as the organizational aspects of the household.

Two very different socio-economic and political conditions have resulted in the increase in the numbers of *de facto* female-headed households during recent decades. Most important of all is male labour migration. This consists not only of the rural-urban migration common in parts of Africa, but also the dramatic flows of international migration such as those from the resource-poor areas of Asia the rich Middle Eastern economies. Female-headed households also emerge under conditions of war, insecurity and disaster, whether 'man-made' or natural.

It is estimated that women head one-third of th e world's households. In urban areas, especially in Latin America and parts of Africa, the figure reaches 50 per cent or more. In rural areas where men traditionally migrate it has always been high, while refugee camps in areas of Africa and Central America it is nearer 80 to 90 per cent. While there are considerable regional variations, the number of *de facto* female-headed households is increasing rather than declining. In many parts of the world this is not a new phenomenon, simply one that is now more openly acknowledged. The reasons for this recognition are twofold. First, attitudes within communities are changing about the stigma of a woman living without a man. This is particularly evident in communities under conflict, where women forced to live on their own have themselves become more confident in confronting criticisms about their status (Weeda 1987). Secondly, there is growing recognition by planners implementing projects, if not formulating policy, that they cannot ignore women who head households if they ar e concerned with the successful completion of their work.

The economic conditions of female-headed households vary considerably. They depend on such factors as the woman's marital status, the social context of female leadership, her access to productive resources and income, and the composition of the household. Some *de facto* female-headed households in which husbands regularly send remittances home are better off than if their husbands were present. In other cases, where men become 'guest husbands' with a series of temporary liaisons, the situation is worse. Nevertheless, it is important not to assume *a priori* that households headed by women are poorer than those with a male heads. Clearly, women house not to marry in some contexts, and in others to marry but live separately from their husband.

The crucial issue here relates to the apparent trend of increasing detachment of women and children from men' income. This results not only from changes in legal arrangements or sexual practices, but because of the economic cost of bearing children. Where these households have a higher dependency ratio and a lower participation rate among potential eaners, as well as earners with less income-earning power, all too often they fall below the poverty-line, and are over-represented at the lower end of the income distribution, disproportionately numbered among the poorest of the poor (White *et al.* 1986). Female-headed households in poverty are poor for many of the same reasons as male-headed households. It is important, therefore, to identify whether it is useful to target female-headed households as a separate category. In reality, the most disadvantaged are those households without adult income-earners other than the mother, and with many dependent children. In such cases children are less likely to attend school and more likely to work with obvious consequences for the inter-generational transfer of poverty. Women who head households are no a homogeneous category. Nevertheless, the problem of balancing multiple roles is excerbated for this group, which can have policy implications in specific contexts.

Household as a Natural Decision-making Unit

The second assumption, and one most commonly made by macro-economic planners working on problems of rural development, is that the household functions as a natural socio-economic unit, within which there is equal control over resources and power of decision-making between adult household members in matters influencing their livelihood. This is based on two critical premises that require detailed examination from a gender perspective.

Families and Households

The first premise, at the liner-household level, is that of

the household as a natural socio-economic unit. This simple but fundamental planning stereo-type derives from the assumption that the family, a social unit based on kinship, marriage and parenthood, and the household, a residential unit based on co-residence for such purposes as production, reproduction, consumption and socialization, are 'naturally' and universally synonymous sun its. In this 'one pot, one roof model' (Lehmann 1986) the family live and work together as the basis labour unit, sharing both work and the proceeds of their labour. As Young (1990) has argued, this is based on a on flation of the two separate concepts of households and families. Many assumptions made about the nature of intra-household relations relate to marriage relationships and relations between parents and children.

The idea that the household functions as a single socio-economic unit, organized as an independent entity with clearly defined boundaries that separate it from other households in the socio-economic structure in which it is located, is not borne out in reality. Although families and household s may overlap in some societies,particularly those that are Western and urban, in others they do not. Wide variations in marriage and kinship systems influence residential and conjugal arrangements. These vary both spatially and temporarily. Internal factors relating to the nature of the marital contract, patterns of inheritance and the difference stages of expansion, consolidation and contraction in the family life cycle influences them. In addition a diversity of external socio-economic and political factors are also important. Whereas planners treat households as static units, in reality they vary widely depending on socio-economic contexts. These are themselves subject to constant restructuring, with their limits and boundaries often difficult to find out.

The concept of the household as a unified economic entity obviously fails to recognise inter-household resource and labour exchanges and systems of reciprocity. The most formalised are those that exist in polygamous households, but they are also widespread in other family structures. Of particular importance for women are the various forms of co-operation and collectivity in reproductive work between households. A common form is where some women undertake such domestic work as the minding of children and cooking or fuel and water collection, in order to release others to engage in wage labour or subsistence production (Harris 1981). Such arrangements may be institutionalised through kinship ties, or else based on informal arrangements of solidarity to meet a joint need.

Household as a Joint Utility Function

A further tendency of household-level analysis, that of looking at households rather than inside them, ignores the importance of intra-household dynamics. The second premise, at the intra-household level, that requires particular scrutiny from a gender perspective, concerns of power and control over the distribution of resources between household members in matters affecting their livelihood.

The household has long been used as the unit of analysis for census, statistical and survey purposes. Since the mid-1960s, however, it has gained a particular prominence among macro-economic planners, because of their increasing concern to develop and apply a model of household decision-making behaviour for several diagnostic and predictive purposes. A number of models of the household as unified undifferentiated units have been developed from very different political perspectives, influnced above all by the work of Chayanov and Becker. From a Marxist perspective, for instance, Chayanov's Theory of Peasant Economy has been used to develop models of household utility maximization under conditions of land and labour constraints. In this the tightly bounded household unit is identified as the operative unit of production and consumption. In contrast, Becker (1965) has combined arguments about the economic rationality of household behaviour with the neo-classical theory of the firm to develop a new theoretical approach, known as New Household Economics (NHE). Here a complex array of relationships and exchanges with households are collapsed into a function that is similar to that of a individual decision-maker.

As Evans (1989) has argued, models based on NHE identify the household, rather than the individual, as the most relevant unit of 'utility maximization'. The family is identified as the basic unit not only of production but also of consumption. Its utility derives not simply from the consumption of goods and services purchased in the market place, but also from the range of home-produced goods and services, the so-called 'Z-Goods'. because they comprise objects of final consumption produced within the household, such Z-goods are often considered similar to use-values. They are goods produced within the household with fixed capital,variable inputs and labour, combined with different levels of labour and capital intensity. The particular combination will depend not only on the level of household technology, but also on the prices of market goods, an imputed rate of return to household capital, and the shadow price of time—in other words, the domestic worker's earnings forgone from the labour market (Hart 1990). Thus the household does not simply maximize profits but rather it maximizes the joint utility of all its members. In addition, welfare maximization is based on the condition that the 'free choices' or preferences of household members are equally represented in the household utility function, such that the welfare of each family member is normally integrated into a unified family welfare function (Schultz 1988). These assumptions will now be examined in more detail. Among the many limitations from a gender perspective of the notion of the household as a joint utility function, Evans (1989) has identified three of particular importance.

Households: Unified Units of Consumption and Production

The basic premise of the NHE model that households are unified units of consumption and production with all choices made by the same decision making family unit is not borne out by empirical evidence. In reality, in the same way that families and households do not necessarily overlap, so neither are production and consumption units necessarily unified at the household level. The unit of production in both agricultural cultivation, as well as in informal sector activities, often extends beyond the household to include others. These are linked by such criteria as kinship, ethnicity, gender or geographical location. Similarly, units of consumption often expand to include extended family or neighours. In such cases consumption decisions are to necessarily made jointly after all production decisions are made. They are more likely to be based on the different production possibilities of various household members.

Joint Utility Function and Substitutability of Labour

The second important limitation of the NHE is its explanation of the household division of labour in terms of comparative advantage. The NHE argument is that since individual labour time is valued in terms of a market wage, it is obviously allocated to tasks in which it is more efficient. Labour is assumed to be perfectly flexible and substitutable, with the gender division of labour between women's household work and men's wage work legitimized as both functional and efficient for household welfare maximization. Low (1986), for instance, argues that it is to the mutual advantage of the 'rational' farm-household to allocate women's labour time to household-based activities while encouraging men to migrate to off-farm employment. However, as Evans has commented, 'this explanation completely obscures the non-economic and ideological factors that discriminate between male and female labour in the market-place, and values their labour differently in market and non-market sectors' (1989: 10). In reality, family labour time is not like other factors of production that can be flexibly allocated based on its comparative costs in market and non-market activities. Gender as well as age and status are all critical determinants in differentiating the mobilizaiton and allocation of family labour to different activities. Not only do the divisions of labour based on gender define reproductive work as women's work but they also segregate the productive work undertaken by men and women in both agricultural and industrial sectors.

The incentives introduced by governments to encourage farmers and entrepreneurs alike to switch from non-tradable to tradable goods have been based on the assumption that households would respond to new opportunities by real locating their labour. In rural areas increased production of export-orientated crops has resulted in increased productive work for women in their roles as peasants. This has been accompanied by a reduction in their subsistence production for household consumption (Feldman 1989). In urban areas it has meant greater unemployment for men displaced from jobs producing non-tradable goods. For women drawn into export-orientated manufacturing or undertaking incresed domestic service to supplement family income this has meant extra paid work added to their run paid reproductive work (Moser 1992a). Where women's preferences in terms of allocating labour do not necessarily concur with that of the household head, conflict is a likely outcome.

Joint Utility Function, Decision-making and Resource Allocations

NHE's third limitation concerns the use of the joint utility function to deal with the issue of preference aggregation in relation to both decision-making and resource allocation. Critical here is the fact that welfare maximization is conditional to the 'free choice' or 'preferences' of household members being equally represented in a single household utility function. How do the single family welfare functions cope with the fact that within households individuals are perceived to make free and voluntary economic choices? this has proved problematic for economists, particularly in relation to who makes the decision.

Becker (1965), for instance, originally used the concept of altruism to avoid confronting the issue of preference aggregation. He assumed that because individual choices are motivated by the desire to maximize total family welfare, household members subordinate individual tastes and preferences in pursuit of common goals. However, the identification of self-interest as the preserve of the market place, with altruism limited to the sphere of th e family, was widely criticized a avoiding the issue of conflict within the family. To explain why individual family members do not 'free-load' on the benevolence of others, and how families formulate goals in the interests of all members. Becker therefore substituted the assumption of *pure altruism* with an assumption that a '*benevolent dictator*' rules the household. In practice this is assumed to be the male head of family. He sets the goals of the household in the interests of the household as a whole, and ensures that conflict or inequality is laminated by working in the interests of all parties. In this way the socio-economic interests of family dependents such as women and children are internalised within the utility function of the husband and father.

The male household head may not have any real understanding of the day-to-day problems associated with household welfare, since provisioning is a reproductive task of women. Men frequently know little of their wives' coping strategies. When men are absent from home in West Africa they remove themselves 'from the children's cries for food' (Whitehead 1981). In some cases, the authority of the male head does not necessarily coincide with the residential family unit, but may lie with kin elsewhere or with some wider economic or political sphere. It cannot be assumed that one altruistic member of the family, for whom the household head is a proxy, cares sufficiently about all members to transfer resources to them. Neither can it be assumed that the presence of an altruist induces other household members to act altrustically.

The fundamental problem with the concept of the joint utility function is that it removes the possibility of exploring conditions of unequal exchange and exploitation between family members. In particular, this is so between men and women, as they relate to decision-making and the allocation of resources. The assumption that the family pools and shares its resources derives not only from the conflation of families and households but also from the stereotypical assumptions planners have about marriage. This is identified as 'sanctum protected from the conflicts that characterize most other social institutions' (Dwyer and Bruce 1988:3). This conception of marriage as a partnership between two persons with reciprocal but unequal rights and obligations to each other, with similar rights over and obligations to the children of the marriage, and with a common set of interests, has resulted in the assumption that marriage produces a unit marked by joint control and management of resources (Young 1990).

The ideological and cultural as well as economic reasons underline the symmetries and asymmetries in intra-household resource allocation. It is questionable whether family labour, income and resources, on the grounds of allocative efficiency, enter into a common fund. Equally controversial is the idea that they are distributed equitably such that all family members have access to pooled resources sufficient to meet their personal and collective needs. Empirical research clearly shows that unequal exchange and inequality exist within households. Intra-household decision-making, management and distribution arrangements vary depending on the household form and the nature of the 'conjugal contract' (Dwyer and Bruce 1988). The household is not necessarily a 'collectivity of mutually reciprocal interests'. Even where an ideology of sharing exists this doesn't necessarily mean that an equal distribution of resources occurs. Within the household, even in non-market environments, self-interest is often the predominant motivation. Since the 'benevolent dictator' does not represent household needs, his welfare cannot be taken as proxy for the welfare of all household members.

This has been most vividly illustrated in the documentation

on the distribution of resources within households. Here the subordination of needs based on gender is often clearly visible. Women regularly eat last, and less (with girl children also discriminated against in the allocation of food) (Chen *et al.* 1981), less frequently get new clothes, or go without luxuries. These are all examples. Whitehead (1984a) has argued, of the 'maternal altruism' that is part of women's obligation to the family. Although women and men often own, and have access to income and resources, this is generally structured differently. Although, wide regional variations exist in women's access to and control over land in Africa, Asia and Latin America, nevertheless in most rural societies women's access is largely indirect. They acquire land by means of their relationship to individual males such as husbands, fathers or brothers by virtue of their gendered roles as wives or mothers. In contrast, men own land in their own right or by virtue of their lineage membership or other systems of inheritance.

Gender based responsibilities also result in differences in the management and distribution of resources with the household. Gender divisions of income allocation vary widely. Cultural traditions determine which aspects of collective expenditure each must occur. Rarely are women's and men's income allocated to the same expenditure categories. In some societies husbands are responsible for housing and children's education. While income for food and clothing can vary, ultimately, almost universally women allocated income to day-to-day food, clothing needs and domestic goods. The fact that they take primary responsibility for household provisioning, means far greater allocation of women's income than men's to everyday subsistence and nutrition (Blumberg, 1988). Studies of 'good mothering' show that a child's nutritional level correlates positively with the size of a mother's income, food inputs from subsistence farming and the quality of family-based child care.

Constraints in the capacity of NHE models to handle the dynamics of intra-household inequalities have resulted in the promotion of other models of the baraning household. These recogise that family decisions are more properly modelled as negotiations among primarily self-interested individuals in which members contend and exchange to gain their individual ends. Manser and Brown (1980) and others have used the work of Bash (1953), because his model of both conflict and cooperation has been identified as particularly relevant to the analysis of household decisions. Household budgets are managed and distributed in a variety of ways, not always obviously rational in economic terms and with varying amounts of conflict and co-oppression between family members. Sen argues that conflicts of interest between men and women are very unlike other conflicts, such as class conflicts. A worker and a capitalist do not typically live together under the same roof—sharing concerns and experiences and action jointly. It is this aspect of 'togetherness' concerns and experiences and action jointly. It is this aspect of 'togetherness' that gives the gender conflict some very special characteristics. The assumption of clear and unambiguous perceptions of individual interests, Sen maintains, misses crucial aspects of the nature of gender divisions inside and outside the family. He asserts that perception is one important parameter in the determination of intra-family divisions and inequalities. The informational base of cooperative conflict must include and recognise two biases in *perception*. The first perception bias concerns assessments of interests and well-being that are imprecise and ambiguous. A person may get a worse deal in the collective solution if his or her perceived interest takes little notice of his or her personal well-being. Thus, if a woman undervalues herself, her bargaining position will be weaker and she will be likely to accept inferior conditions.

The second perception bias concerns perceptions of contribution, which have to be distinguished from actual contributions since they may be asymmetrical. If a person were perceived as making a larger contribution to the overall well-being of the group than their actual contribution, then the collective solution would be more favourable to that person. It is important to note that perception as tends to relate to the size of direct money-earning, rather than the amount and time and effort expander (or to the role of non-market activities by other members of the family, who indirectly support such activities). As an example of this, Sen cites the disadvantages of women with frequet pregnancy and persistent child bearing. This makes the outcome of co-operative conflicts less favourable to them, through a lower ability to make a perceived contribution to the economic fortunes of the family. Thus rules governing intra-household distribution appear natural and legitimate although they often embody spectacular inequalities, with gendered perceptions tending to support and sustain them.

Research by feminist economists provides an important addition to this work. For example, in contrast to the 'one pot, on e roof' definition of the household mentioned at of this section, a useful one is that of Feldstein (1986). She identifies it as a system of resources allocation between individuals, in which members share same goals, benefits and resources, are independent on some, and in conflict on others. This researche focused on the causes of widespread intra-household gender inequality, attempting to find out the extent to which this is determined by economic factors as against 'exogenosly given' non-economic factors, and the capacity of neo-classic as well as Marxist economic analysis to deal with social and economic relations beyond the market place.

The most important policy-related issue raised by this debate concerns the extent to which intra-household inequality relates to systematic differences in the economic bargaining power of different family members, and consequently the extent to which employment enhances women's domestic decision-making power in cooperative conflict.

Policy-makers recognise that fundamental gender-based asymmetries in access to welfare and productive resources with households often constrain women's capacity to develop or expand income-genderating enterprises. Increasing income is identified as important. Not only does it help women increase their power to negotiate overhousehold assets and thereby decrease intra-household inequalities, but also because it will more effectively influence household welfare. A particular concern is to provide women with greater access to paid employment on the basis that this will increase their control over resources. Evidence clearly shows that working women have more control over the allocation of household resources than do non-earning wives. However, the connection between income-earning and power is not as straightforward as many policy-makers assume.

Not only do husbands frequently under-value the economic contribution of women's income to the household. The normative expectations that their husband will control their income also often influence women. The question as to who define 'objective' needs and interests, therefore, is itself highly political, as are questions of whether they will be recognized and on what terms. As Hart (1990) has argued, instead of perception bias it may be useful to focus on how domestic consent is produced and maintained and the confitions under which household members are likely to challenge and redefine rules (rather than measuring 'perceived contribution bias' from some 'objective' norm). 'To come to grips with intra-household bargaining and contestation we have to engage directly with questions of ideolog and meaning, and recognise how struggles overseers and labour are simultaneously struggles over meaning' (Hart 1990: 25). Thus Whitehead (184b), in her comparative study of the politics of domestic budgeting, shows how the relative power of husbands and wives cannot simply be read off wages commanded in the labour market, or labour inputs in agricultural production. Incomes earned by women do not necessarily translate into the same kind of power as that of men. Practices, such as the gender division of responsibility for specific consumption needs, render women's income defined as less important and therefore non-commensurate with that of men. Feminists also recognise that fundamental changes for women cannot be based solely on increased income. Self-esteem play an important role in women's potential to mobilise external strengths (such as wages, the persuasion of kin,community opinion). In addition, internal constraints (such as improving their health, education and income-earning capacity) are also important in changing their situation (Dwyer and Bruce 1988). For Sen, along with women's involvement in so-called gainful employment, it is the process of politicisation—including a political recognition of gender issues—that can itself cause sharp changes in gender perceptions. The critical issues of incrasing women's self-perception of their status and personal power has led to a focus on the role that the collective action of women's solidarity groups play. In the confrontation of the persistent reinforcement of inequalities, their activities are vital.

Triple Role of Women

Of the three planning stereotypes, the most problematic is the third, which relates to gender divisions of labour within the household. While they typesetting of women as 'home-makers' is true, this is only one of three roles that they perform. Almost low-income Third World households women have a triple role. 'Women's work' includes not only *reproductive* work, the child bearing and rearing responsibilities, required to guarantee the maintenance and reproduction of the labourforce. It also includes productive work, often as secondary income earner. Is rural areas this usually takes the form of an agricultural work. In urban areas women frequently work in informal sector enterprises located either in the home for the neighhourhood. Also, women undertake community managing work around the provision of items of collective consumption, undertaken in the local community in both urban and rural contexts.

In most developing societies the stereotype of the man as breadwinner — that is, the male as productive worker—predominates, even when it is not borne out in reality. Invariaby, when men perceive themselves to have a role within the household it is as the primary income-earner. This occurs even in those contexts where male 'unemployment' is high and women's productive work actually provides the primary income. In addition, generally men do not have a clearly defined reproductive role. This does not mean empirically that they do not play with their children or help their women partners with domestic activities. Men also undertake community activities but in markedly different ways from woman, reflecting a further sexual division of labour. While women have a community managing role based on the provision of items of collective consumption, men have a community leadership role, in which they organise at the formal political level generally within the framework of national politics.

Feminist Debates and Triple Role

The concept of the triple role is not an arbitrary categorization. It derives from the predominantly feminist debates in the extensive literature on gender relations from both the First and Third World, as well as from the research on women in the Third World. This provides the knowledge base for the new tradition of gender planning. This literature is complex and contradictory. Nevertheless, it is universally agreed that the central problematic remains the concept of power and its opposite, oppression, articulated in gender relations in terms of the subordination of women to men. Furthermore, it is the gender divisions of labour that are identified, above all, as embodying and perpetuating female subordination. This phenomenon, more commonly, if in accurately, is termed the sexual division of labour. The fact that some tasks are allocated predominantly or exclusively to women, and others to men, is persistent in human society. Until recently such divisions were perceived to be rigid and universal. The fact that this is not true is now clearly accepted. Divisions of tasks at a point in time vary from one country to another. As countries undergo economic change and the nature of work changes so does its distribution between men and women.

It is this recognition that has caused feminists to challenge two basic premises of the gender division of labour, first, that it is 'natural'; second, that the division between the male breadwinner and the female home-maker is based on a perceived complementarity of roles for men and women, who are different but equal. Feminists argue that there is no reason why gender should be an organizing principle of the social division of labour, except the physical process of child bearing. It is the penetration of Western capitalism with its historical separation of production and reproduction that has resulted in such an artificial division, and its ideological reinforcement.

In examining the different roles of women and men, the gender division of labour provides the underlying principle for separating out and differentiation the work men and women do. it also provides the rationale for the difference in value placed on their work. This accounts for the link between the gender division of labour and the subordination of women.

1. *Reproductive work*

The reproductive role comprises the childbearing/rearing responsibilities and domestic tasks undertaken by women, required to guarantee the maintenance and reproduction of the labour force. It includes not only biological reproduction but also the care and maintenance of the workforce (husband and working children) and the future workforce.

Why is it that the reproductive role is naturally considered women's work? The obvious answer lies in the fact that women bear children and that this connects naturally to the reproduction of all human life. There is no reason why this should extend to the nurturing and caring, not only of children but also for adults, if they are sick or aged through the daily provision of a range of domestic services. This contradiction reflects the diversity of definitions and meanings of reproductive work.

While 'biological reproduction' refers rigidly to the bearing of children, the term 'reproduction of labour' extends further. It includes the care, socialisation and maintenance of individuals throughout their lives, to ensures the continuation of society to the next generation. This daily rainwear and regeneration of the labour force has been termed 'daily' or 'physical reproduction' or 'human reproduction'. It is important to distinguish this term from that of 'social reproduction. Mackintosh (1981) defines this to include the far broader processes by which the main production relations in society are recreated and perpetuated. These include not only the production and maintenance of the wage labour force but also the reproduction of capital itself.

Feminists argue that the strict division of labour that makes reproductive work women's work is a consequence of capitalism. Clearly, there are many examples of pre-capitalist societies where such rigid divisions did not exist. However, despite the esoteric examples of the flexible child-care arrangements of pre-colonial and 'traditional' societies provided by such anthropologists as Margaretmead, the extreme drudgery of domestic work experienced by the vast majority of Third World women, whether they are rural peasants in Asian subsistence production or urban slum-dwellers in Latin American petty commodity production, is also only too apparent.

As the modern cash economy became increasingly divorced from subsistence economy, women lost economic autonomy in their own right as farmers, craftworkers and traders. In this way they increasingly depended on the wages of men. She comments that in such societies gender distinctions are commonly rationalized by beliefs about the central importance of women's role in childbearing, and the imputed operation of 'maternal instinct'. Western male ideology has been of critical importance in emphasizing the exclusive role of the biological mother in nurturing infants and children. This has reinforced the concept of maternal deprivation and promoted the domestic science movement as a vocation justifying the unemployment of women to serve men. Domestic ideology has rephrased the identification of the domestic sphere and the house as the women's place. Even when they have a waged job outside the home, women's primary occupation is as wife and mother.

A crucial issue relating to women's reproductive work concerns the extent to which it is visible and valued. For despite its actual character, because it is seen as 'natural' work it is somehow also not real 'work' and, therefore, invisible. This is most graphically illustrated around the issue of rest. When men finish work, be it from the farm or the factory, and return home, they are tired. They therefore rest, whether this takes the form of sleeping, drinking with other men or watching TV. In contrast to this, domestic labour has no clear demarcations between work and leisure; caring for young children is without beginning or end. Because reproductive work is not 'real' work, women very rarely rest except at night. Consequently in most societies women tend to work longer hours than men. Not only are they the first to get up to prepare the household for the working day, but also last to go to sleep.

Lack of recognition of the economic cost of reproductive work under capitalism has resulted in the separation of paid work, which is allocated an exchange value, from that of unpaid 'domestic' work, which is allocated only a use-value. The fact that this occurs not only in Western but also in non-waged economies, however, suggests that capitalism is not the only explanation. In both capitalist and socialist societies, men do not have clearly defined reproductive roles. In contrast, women's allocation of domestic work, particularly child care, remains extraordinarily rigid and persistent at a global level. Why is it that the gender divisions of labour around human reproduction are so rigid? This question requires an understanding of the relations under which reproductive work is done. Marriage-based households are constructed by definition on the basis of gender, with economic relations within such households also structured by gender. Housework and child care are the activities most influenced by the relations of marriage. It is this that provides the critical link between productive and reproductive work. As Mackintosh so succinctly argues.

> The household has become a kind of mediating institution, mediating that is two sets of social relations; that of marriage and foliation, which act to constitute the household and determine the context of much of child-care, and the wider economic relations of society. Women's performance of domestic work, especially the care of children within the home, both expresses their dependence and subordination within marriage (since men actively benefit from this work) and also weakens their position within the labour market, contributing to their low wages and poor conditions as wage workers. (1981:11)

2. *Productive Work*

The productive role comprises work done by both women and men for payment in cash or kind. It includes both market production with an exchange value, and subsistence/ home production with an actual use-value, but also a potential exchange value. For women in agricultural production this includes work as independent farmers, peasants' wives and wage workers.

Whereas the ideology of patriarchy has served to reinforce the popular stereotype of the male breadwinner, reality does not bear this out. Throughout the Third world most low-income women have an important productive role. Nevertheless, the rigidity of gender divisions of labour has ensured that although this is the one area in which both men and women work, they do so unequally. Ideological masked asymmetrical gender relations in productive work, whether it is in the formal or informal sector, rural or urban production, means that against women as a category are subordinated to men.

Definitions of 'productive' work are fraught with complexities. This is most visible in cash economies, and by contrast, least so in subsistence production. It includes work in both the formal and informal sectors, as well is in family enterprises. In the latter case it may not be perceived of as work with an exchange value, since work undertaken does not get a wage.

Many feminists have argued that since the reproduction of labour involves several productive tasks, a dualist division, such as that between production and reproduction,is not helpful. They claim that reproductive work is also productive. because its domain its the production of use-values under non wage relations, it is not identified as 'productive' work. It is recognized that the use of the term 'productive' work as referring only to work with an exchange value is an over-simplification of reality. Neverthless, in developing the conceptual principles for gender planning the purpose of distinguishing between women's productive and reproductive roles is precisely to highlight the multiple forms of women's work. Thus reveals the severe limitations of contemporary planning categories which in emphasixing the difference between men's productive work and women's reproductive work, have so effectively rendered women's productive work invisible. The purpose of this simplification, therefore, is not to undervalue or ignore the importance of production for use-value. It is to identify how the complexities of women's multiple interdependent roles can be unplified into methodological tools that planners can translate into practice.

In recent past a veritable explosion of research on the complexities of women's productive work in withnessed. This has clearly identified the extent to which gender divisions of favour continue to reinforce women's subordinate position in productive work. Despite structural transformations in systems of production in both urban and rural area, this continues. Although patterns of segregation run through all societies, exactly which job falls to men, and which to women, has varied enormously. In essence, however, it is still the fact that 'women pick up the work men wont' do'. This is most visible where men and women both work for wages.

Segregation of the labour market means that in all economies women predominate at the lower end of the labour market. They cluster in certain industrial and agricultural sectors, and within these and to have certain occupations. Not only are they distributed vertically, that to say, sex-segregated based on gender hierarchy, into lower-paid and lower-skilled jobs. They are also distributed horizontally within particular sectors, with few women in managerial positions and most in those occupations that are an extension of domestic labour.

Even where entirely new areas of enployment are created, new forms of 'women's work' are established, there perpetuation women's subordination. This is most visible in the processes of the internationalisation of capital, when production relocates to avoid trade union regulations in Free Trade or Border Zones. It takes advantage of lower employment costs with matching or even higher levels of productivity. Most frequently this is youth, single women's labour. Elson and Person (1981) have identified that such women are often recruited because of their so-called 'number finger's. In reality, they form the cheaperst, most docile labour force best suited for tedious, monotonous waed work, whose lower wages are attributed to their secondary stats in the labour market, which is itself identified because of their capacity to bear children.

Neither is the situation generally and better for womenoutside waged work, whether self-employed or working as members of family enterprises. Small scale 'petty commodity production' within the so-called informal sector is both dependent and involutionary in nature. Its relationship to large-scale formal sector production is exploitative interms of issues such as access to credit, between remunerated and non-remunerated work, and therefore do not perceive it as work.

Gender divisions of labour also continue to structure work relations in rural areas. In agricultural production in Africa the common policy stereotype is still the dichotomy popularized by Boserup's seminar research; women work on subsistence food production while men produce cash crops. This results in a high level of invisibility of rural women's work has identified, the gender divisions of labour are more complex. Although there are clear gender demacrations of tasks, women generally have a dual productive role, and sometimes even threefold. In cases where women have separate access to land it is common for them to work both as 'independent farmers' on their own small holder plots, and work as 'peasant wies', contributing to household production as unremunerated labour in the fields of male household members, where they work in planting, housing and weeding, the tasks designated in the gender division of labour as women's work. Women also work as wage labourers, most frequently seasonally, to supplement household income. Finally, the commercialisation of agriculture an concomitant transformations in production systems and technology have influenced the so-called 'separate but equal' status of women in several fundamental ways. These relate particularly to time ad access to resources. Capital in agriculture has put increasing pressure on women to spend more time working on their male kin's farm. This reduces the income, in cash or kind, from a women's own small holding. The change of ownership from collective to market systems of private ownership,with state-codified individual forms of lad allocation and resettlement, has frequently resulted in blindness to, or ignorance of, women's land rights.

Community Managing and Community Politics

The community managing role comprises activities undertaken primarily by women at the community level, as an extension of their reproductive role. This is to ensure the provision and maintenance of source resources of collective consumption, such as water, health care and education. It is voluntary unpaid work, undertaken in free time. The community politics role in contrast comprises activities undertaken by men at the community level organising at the formal political level. It is usually paid work, either directly or indirectly, through wages or increases in status and power.

Recognition that women have a community managing role is still far from widespread, such that it is still most frequently identified as part of reproductive work. This may well relate to the fact that feminist debates around issues of consumption are preliminary. In outlining the conceptual principles of gender planning, however, it is essential to define this as a clearly identified role in its own right./For, like reproductive work, community managing is seen as 'naturally' women's work. The importance of giving recognition and visibility to this form of work, as an activity in its own right, is of particular significance in the current economic climate where low-income households are increasingly resolving community-level problems through self-help solutions.

'Community managing', then, is defined as the work undertaken at the community level, around the allocation, provisioning and managing of items of collective consumption. A wide diversity of consumption needs for the reproduction of labour power have been increasingly socialized at the level of the community. The fact that women,in their acceptance of the gender division of labour, see the house as their sphere of dominance and take primary responsibility for the provision of consumption needs within the family has already been discussed. However, these needs include not only individual consumption needs within the household, but also the consumption needs of a collective nature at the neighborhood or community level. Thus, for women the point of residence includes not only the home but also extends into the surrounding areas. Social relationships include not only household members but also neighbours. Mobilisation and organization at the community level is a natural extension of their domestic work. Where there is open confrontation between community-level organizations and state or NGOs for infrastructure provision,women most frequently take primary responsibility for the formation, organisation and success of local-level protest groups. This phenomenon has been most widely documented in urban South America (See Barrage and Fort 1987: and Moser 1987b). It is, however, neither uniquely South American no urban.

It is now widely recognised that the serious deficit in housing,infrastructure and social service provision experienced in most third World countries is not simply a problem of rapid urbanization. In the late 1970s Castells (1977) described these gaps in provision as a 'crisis of collective consumption;. He argued that while the capitalist system requires the adequate reproduction of labour power as a prerequisite of continued production and accumulation, private capital finds it less and less profitable to invest in the means of collective consumption. In order to deal with this contradiction the state interences (directly or indirectly) and takes responsibility for the reproduction of labour power. This may have provided an interpretation for increased top-down state provision in the 1970s through such policies as basic needs. A decade later diet, recession and structural adjustment loans have resulted in severe cutbacks in state provision of infrastructure and services. For low-income women this has meant increased time pressure in their role as community managers. They engage in bottom-up struggles manifested through self-help community-based solutions to obtain food, health and education. In contexts where NGOs with highly 'participatory' programmes are helping with service delivery these are most frequently designed on the assumption that women will provide the necessary (unpaid) labour.

Gender divisions of labour are equally important as they are at the household level. The spatial division between the public world of men, and the private world of women, means that for women the neighhourhood is an extension of the domestic arena, while for men it is the public world of politics. This means that while women in the gender-ascribed roles of wives and mothers are involved in community managing, men are involved in community politics. In low-income communities throughout the world there is a consistent trend for political organizations to be run by men with mainly male members, and for collective consumption groups to be in the hands of women. For example, in Lima men control and lead the Junta Communal, while women organise the Community Kitchen Associations; in Manila a man is generally the Baranguay Captain, while a woman obviously leads the Women's Club; in Bombay, the National Slum Dwellers Association local representative is a man, but the Mahila Mandal leader is a women.

In organizations in which these two activities overlap, especially in societies where men and women can work alongside each other, women most frequently make up the rank-and-five voluntary membership. Men tend to be involved in positions of direct authority and often work in a paid capacity. The fact that male leaders are frequently paid for their work is legitimized by the fact that 'a man has to work'. Women by contrast, are expected to be selfless and pure. Their participation is justified in their render-ascribed role of being a good mother, working to improve living conditions for their families. This gender division at the community level between paid men's work and unpaid women's voluntary work has been extensively reinforced by governments, internal agencies and NGOs alike.

As long as women mobilise around issues relating directly to their social sphere and outside established political organizations, they can become very powerful, precisely because they do not challenge the nature of their gender subordination. Once they move into the 'masculine' world of public politics confrontations are virtually inevitable. These are personal, with women friends and husbands, as well as political, with male politicians; women only avoid conflict by rigidly conforming to their gender-ascribed roles. This is one important reasons why women with their particular responsibilities for social and welfare politics often choose to remain involved in community managing.

CHAPTER 11

Gender Planning: An Institution

Lack of appropriate administrative structure is identified as an important hurdle by the organisations concerned with incorporating WID/GAD policy into planning and practice in the recent past. The strategy frequently adopted has been the creation of new structures. Their specific mandate then is to translate gender policy into planning and practice. Globally, a proliferation of new organisations has emerged. These include ministries of women's affairs in national government, gender units in NGOs, and women's divisions in donor agencies.

The institutionalisation of gender and women and development policy, identifying constraints and opportunities in current strategies are examined here. It provides a brief historical background before describing the comparative strategies of several institutions currently integrating a WID/GAD policy within their institutions during the 1980s. These include national governments such as the Caribebean CARICOM countries. Besides, it includes bilateral donors, such as the UK Overseas Development Administration (ODA) and the Swedish Development Agency (SIDA). Finally, it also refers to multilateral donors, such as the World Bank and the Food and Agriculture Organisations (FAO), and UK-based development NGOs such as Christian Aid and Oxfam.

Institutionalisation of WID/GAD

It is important to highlight the extent to which the

institutionalisation of WID/GAD is simply a technical problem relating to existing institutional structures, or whether it is a political problem requiring change in the nature of institutions themselves. This raises two fundamental questions concerning meaning of institutionalisation. First, is possible to gender' an institution? Second, is the purpose to create a 'gender-aware' organization, or a 'gendered organization'? the first question has implications for the relative success of the two different organisations strategies, that of creating new, separate institutions of mainstreaming within existing structures. Whereas the tendency in published research has been to focus on the technical nature of institutional components, Staudt (1983) has pointed out the essentially political nature of institutionalisation. According to the 'bureaucratic politics' model, organizational action is a result of the bargaining that occurs between hierarchically positioned players in an organization. The probability of success in bureaucratic games depends on bargaining advantages, skill and will in using resources. Prospects for effective bargaining depend on power resources, which include expertise, control over material resources, structural location and internal alliance building.

To institutionalise WID/GAD, not only do organizational strategies often differ, but so also does the mandate as to what 'institutionalising' effectively involves. This raises a second fundamental question. Can it be assumed that an institution that is gender-aware (because all those working within the institution recognise the importance of gender) will act in a 'gendered' manner? Two issues are relevant here. First, although an institution may be gender-aware, it may nevertheless still be structured as before. To have a gendered institution, as many feminists have argued, it may be necessary a priori to change the institutional structure. Secondly, it cannot be assumed that a gendered institution will act in a neutral, objective manner. This assumes that once technically perceived problems of lines of responsibility and gender-awareness are ironed out, successful implementation can occur. Do organisations operate 'objectively', such that institutionalised interventions are 'neutral', in effect, or are decisions made in the interests of particular groups?

Staudt (1983) has argued that bureaucratic resistance to women's programmes may be greater than the usually resistance to new mandates. In her analysis of the 'bureaucratic mire', she maintains that institutions are political factors in their own right. Consequently, bureaucratic resistance must be seen in terms of the fact that the prospect of female emplorement threatens male privilege (1990). The creation of new institutional structures, or the gendering of existing structures, may both in themselves ensures successful implementation. From the outset it is necessary to recognise that political constraints and opportunities may determine the extent to which the institutionalisation of WID/GAD makes any fundamental change sin the planning process.

Historical Background

In the history of planning, new organizational structures commonly develop for the institutionalisation of new planning procedures. Once established, such organisations very rapidly tend to become the legitimized 'home' of a particular sectorial issue or planning concern. This makes it difficult for them to absorb new issues. It also means that once a planning concern is identified with a particular administrative structure it is difficult for other organisations to institutionalise it.

For these reasons, the recent institutionalisation of WID/GAD must be viewed in terms of its historical origins. Colonial and post-colonial governments first identified the problems of Third World low-income women as a policy concern. Residual welfare social policy during this period considered women, along with other 'vulnerable groups', as a marginal issue. If they institutionalised such policy at all, it was into weak, under-financed ministries of social welfare.

Prevailing macro-economic and social policy has resulted in the institutionalisation of low-income women's needs into peripheral and under-resourced organisations. In addition, it is the result of the difficulty experienced in location women, a category of people with cross-sectorial importance, within planning machineries based on sectorial priorities. Despite the widely acknowledged problems this poses for non-sectorial concerns, most planning procedures, particularly those at government level, continue to plan with a sectorial approach. The problem, thus, is not unique to WID, but has also dogged other cross-sectorial concerns such as community development, rural development and, most recently, the environment. Despite the obvious lack of analytical logic, these are frequently identified as sectorial concerns (Moser 1989b; Conyers 1982). One successful institution to cope with cross-sectorial planning is UNICEF. Their mandate is to plan for children, although interestingly enough over time they have extended this limited target to include women and others concerned with children's welfare.

The institutionalisation of WID concerns into welfarist, under-resourced organisations whether at national, international or donor level, was a legacy inherited by the UN Decade for Women. Until 1975 most Third World countries had not addressed women's concerns in their own right. Yet, as early as 1962 the UN Commission on the Status of Women first identified the value of appointing national commissions on the status of women. These made recommendations for improving the position of women in their respective countries (UNCSDHA 1987). Subsequent UN meetings focused attention on institutional mechanisms as an important part of national strategies for the advancement of women. However, it was not until the first major conference of the UN Decade of Women, in 1975, that the endorsed World Plan of Action identified national machinery in the following terms:

> The establishment of interdisciplinary and multisectoral machinery within government, such as national commissions, women's bureaus and other bodies, with adequate staff and budget, can be an effective transitional measure for accelerating the achievement of equal opportunities for women and their full integration into

> national life. The membership of such bodies should include both women and men, representative of all groups of society responsible for making, and implementing policy decisions in the public sector.

It recognised the cross-sectorial nature of the concern and identified that representation should include government ministries and departments responsible for education, health, labour, justice, communications and information, culture, industry, trade, agriculture, rural development, social welfare, finance and planning.

During the 1976-85 Decade of Women, 'machineries' were more clearly defined. This involved a shift from the early emphasis on advisory bodies to a broader idea of machinery in multiple and more complex forms, intended to emphasise official institutionalisation within government. Its popularity with international donors has been explained in the following terms:

> At the time it was also believed, it seems, that WID belonged to that group of trendy issues that the UN introduces from time to time to stimulate the imagination of the international community to strengthen its sense of solidarity with less fortunate members, and to prevent opinion leaders from losing interest in matters of global concern. (Himmelstrand 1990: 104)

By 1985 most countries identifies some form of national machinery, 50 per cent of which they set up during the decade. Of the 127 member states listed, approximately 22 percent had organisations for women located in ministries of social affairs or social welfare. A further 20 per cent were in NGOs, about 16 per cent in separate ministries, and about 17 per cent located in the office of the prime minister.

More recently, bilateral donors have also addressed the institutionalisation of WID. All nineteen members of the OECD's Development Assistance Committee (DAC) have adjusted to facilitate the implementation of their WID policies. Centralized WID Units work as catalysts for WID issues within the organisations, giving WID assignments to designated officers in the various departments/divisions of the agency concerned. While each agency has the minimum of one permanent WID adviser, twelve have WID Units. These comprise several professionals and support staff, located in strategic positions to provide WID expertise to those departments or divisions involved in policy-planning and operations (OECD 1990). A recent survey of European NGOs working in the South showed that 31 per cent had a person, group or department dealing with gender issues. This figure ranged from 4 per cent of French NGOs to 61 per cent in the Netherlands, many of whom are part-time or volunteers (LCD 1989). Despite such an array of new administrative structures, clearly women's 'machineries' have not fulfilled their expectations. Even by 1985 the UN, one of its greatest proponents, had expressed doubt concerning the efficacy of the mechanism in place. National machineries were expected to have a multiple function, with both a planning and advocacy role, carrying out decisions and playing catalytic role. The UN, therefore, concluded that 'Looking back it is clear that too much was expected too soon from widely disparate bodies, in very different locations' (UNCSDHA 1987: 7).

An INSTRAW assessment of the 'failure' of women's machinery in seventy-nine countries identified a number of factors responsible. These included small budgets and staff, attitudes that legitimize female subordination, mandates that focused on welfare, under-funding of women's projects and separate women's divisions, and ministries lacking the resources and time to influence other government ministries. Similarly, Northern NGOs list lack of resources, internal decision-making structures, internal staffing policies, insufficient awareness of gender issues, and lack of willingness to change as the most frequently encountered problems (LCD 1989). Finally, the OECD (1990) reported that limited staff resources have been a major constraint against the adoption of WID policies.

Staudt provides additional evidence to support the

assertion that such machineries have 'failed', citing the budgetary allocations of multilateral and bilateral donor agencies. In the UN agencies, less than 4 per cent of project budget allocation benefit women, with a cursory 0.2 per cent of budget allocated directly to them. Less than 1 per cent of FAO projects contain strategies to reach women. Finally, of the $700 million budget of the UN Development Program, UNDP, UNIFEM receives only $5 million (Staudt 1990). Nor is the situation of Northern NGOs working in the South more encouraging. One 1988 survey showed that 93 per recent of European NGOs it not have a separate budget line for women's projects. Of those which did, the women represented an average of 9 per cent of total budget (LCD 1989).

It is now widely agreed that the creation of women's 'machineries' in governments, donor agencies and NGOs raised expectations that women's needs would be addressed. It also manipulatively gave the impression that the creation of separate institutional structures met such needs. This has often resulted in a total reduction in the resources reaching women.

Northern NGOs Experience

Most governments, donor agencies and NGOs have set up separate organizational structures to institutionalise WID. The first question concerns whether this marginalises the issues. Is its an appropriate institutional strategy to mainstream within existing structures? As Anderson and Chen (1988) have identified, the underlying rationalise for the two strategies differs. One strategy establishes specially designated WID offices, whose responsibility it is to raise the issue of WID for the institution as a whole, and to carry out WID programmes.

This strategy requires gender specialists to take responsibility for the institutionalisation of WID, from a separate institutional structure.

By contrast, another approach prioritises the integration, or mainstream, of WID within existing institutional structures, into established programme areas and sectorial activities. It argues that institutional responses will only be significant and convincing if, and when, the core staff and programmes of the organization accept and integrated WID. Institutionalisation will be more effective if carried out by gender aware generalists from their particular positions within the organization.

The comparative experience of two Northern international NGOs based in the United Kingdom and funding third World development projects highlights some of the advantages and disadvantages of these two alternative strategies. Oxfam is one of the largest UK NGOs with a staff of more than 1,000. It has created a designated WID office, the Gender and Development Unit (GADU), emphasizing the importance of gender specialists. In contrast, Christian Aid, a smaller organization numbering about 230 staff, has chosen a mainstream approach. In Oxfam the impetus to create a special WID focus came 'bottom-up', from a group of women field officers. Working in collaboration with regional and headquarters staff, they proposed the establishment of a separate unit. In Christian Aid, its Women's Group (an advisory body of women working in the organization) drew up a set of organizational recommendations in 1983. These identified constraints and blockades to WID. In 1987 a second set followed, when the group formalized itself into a Women's Forum (Christian Aid 1987). Thus, in common with most organisations, in both cases the original catalyst came in the early 1980s— 'bottoms and from women within the organization.

GADU was established in Oxfam in 1985 as one of the first initiatives of a new overseas director, with its purpose 'to tell people about the gender issues. He perceived this as a short-term initiatives that would cease once everyone had understood the issue. In Christian Aid one of the divisions, the Aid Sector, responded to the women's Group's recommendations. This came, from a concern that the organization's project documents did not adequately incorporate gender issues. In Oxfam the final impetus for the creation of a separate institutional structure was a top-down directive from a sympathetic senior male staff member. In Christian Aid the planning preoccupation of its division directly concerned with the allocation of project finance was particularly important in endorsing the initiatives to mainstream gender. At its inception, Christian Aid's support for a WID initiatives had a broader support base than that of Oxfam, where one senior-level staff member played a deciding role. Different policy approaches in these two NGOs, therefore, influenced the particular procedures and methods used to institutionalise gender.

In Oxfam GADU was one of several specialist units which also included research and evaluation, technical and health units. In a management structure which excluded them from the main line, their function was an advisory one. Because Oxfam defines itself as a 'field-led' organization, with most of its staff working in the Third World, GADI, like other units has a responsive approach. It started by focusing its work at the field level, responding to requests for advice and funding. This was followed by the promotion of the employment of gender project officers in the field to do the work 'in situ', and more recently the endorsement of the need for regional offices to develop a gender policy. It identified networking through regional workshops as a means to influence the attitudes and working practices of staff in their Oxford headquarters. Given its advisory mandate, it did not initially prioritise training.

Christian Aid, as a smaller organization without field offices or a structure of advisory units at headquarters, from the start prioritized gender planning training of all staff with responsibility for project funding divisions. It saw this as a long-term process and, therefore, institutionalised it through three gender-aware generalists and a trainer. They all took on the responsibilitity for training as one of their mainstream activities. In addition, planning procedures changed because of redesigned checklists and the introduction of project-level gender guidelines. Both planning tools used the concepts and planning methodology introduced through training.

Both organisations say they have made progress in institutionalising gender, but still have a long way to go. Both confirm that at the time the strategy adopted was the appropriate one for their particular organization. The strength of a WID unit such as GADU is that it can act both as a monitoring unit to ensures integration, as well as a pressure group to ensures that WID is constantly on th e agenda. A recent survey of NGOs in Europe confirms these findings. It shows there was a correlation between the existence of a person, group or department dealing with gender issues and the formulation of WID policy documents (LCD 1989). In the same vein, proponents of separate organisations argue that the strategy to mainstream hides the fact that WID is not a sufficient priority to warrant a separate unit. Reliance on mainstreaming also can mean that WID has to challenge over-riding concerns in each sectoral interest. It therefore is more likely to be institutionalised into areas in which women already predominate (such as health, education, welfare and nutrition) than the more technical sectors of the institution.

While it may not decide the outcome, the type of institutional model chosen reflects organizational 'culture. The evidence suggests that a mainstream approach is more likely to occur in organizations with an organizational 'culture' of consensus management. The creation of a separate unit is far more likely to be advocated in organisations with a 'culture' of conflict management. The creation of a separate unit frequently results in higher levels of organistional tension and trauma than does a Mainstream Strategy. The holder of the WID post has a mandate to confront those not delivering, but also must be prepared to be on the receiving end of abuse. The staff of GADU are clear that the creation of a separate institution has been critical in providing the necessary space to think through WID policy.

They acknowledged that it has not been smooth riding.

One staff member commented that it was a miserable job and could have been called the moan and groan unit. Staudt argues that 'Gender redistributive politics are as conflict laden as any other redistributive issue, but are subtle in the personalized resistance they incur, and complex in their confusion with cross-sex interpersonnal relations' (1990: 4). Where the issue is indentified in terms of a individual, generally a woman, the conflation of the professional and the personalise often far greater. Open displays of conflict may be more cathartic in changing attitudes, but are certainly more painful. A clear cycle of changing attitudes is visible in many organizations, and Oxfam is by no means unique in this. When gender is first raised as an issue it is often dismissed as a joke; them personal attacks occur that question the sexuality of individuals; finally, acceptance manifests itself in a pretence of agreement. A member of GADU commented that 'When GADU started many people laughed; one or two called us lesbians, dykes; that is no loner acceptable. Now the most difficult problem is one of people pretending they agree.

This pressure to personalise is widespread. Staudt provides an example in a case study of USAID. She cites testimony before Congress in which a Representative repeatedly tried to prompt and extend the words 'malechauvinism' and 'male chauvinist pigs' to the WID co-ordinator's comments. In response, she replied, "It's your term, not mine. Open displays of conflict are disturbing for both men and women. men employed is WID units often experience a very particular form of trauma. The evidence suggests that a mainstream approach does not seem to provoke such problems. Here the concern is to identify who has responsibility for WID. The danger is that issues will not be monitored because everyone simply passes the buck. As a staff member of Christian Aid commented: 'The fact that people pay lip service to the rhetoric of gender does not mean they necessarily take on the issues in practice. They are not necessarily fully on board.

It is still important to clarify principles. Nevertheless, it has become clear that the amount of action on WID at the international level has lessened the relevance of the debate concerning alternative institutional strategies. The adoption of the Nairobi Forward Looking Strategies (NFLS) requires governments to set up separate 'machineries'. The OECD DAC Revised Guiding Principles on WID mandates administrative adjustments to help implement WID policies. Both require the identification of personnel with WID responsibility. This has meant that evening those organizations with a mainstream policy, representation at international monitoring meetings requires a designated individual, by default if not design, to wear the designated WID hat. At the NGO level similar trends have emerged. In Christian Aid the generalists in the gender planning training team have to resist very hard not to become, de facto, the WID Unit. The lack of a person with full-time WID responsibility has implications for Christian Aid's impact at the level of the inter-NGO lobbying and networking. In some instances staff members represent Christian Aid as a function of their job, while in other cases it is the Women's Forum's responsibility to be involved.

If the issue is not the validity of WID units as such, then the critical questions is the determination of WID's power, legitimacy and mandate. Obviously, there is no single factor but several causally interrelated constraints and opportunities that have effectively determined the capacity of women's units to institutionalise WID. The following section discusses each separately to show the manner in which each influences the other.

Experience of Government Women's Bureaus

Anderson and Chen argue, 'it is not the institutional machinery per se that makes the difference...what is important in whether WID is taken seriously is the institutional strategy that its proponents adopt' (188:4). If the creation of a separate unit is not the problem, its location within the planning structure is often the first important decision in the institutional strategy. In government women's bureaux, Gordan (1984) has argued that ministerial location reflects the extent of the government's commitment to the notion of integrating women into national life. It also reflects its ideological opposition about the role of women and, therefore, its perception of the role of the machinery itself. Power and legitimacy relate primarily to the machinery's access to the planning, policy formulation and funding sectors of the government. These determine its ability to have any significant impact on the direction of development in the country.

Women's 'machineries' of government were created 'top-down' by the political leadership as a response to the demand from the international community during the Women's Decade. This meant that the creation of a women's bureau' was often more a symbolic gesture than a legitimization of women's activities (Gordan 1984). Nevertheless, its structural vocational community during the Women's Decade. This meant that the creation of a women's bureau' was often more a symbolic gesture than a legitimization of women's activities. Nevertheless, its structural location was the logical consequence of the current policy approach to women by the government concerned. Since this was almost without exception welfarist in orientation, the common pattern was to locate women's bureaux in ministries of social affairs or welfare. One exception, however, was the location of nearly a fifth of all bureaux in the prime minister's office. This was largely a matter of short-term political expediency. Only recently, with the shift towards an efficiency approach, have governments begun to consider the importance of women's units in such ministries as agriculture or industry.

The structural location in ministries of social affairs or welfare over the past decade has been highly problematic for two main reasons. First, there is a fundamental contradiction between the UN Decade's objectives for machineries to improve the status of women by ensuring their full integration into national life, and the welfarist objectives of social welfare ministries. Their concerns, in contrast, are to ameliorate the position of women as passive beneficiaries of development, while reinforcing their subordinate status. Secondly, because ministries of social welfare, as 'soft', marginal ministries, have traditionally lacked power, status and associated financial resources, these same problems have been transferred to women's bureaux. Not only has structural location proved problematic for women's bureaux.

Not only has structural location proved problematic for women's bureaux, but in some countries the constant moving of location has probably been even more so. In her 1984 study of six Caribbean countries Gordan identified that the three earliest countries to set up their women's machinery had each had four changes of location. This might be expected in the early stages of institutionalisation of WID, particularly with the high profile expected in 1985. While the average for all nine countries was approximately three location changes, five of the nine countries had experienced four or more. This may be the consequence of political expediency, and reflects the continuing marginality of the women's bureaux. It also suggests that governments have experienced considerable problems in integrating the cross-sectoral issue of women's concerns into sectoral-based planning systems. The constraint can be identified as both political and technical in nature.

The Grenada government, for instance, has repeatedly redefined the sectoral basis of women's concerns. It moved this Department of Women's Affairs first from the Ministry of Education and Culture, to Health, then to Housing and Community Development. Communications and Works followed, and it has ended in Tourism and Civil Aviation. Equally, Trinidad and Tobag has struggled to redefine its cross-sectoral ministerial concerns. It has moved its Women's Bureau from Social Security and Cooperatives, first to Health, Welfare and the Status of Women, and most recently to Social Development and Family Services. Those women's machineries with a lower level of mobility, such as in Belize and the Bahamas, have located them from the starting ministries broadly concerned with social development.

UNCSDHA, among others, has argued that because the issue of location is obvious it has received more attention than it merits. The real issue is the more basic one of access to power, achieved by a variety of means, only one of which is location (UNCSDHA 1987). Despite their specific location, women's bureaux work within an operating bureaucratic system. In principle, this gives them the right of access to available resources of services, personnel and machinery within the system. Gordan (1984), therefore, concluded that political support for WID may not be as important for progress as appropriate strategies. Bureaux' success depends on an administrative framework that permits collaboration with the top bureaucrats and technocrats in all relevant ministries. One important measure has been the identification of administrative arrangements emphasizing multisectoral bureaux functions. The extent to which this has been successful has depended, above all, on the policy framework of the women's bureaux.

Lack of Coherent Policy

These have important organizational implications. Clearly, many organisations that created 'top-down' women's bureaux and units lacked a clear policy approach to WID. So did most WID units when first formally constituted. Their broad goals reflected the popular international rhetoric of the Women's Decade more than specific country-level priorities. The Decade's extensive goals of equity, peace and development all concurred in their aspiration to improve the 'overall status of women's (equity) and to 'integrated women into development' (development). However, no clear consensus existed as to the strategies by which this might be achieved. the 1985 Forward Looking Strategies provided more specific objectives and were important starting points for government-level women's organisations. Nevertheless, it was the responsibility of each individual government to develop its appropriate strategies. To date, in many countries all that exists are broad policy statements. These lack specific goals and priorities, or the relevant planning procedures and management support structures necessary to transform them into practice.

Where goals, objectives and strategies have been defined, there is often conceptually a lack of internal consistency. For example, although endorsing the rhetoric of equity, few women's bureaux have understood, or acknowledged, its implications in terms of its top-down priority of women's strategic gender needs. In practice it results in goals of equity combined with strategies of welfare. The reasons are obvious. Welfare policy is still the common WID approach. Many governments, and the personnel recruited into the women's bureaux do not acknowledge that welfarist measures help low-income women meet practical gender needs, but reinforce their subordinate gender position. These approaches are unlikely to reach the strategic gender needs agreed in the overall goals.

Of late organisations have structured to define specific goals, objectives and related functions. For many bureaux, established because of government lip-service to the Decade, their high profile and the level of expectation to deliver on every front exacerbates the situation. A common tendency has been the simultaneous adoption of numerous strategies, with activities ranging from research on women, through policy formulation to project implementation. In reality, however, one institution cannot be expected to provide the full range of policies, programmes or projects necessary to accomplish WID goals. Anderson and Chen (1988) argue theat agencies differ in their capabilities and limitations. Each may have relative advantages over others in terms of the level at which it works. They distinguish between three types of institutions, government, professional intermediary institutions and private voluntary organisations (NGOs), and summarise the relative strength of each. NGOs are strong as advocacy an promotional agencies. They have organizing skills but fewer technical and managerial skills and, therefore, can play an important advocacy role in raising and polarizing issues. The strength of professional institutions is in the their research and ability to provide technical and managerial assistance and, therefore, their importance is in providing assistance for targeted programming. Finally, governments have greater access to financial resources and specialized expertise. This gives them advantages in terms of scale and coverage and infrastructure development necessary for integrated, mainstream and broad-scale programming.

The 1990 survey of women's bureaux in nine Caribbean countries revealed that all implemented projects. The majority also undertook research and advised other ministries, and about half also undertook government policy formulation. Although in theory different organisations have relative advantages in terms of their mandate, in practice political legitimacy forces women's bureaux to undertake a wide diversity of strategies. A fundamental policy problem for women's bureaux is the lack of integration of WID policy into national policy objectives. Although paying lip-service to WID policy, governments in the main have continued to see women as an add—on or separate matter, purely the concern of th e women's bureaux. The failure to establish women's priorities in terms of other national priorities has important institutional implications. It means that the women's bureau operates in a highly hostile environment in the ministry where it is located. Other departments assess it as an imposition and drain on resources, rather than as a contribution to the profile or status of their ministry. They therefore do not make the arrangements necessary to ensure collaboration between the bureau, its parent ministry and other governmental bodies. Without defined lines of responsibility and accountability professional staff cannot operate. Gordan's (1984) assessment showed that difficulties experienced in getting regular contact with the Permanent Secretary of their particular ministry was one important problem identified.

The failure to integrated WID policy into national policy objectives results in a lack of clarity as to the role of other government agencies in carrying out policies relating to women's needs. Problems in persuading other bureaucracies of the fundamental need to link welfare concerns about women with the major economic, social and political concerns of their country are widespread. Finally, in the creation of intra-organizational linkages, so critical if women's bureaux are to move from project—to policy-level, WID units have experienced severe problems. these relate both to identifying administrative structures for intra-governmental linkages as well as those with relevant NGOs. Ministries often lack the necessary consultation processes to ensure that they incorporate women's concerns into their work. They often achieve more effective programme coordination when they institute routine administrative arrangements such as steering committees and working parties. However, these are only successful if officially validated with precise objectives specified. Even where such legitimacy is provided, there are enormous organisational problems associated in the co-ordination of cross-sectoral planning in ministerial structures based on sectoral planning procedures.

Since power and status within organistional strctures is most frequently determined in terms of control over resources, this is commonly identified as the most important factor in institutionalising WID. Within organisations different parts complete for budget allocations. Consequently, the size of the budget has come to exemplify the organisations' perception of the importance of the work of the WID Unit. Many governments regard the budget statement as the annual declaration of its policy. This means that the only other important source of leverage for women's machineries is external funding from either official donors or NGOs.

There is a consensus that all women's machineries are severely under-funded, with participation in their organistion's budgetary planning marginal, if present at all. The evidence is not only fragmentary but also difficult to evaluate. Budget allocations vary depending on how far the bureau has an implementing as against advisory function. The 1990 Caribbean survey,for instance, showed that all the women's machineries had an annual budget allocation. However, the amount involvedvaried very widely,in relation nto only to tits status, but also its mandate.

Only consequence of limited budget allocation is that it has force women's bureaux to rely increasingly on external funding. This in turn has meant less control over their preferred policy direction. The fact that some donors prefer to allocated resources to projects, particularly income-generating projects, forces bureaux to become more project-orientated than their mandate designates. This reduces their capacity to fulfill other objectives. It is important, however, not to over-exaggerate the size of resource allocation made by donors to women's projects. In the United Kingdom, ODA resource allocations for WID-specific projects increased from four in 1987/88 to six in 1988. For WID-integrated projects it increased from two in 1987/88 to sixteen in 1988 (ODA 1989). There are considerable problems caused by fixed short-term project funds, that leave bureaux to carry on without adequate support. External funding, however, is often critical for political large to obtain recognition and consequently funding from internal sources. Consequently, bureaux constantly make difficult decisions in terms of very different priorities.

As the mandates of women's units and bureaux shift more towards influencing policy than carrying out projects, their concern becomes less their own budget allocations, and more the WID allocations within other parts of the organization. In ministries of agriculture, for instance, what are the budget allocations for projects involving women heads of households? In ministries of health, how are resources allocated between large curative teaching hospitals and mother and child health centres? As the mandate of the women's unit becomes one of advising, monitoring and evaluating that the organization integrated gender in all work, their biggest budget expenditure then becomes staff salaries.

Budget allocations vary depending on the extent to which the women's unit is an implementing agency. Consequently, the best indicator of status and power is that of staff size. Despite the nature of the institution staff allocations to WID are universally pathetic. The 1990 survey of Caribbean countries reveals an average staff size of our (excluding Jamaica, with the usually large staff size of fifteen). A recent OECD survey of WID officers employed full-time in thirteen countries with WID Units shows an average of 2.4 (excluding the United States with its atypical number of sixteen) (OECD 1990).

Other important issues need to be mentioned in relation to staffing: first, the role of the director. Much has been written of the deciding role of the director whose charismatic power or hopeless incompetence influences the unit's outcome. Clearly, an inordinate amount of responsibility for the potential success of failure of the women's unit is vested in the hands of one person. Her (or his) job description covers everything from academic knowledge of WID policy, through management skills to competence in publicity, funding and international relations. Yet the status and salary level of this job does not make it necessarily very attractive to many professional women unless they are ideologically committed to working on women's needs. In the 1990 Caribbean survey, the average age of the head or director of women's bureaux is thirty-seven years of age. Of these, 55 per cent have higher educational diplomas or certificates with the remaining 45 per cent holding university bachelor degrees in the social sciences.

In many agencies, government and donors alike, women can become stigmatized and stuck if they work too long on WID issues. The labeling of women WID officers with their work is an example of the conflation of the personal with the professional that so dominates this career structure. In the case of donor agencies it is not the aid agencies that suffer, although they become duller places in which to work. It is women in developing countries who will lose badly needed allies in the donor community (Himmelstrand 1990: 111).

An indicator that also highlights the hypocrisy of the

WID mandate of a many donor agencies is the small number of women employed on their staff. In her discussion of the bureaucrats who bring life to an institution, Staudt argues that there is sufficient evidence to be optimistic that more feminists inside bureaucracies can make a difference for women outside. This is particularly the case when they incorporate and combine their own agendas with other activist agendas (Staudt 1990). However, it is important not to assume that women by definition are feminists. There are many examples of women who have not necessarily served women's interests, such as those described by Yudelman (1990) in the Inter-American Foundation, and Helzner and Shepard (1990) in Population private Voluntary Agencies. Equally, the co-operation of women's organisations into political parties is both widespread and well known (Hirschmann 1990).

In spite of the problems identified above, it is still salutary to identify not only the number of women in such organisations, but also the positions in which they are located. Examples from donor agencies in the United Kingdom illustrate this point. In the Commonwealth Secretariat, for example, although women comprise half the total staff, only a quarter are professionals, of which top management comprise 10 per cent. As in the majority of organisations,women predominate at clerical and secretarial levels. Of the consultant technical co-operation officers (TCOs) recruited by the UK ODA to adviser governments and parastal organisations in 1987/88, some 11 percent were women, increasing to 12 per cent in 1988/89. Even an NGO with a very specific equal opportunity staffing policy such as Christian Aid has had problems. In 1983 the Women's Group put forward the recommendation that equal representation in area secretaries, board members and regional committee members should be achieved in five years. However, by 1987 only 35 per cent of area secretaries were women, as were 32 per cent of board members, and 35 per cent of regional committee board members. Although these figures were below the target set, they are far higher than in any other UK NGO, except in NGOs targeted specifically at women such as Woman kind and opportunities for Women.

For donors, another important indicator of the responsiveness of national governments to WID is the number of women sent on overseas training. The Technical Cooperation Training Programme (TCTP) of the UK ODA, for instance, in 1987 had a total budget of £65 million sterling. It involved more than 110 countries and 11,500 students, of who some 15 per cent were women, with this number declining slightly in 1988 (Holden 1988; ODA 1989). The Canadian International Development Agency (CIDA), even with a much more specific positive discrimination policy, has only been able to increase slightly its numbers of female sponsored trainees and students. In 1985, its global figure ws 23 per cent, and although it increased to 32 per cent in 1986, in 1987 this was down again to 29 per cent (CIDA 1988).

There are obviously several interrelated reasons for the appalling problems experienced with funding. Lack of adequate policy influences the level of resources allocation. Typically, all that exists are broad policy statements, without any clear definitions of goals and priorities. Associated arrangement for the poison of proper levels of resources and management support structures do not exist. Furthermore, the institutional location of WID Units influences resource allocations. Women's bureaux located within welfare ministries are not only last to be allocated money but also the first to be cut. Here the problem is less the status of the until itself, and more that of its ministry. Besides such administrative problems, there are more fundamental political and ideological reasons for the severe budgeting consternates widely experienced. Budget allocations are clearly the ultimate verification of legitimacy, when lip-service must be converted to practice. Consequently, it is the biggest challenge and the most effective way in which male privilege blocks women, and reinforces their subordinate positon. Well-financed units, provided with adequatate supportive structures, serve as crucial institutional structures to ensure positive discriminatory practices and oversee the integration of WID into the institutional structure. As such, they are consequently threatening the existing institutional system of power and control that effectively marginalises women's gender needs, both practical and strategic.

Problem of Lack of Awareness of Gender Planning

Recently, as more technical constraints in the institutionalisation of WID have sorted themselves out, attention has increasingly turned to the more entrenched political constraints. Gender-blindness of both male and female colleagues working within such organisations, has increasingly been identified as one important problem. Training in gender analysis, gender-awareness or gender planning has become an important solution, particularly in those organizations that have adopted a mainstream approach.

Opportunities in Current Strategies

If it was politically naive of women to think that the creation of a new institutional structure would ensure the institutionalisation of a new planning concern, it was also politically expedient for planners to believe that these palliative measures would be sufficient to keep women quiet. A number of different stages in the process of institutionalisation can be identified. The 1970s was the 'introduction' stage, when the WID issue was first legitimized within government bureaucracies with WID structures defined. This was followed in the early 1980s by a second 'fashionable' stage, during which a few women were appointed to small, 'co-option' stage followed, with the recognition that WID was not a short-term tried (Himmelstrand 1990). Organisations began to define their demands so that they fitted into established structures without requiring organizational changes. WID units were integrated into the co-opting establishment, and accepted by them as a regular, if peripherally important, member.

WID in a diversity of institutions in government, donor agencies and NGOs. The experience in each is obviously unique, with different constraints determining success.

Nevertheless, most institutions are now involved in the third, co-option phase, with 'gendered bureaucratic subversion' the most problematics issue. A decade of experience has shown that the 'top-down', product-oriented creation of the WID Unit has not institutionalised WID. Most frequently, it has simply been co-opted into the dominant organisational structure. In the past few years, therefore, organisational structures have focused attention on the development of collaborative, bottom-up processes within their structures. These are attempting to identify blockages, and to use combined strategies. These include the creation of new, more effective organisational structures and alliances. Women's machineries have been forced to understand more about the nature and content of bureaucratic politics, while focusing less on the performance of their own WID Unit.

Combined Strategies as an Institutional Strategy

The institutionalisation of WID occurs through a strategy that combines the creation of a WID unit with a mainstream approach. A successful strategy generally has two main components. First, mainstream departments, field offices and other important parts of the organisations appoint designated WID specialists. Secondly, the role of the WID Unit gender specialists changes. They give less emphasis to controlling the WID mandate, and more emphasis to creating the necessary networks and alliances with gender-aware sectoral specialists. Through the development of effective coalitions and lobbying pressure they give up their WID mandate. The most critical institutional issue then becomes the identification of gender entry points, with the best tactic to operate on several fronts simultaneously. Combined strategies are not necessarily new; what is, is the precise level of definition.

Again problems can easily occur, with combined strategies not necessarily successful. WID specialists can be as marginalised in mainstream departments as they were in the WID Unit if they lack the necessary collaborative support and networks. The long-term WID Unit gender specialists often have problems letting go of their ownership of WID, which has so long provided them with the basis of their legitimacy.

The experience of a bilateral donor such as SIDA provides a useful example of the process that has to be undergone in order to achieve a combined strategy. The WID Unit was established in 1979. Like Oxfam's GADU, it was a temporary arrangement to exist ony until all SIDA's programmes under the supervision of programme officers had integrated the 'women's dimensions'. Commenting on this, a recent head of the WID Office said, 'This was the watchdog period.' In the past few years its status has been confirmed as permanent, due to pressure, from both inside and outside the organization, that 'WID is not a trend of short duration' (Himmelstrand 1990: 110). It considers its location within the Planning Secretariat a good position since it has direct access to the Director General. Nevertheless, the Gender Office has only five full-time appointments in Stockholm. Identifying themselves as catalysts, their institutional strategy comprises three clearly identified, interrelated priorities. First, they have focused on building up a support structure for WID personnel in the country-level Development Cooperation Offices (DCOs). The role of country-level Development Co-operation Offices (DCOs). The role of country-level officers is to ensure that sector programmes integrated WID, as well as administering direct support. In 1990 there were twenty field-level personnel responsible for WID. They were mainly local, part-time appointments with rapid turnover (many of them Swedish spouses of Swedish overseas staff). The problems with junior-level appointments are not solely that officers lack knowledge of SIDA's structure and procedures; of greater importance is the fact that their low status impedes them when trying to challenge more senior staff on controversial gender issues. To counteract these tendencies, the Gender Office would like to have two positions at programme officer level. This would consists of a Gender Officer responsible for integration aspects until all SIDA staff are sufficiently gender-aware, and a Gender Adviser who ideally should be a national, responsible for work on direct support and acting as a long-term adviset on all programmes.

The second component is training in gender-awareness and gender planning methodology based on SIDA's case studies and related to SIDA's planning cycle. Heads of Sector Bureaux, Heads of Section is Sector Bureaux and Heads of DCOs, as well as programme officers and consultants all undertake such training. The purpose is not only to make them gender-aware. It is also to introduce a planning methodology to them, which includes identifying the institutionalisation of the WID officer in the mission's work. WID officers also undertake gender training. This helps professionalise them in them in their job, as well as assists them to identify critical entry points for WID strategy in the SIDA planning cycle.

By way of comparison with SIDA's strategy, the OECD in its Monitoring Report assesses the creation of full-time positions for WID experts in the field to be one major achievement accomplished. Five countries currently appoint full or part-time positions (ranging from the United States with seventy part-time positions to Denmark with four full-time). However, while the report states that there has been a noteworthy expansion in the countries undertaking this, the number of personnel is the same as two years previously NGOs also comment that where a WID field officer has been appointed the likelihood is that gender issue will be more effectively integrated into projects, and more resources allocated to women's projects. While this is obviously a critical move to mainstream, clearly the importance of WID field officers relates directly to their status, and legitimacy both from the local field office as much as from headquarters. If their mandate is simply collecting information on women, this does not necessarily in any way impact on major policy decisions or programme- and project-level resource allocations.

The third component in SIDA's strategy is the development

of methodological tools to be used in the different stages of SIDA's planning cycle (SIDA 1989). The Gender Office has its own small budget for supporting initiatives at national, regional and international level. However, inputs made within sector programmes are normally financed within the existing country frame. This means that budgetary issues therefore have become mainstreamed.

Combined strategies, such as those used by SIDA, clearly reduce many technical constraints experienced by those adopting single strategies. Indeed, combined strategies have been adopted widely, especially by multilaterals such as FAO and bilaterals such as Canadian CIDA and USAID. These latter two, in particular, now have comprehensive, widespread institutional strategies that also include the three components described above. Nevertheless, they are still essentially technical solutions and in themselves are often necessary but insufficient for fundamental changes in instituonalising WID. Other measures are required if more fundamental political constraints are to be challenged.

Focus on Intra-organisational Networking

The importance of intra-organisational networking has long been recognised. Such alliances are necessary to create leverage in bureaucratic politics. However, networks are only useful if structured to contribute to mainstream institutional procedures. Many intra-organisational WID networks of governments, donor agencies and NGOs alike, were set up simply to legitimise WID, and are considered time-wasting and irrelevant by those involved.

In addition, different types of networks are simultaneously required. For instance, a recent monitoring report of the OECDDAC/WID group identified three different institutional structures, set up as support to WID units. Four OECD member countries have established high-level WID steering committees. These are hierarchically structured and composed of senior policy and operations departments staff entrusted with the responsibility for overseeing the implementation of WID policy, in both an advisory and monitoring role. Their purpose is to show a strong and visible commitment by the senior management to integrated gend‹ needs and interets in bilateral concerns (OCED 1990)

Secondly, nine countries have set up Inter-departmental Task Forces on WID. These are horizontally composed of relevant policy and operations department WID liaison officers,with responsibility for different regional or sectoral divisions. their purpose is to ensure the integration of WID policy into practice through the entire spectrum of aid activities. Finally, three countries have established ad hoc Working Groups, to work on specific WID-related issues as needs arise.

The location of WID Units has important implications for intra-organisational alliances. Set up as an advisory unit, Oxfam's GADI, for instance, has no mandatory power and influences procedures and policies through networking. The Unit initially assessed the blockages they encountered to be the consequence of the threatening nature of WID. Over time, however, they witnessed other advisory units on such non-threatening issues as health endure a similar fate. They have recognised that some constraints, although exacerbated in gender issues, relate to the structural problems inherent in the status of a Unit.

The last decade has witnessed the growth and consolidation of inter-organisational networks and the development of a wider strategy to ensure effective organisational leverage. These work at different levels, involving different combinations of the three organisational groups, donor agencies, national governments and NGOs.

Adoption by the DAC of the 1983 Guiding Principles on Women and Development as well as annual monitoring of progress, both provide important means by which pressure is quite clearly exerted on 'reluctant' governments, with particularly recalcitrant members invited to join the steering committee. The fact that nearly all member states now have

WID mandates, have adjusted administrative and personnel arrangements to 'ensure the integration of WID concerns into their AID programmes', and have laborated comprehensive Plans of action has not necessarily resulted infundamental changes. The 1990 Third Monitoring Report notes that the implementation of the measures stipulated in WID action plants still depends on the interest, un derstanding and willingness of individual staff members, with the changing of attitudes of some staff members still a slow process.

A similar inter-organisational network to assist the implementation of the Forward Looking Strategies is that of Commonwealth government. The Commonwealth Plan of Action accepted in 1987 by all Commonwealth governments contains guidelines for national governments as well a s national plans of action for WID bureaux. The Women's Development Programme (WDP) at Commonwealth Secretariat headquarters in London monitors progress through an annual questionnaire. In addition, the WDP provides a funded extension service in response to requests for assistance from governments formulating their WID policy and Plans of Action. The Commonwealth Secretariat has a certain ability to pressurize national governments. However, compliance is still dependent on the political will of national governments, many of which do not respond effectively.

For many organisations it is the inter-relationship between the different types of inter-organisational pressure that effects changes. In the late 1980s the UK ODA Social Advisers were able to use the DAC principles as the leverage to enable the then Minister of Overseas Development to maintain momentum in his 'top-down' pressure to more the debate with in a reluctant ministry. However, the simultaneous 'bottom-up' lobbying of the UK women's NGO group, the National association of Women's Organisations, provided the final impetus for carrying out important changes to institutionalise WID within ODA. Just as lobbying of senators was important for the legitimization of ISAID WID, in the same way the lobbying of Members of parliament with questions in the

House of Commons has put pressure on the ODA to shift its approach to WID. Similarly, Swedish SIDA acknowledges the critical bottom-up pressure provided by the NGO Council of Sowdish Women for WID, whose monitoring of SIDA's progress with their WID agenda provides an important form of leverage. Finally, inter-organisational groups are important between First and Third Worlds. As a staff member of a Northern NGO commented, 'When a woman from a Palestinian NGO says "Palestinian women are concerned about feminism" it's very helpful for us.'

Confronting blockages in bureaucratic resistance widespread criticism of women's bureaux, organisations and units have concerned there lack of policy goals, objectives or strategies. In the past decade, an important priority for most agencies, therefore, has been the clarification of policy. accompanying this has been the development of timetable objectives, and specific proposals for action. It is also important, however, to identify the extent to which increased professionalism of policy and planning has had an impact on the institutionalisation of WID.

Professionalisation of Policy

Many professionals working on WID are clear that clarification of policy has assisted them considerably in challenging blockages on a sounder professional footing. For instance, clear articulation of the different policy approaches to WID has enabled them much more effectively to identify and confront colleagues using inappropriate WID policies, particularly welfare. It has also allowed professionals themselves to develop a much wider strategy in the policies they endorsed. It is here that the difference between WID and GAD has significant political implications. Some agencies, such as USAID and the World Bank, still tend to use a WID framework, focusing on women as separate target groups, and identifying effeciency as synonymous with equity. Others, such as SIDA and ODA, have worked to adopt what they define as a 'gendered' efficiency approach, while also recognizing the different tactical advantages of both the empowerment and equity approach.

At the other end of the spectrum are NGOs, some of whom perceive a priori that all their interventions empower their target groups. They have rudely workmen up to the fact that this does not necessarily include women. Obviously, the culture of the bureaucracy influences the tactics adopted, with concern focusing on the relative advantages of flexible as against highly structured, institutions. While an ad hoc policy means that individuals have a greater scope to create new systems, they also are less accountable and have a greater capacity to block policies. In one Northern NGO, the WID officer named three individuals (all men) whose autnomous control over important areas of the intitution, such as research, communications and evaluation, meant that they effectively blocked critical areas for WID policy. The problem with much of the professionalisation of policy is that it depends above all on the skills of individual professionals. A very thin borderline separates playing the system with unstated agendas, cooption or blockage.

Confronting the Resistance of Men and Women in the Bureaucracies

Ultimately the professionalisation of policy raises the impossibly sensitive issue of how to confront male bureaucratic blockages. Staudt has commented, 'For redistribution to occur, advocates will probably need to ally with men who are either unthreatened by power sharing or supportive for ideological, professional or technical reasons' (1990: 10). Certainly, the anecdotal experience of women in different agencies is full of examples of the critical, circumstantial as against structural leverage that a sympathetic man in a gate-keeping position can provide. The are, however, severe problems with the patronage that this type of lever are created. The reverse is also true of women with in the organization. Not all of the necessarily wish to represent women's interests. This provides yet another example of the conflation of the professional and the personal. In one UK NGO, for example, the intra-organizational women's group has the official status necessary to challenge critically and to monitor the organization's policy organisation chose not to be members considerably reduces the power of this group. This is a classic example of contradictions in the decomposition of intra-organisational groups, which concern not only status, but also the sex of participants.

One serious problem faced by donors and Northern NGOs alike is the fact that male staff still identify feminism as a Western concept. They themselves often have little idea of the prevailing attitudes of wo·en in the Third World countries in which they work. A senior adviser in one donor agency has introduced the concept of 'environmental scanning' other male colleagues. This is a polite method to invited them to 'test the water' and identify with greater rigour the status and position of women in the countries where they allocated aid. It would appear that middle management generally the biggest problem, least willing to take the plane and most likely to export their own role models into the contexts in which they are working. This is one are in which training has played an important part in changing attitudes.

Those whose experience has taught them that change only comes out of self-interest dismiss the long list of issues discussed above as of limited impact, or useless in institutionalising WID. For them the only recourse is to introduce incentives to encourage new attitudes, or sanctions to prevent the worst of bad practices.

Staudt (1983) argues that implementation occurs in response to appropriate incentives. The strength of positive incentives ranges on a continuum from prescription, to resource provision alone, to resource provision tied to performance. Negative incentives, such as sanctions in the form of veto capability or funding termination are potentially strong in molding behaviour. However, the often incur ill will and new, more subtle forms of resistance. Moreover, they are vulnerable to political pressure and rendered meaningle if applied inconsistently or infrequently. There has been an extreme reluctance in organisations directly to introduces incentives or sanctions to encourage new attitudes. One agency embarking on this sensitive path is Cadadian CIDA. It has introduced WID as one of nine criteria on which supervisors and managers are evaluated in their performance review and appraisal report. Since management responsibilities include 'ensuring that policies relating to Official Languages, Employment Equity, Performance Review and Employee Appraisal are followed with there area of responsibility', supervisors and managers are rated from one to nine on their 'Employment Equity'—namely, action on policies relating to under-represented groups, such as women, aboriginal peoples, visible minorities and the disabled. It is still too early to measure the effect, if any, of this one changing resistance within bureaucracies.

Conclusion

Ultimately, however effectively an institution has become gender-aware, or gendered, its institutional structure may still not have changed. Gender has simply been grafted on to the existing structure. This raises fundamental questions,still largely unresolved, concerning the extent to which engendering an institution ultimately requires a fundamental transformation in the structure itself.

The principle by which women's groups operate is one of the few areas in which women's libation has specified the application of its ideology. This includes principle such as self-relation, equality or anti-elitism, sisterhood and authority of personal experience. All have encouraged strctureless groups. 'Union habited' by set agendas. The superiority of groups such as these lies in their being a non-competitive, supportive forum conducive to confidence-building and equal participation (Button 1984)). This is in direct contrast to bureaucracy, the most traditional form of organisation through which legitimate authority is exercised. In its ideal form, Blue (1956) characterizes it as a hierarchy of authority a system of rules, impersonality, employment base do technical qualifications and constituting a career. Feminists argue that hierarchies are antithetical to feminism. However, the degree to which women's organisations and hierarchies can coexists is not proven. At the end of the day, some level of hierarchy, with accountability and effectiveness, is necessary. To date, the non-hierarchical structures of feminist institutions have made few inroads into existing structures, nor sufficiently proved their professional competence to deliver and implement in practice.

Women's organizations recognise the need to talk to bureaucracies to keep their interests and needs on the political agenda. To do so, organisational forms acceptable to both groups, which can articulate their demands, need to be developed. Freeman has argued that while the leaderless, structureless group was part of the evolution of the women's movement, as the goals change from consciousness-raising to social action so also must the organisational form change. However, to suggest that women should be prepared to formalize their organisations is not to agree that traditional forms are superior. There must be other frameworks for building organisations based on democratic structuring and political effectiveness.

CHAPTER 12

Gender Planning: An Emancipation Approach

Of course, Gender Planning is both political and technical in nature; as with all other planning traditions, the context in which it is situated determines its content. The differentiation between practical and strategic needs provides the most important principle of gender planning, allowing for the distinction between two sets of planning needs. The planning methodology to meet practical gender needs is primarily 'technical' in nature, requiring the necessary tools and techniques to assist women to do better what they are already doing. In contrast, the planning methodology required to meet strategic gender needs is clearly 'political' in nature. Secondly, as a transformative planing tradition, gender planning assumes conflict in the planning process.

In fact, Gender planning is not an end in itself but a means by which women, through a process of empowerment, can emancipate themselves. This is best achieved through a process of negotiated debate about the redistribution of power and resources within the household, civil society and the state. Obviously in such a debate participation of women, gendered organisations and planners is essential. It is important to emphasize, however, that the identification of constraints and opportunities for gender planning, in terms of both structure and agency, is itself an extensive topic.

In examining the way that changes in the position and status of women in developing countries have occurred, an important distinction has been made. Change instigated through 'top-down' interventions of the states as the dominant 'structure of power, control and domination is distinct from change achieved through 'bottom-up' mobilization of 'agency' in civil society. It described the ambiguous manner in which the state, in particular contexts, both provides for, and controls, women, either directly through legal means, or indirectly through its control over institutional structures and planning procedures. This has shown only too clearly the limitations of both its political will and its ability to confront fundamental issues of women's subordination. The development of gender planning comes out of the powerful social political movements that women themselves now generate, rather than because of state interventions. As a new planning tradition, necessary to respond to this call for emancipation, gender planning is simply the engine to operationalise this specific political concern so habit becomes accepted as institutionalised practice, in what is an emancipation approach. As a transformative planning tradition, gender planning recognizes that emancipation can ony be achieved by identifying contextual specific enter points. This defines where there is 'room for manoevuvre' for debate and negotiation, at the conjuncture of the state and civil society. In challenging rather than ignoring or avoiding conflict and tension, gender planning seeks to identify such political appropriate points of entry.

Planning can no longer be neatly compartmentalized into separate, isolated, 'top-down' or 'bottom-top' interventions means that criteria governing who is involved in the planning process, the relations between those involved, and the judgment as to what is an acceptable decision all become critical considerations. If negotiated debate is ultimately be most important way to ensure the implementation of gender policy, will 'voice', and the confrontation of those who hold power, at the level of ideology as well as materially, achieve it? Or is the use of 'exit', withdrawal and the creation of alternative planning interventions, a more appropriate strategy? There in no easy, one-off solution to this problem. Ultimately it will depend on the costs against expected returns whether 'voice' or 'exit' is the more appropriate solution.

If the success of gender planning depends on the participation of women, then it is the organisation of women within civil society that requires examination. Because of their capacity to reach the 'grass-roots' where 'real people' are, organisations outside government have increasingly been identified as the institutional solution for 'alternative' development models. This is equally true of women's NGOs. However, this has also resulted in a reluctance to examine critically their limitations and potential in challenging existing structures or in providing alternative institutional structures for planning. It examines the potential of such organizations to influence change through 'voice', developing strategies for negotiating successfully, with those currently controlling resources and power, to ensure that they implement change. What are the choices that women make, both individually, as well as in groups? Where does the family end and the public domain begin? Here we describe the mixed experience of women's organisations in raising consciousness to confront women's subordination, creating alliances and linkages to ensure the success of planning processes. In addition, it highlights entry points identified by women's NGOs for negotiation and debate around women's needs at four different levels: household; civil society; the state; and the global system.

NGOs as Alternative Organizational Structures for Development

It is important to recognise that developments among Third World women's organisations in the past decade have not occurred in isolation. Although many experiences of such organisations are unique because they are specific to women, nevertheless they have occurred with in a wider context in which the role of NGOs in the Third World generally has undergone fundamental changes. It is useful, therefore, to start by mentioning very briefly the relevance of some pertinent NGO debates to women's NGOs.

The 1980s saw the explosive growth in the number of organisations outside government. It has been argued that, if the 1960s was the development decade of growth with 'trickle-down', and the 1970s the decade of Basic Needs, the 1980s was the decade of the NGOs (Fowler 1988). This has certainly been true for women's NGOs. For example, a 1984 estimate identified 15,000 women's groups in Kenya alone, incorporating about 10 per cent of the counters adult women. In this context, the proliferation of women's NGOs seems no more than part of a broader phenomenon that recognizes NGOs as important actors in the development process. Official endorsement of their role is now widespread from governments, donor agencies and international organisation alike. A typical view, provided by the Bruntland Report, identifies the critical function of NGOs to ensure sustainable development. It recommends that government should establish or strengthen procedures for official consultation and more meaningful participation by NGOs (WCED 1987).

Social and Political Development Agendas of NGOs

Voluntarism into an organised structure by the NGOs results in a potential 'to mobilize people into organised structures of voluntary group action for self-reliance and self-development'. Traditionally, their role has been identified as an alternative entry point for local-level social development. Their comparative advantage over government lies in the ways they relate to beneficiaries, as well as their freedom in organising themselves (Fowler 1988). If government's relationship with intended beneficiaries is one of control, for NGOs it is one of voluntarism. This means that NGOs have the potential to adopt an unambivalent position of support, mutual trust and equality of interest with the intended beneficiaries. For governments, an authoritarian stance and dominance is particularly purulent in the 'economically and socially stressed' third World. It is this control orientation that has resulted in hierarchically structured bureaucracies. However, their incompatibility with the needs of Third World micro-development results in structural inconsistencies. The identification of voluntarism as an essential characteristic of NGOs raises questions concerning the objectives of so-called 'community participation' within such organisations, and the extent to which it empower women in the community.

To examine the potential of women's NGOs as alternative institutional structures in the planning process, it is necessary to mention the conventional wisdom concerning the comparative advantage of NGOs over government. Economic, organisational and political factors highlight this. Economically, NGOs with their component of voluntary unpaid labour can allow for greater co-sharing. Since the early community development programmes of the 1950s and 1960s, carried out in Africa and Asia by post-colonial governments with the assistance of local NGOs, this has been widely critiqued as 'development on the cheap' (Mayo 1975). Later community participation projects of the 1970s and 1980s became more politicised in their concern to ensure participation in decision making as well as in implementation. However, this fundamental critique remains. Economic reform policies have resulted in cut-backs in state service delivery. This has increased the neo-welfarists role of NGOs as alternative service delivery mechanisms, relying heavily on unpaid labour, particularly of women.

Organizationally, because of the different ways they relate in intended beneficiaries, NGOs have the comparative advantage of more efficient and effective structures for local-level service delivery. Recognition that NGOs play a key role representing community interests relative to the state has resulted in a variety of attempts at decentralization. This includes the delegation to semi-autonomous or para-statal agencies, devolution to local government and the transfer of functions from public to non-government institutions or joint exercise of functions. Economic events in the past decade make it particularly important to raise such issues, as buzz words such as 'democracy', decentralization' and 'participation' again enter the planning agenda.

Decentralization is also liked to increased democratization, and the political processes through which local communities can more effectively challenge the state to meet their needs (Diamond 1989). This shift in NGO agendas relates to changing agendas, the state reduces the level of public control. It includes a shift in service provision from the public to the private sector, and from central to local government.

The stress on appropriateness, decentralization, self-reliance, popular participation, sustainability, the building up of local institutions and getting rid of excessive and oppressive bureaucracies, all show a potential willingness to identify more appropriate managerial and institutional structures. Across very different contexts, the re-alignment of government interests, required by fiscal constraints,has institutional implications. Debates are taking place over cut-backs in public expenditure, the rationalisation of service delivery and devolution to the 'private' and 'voluntary' sectors. This renegotiation of the boundary of state interventions has important implications for the NGO sector generally and women's organisations in particular.

Not only has the nature of government interventions changed. In many parts of the world the capacity and capability of organisational structures outside government have increased during the past decade, as NGOs have renegotiated their relationship with the state. The impetus for this comes from hands-on, 'bottom-up' practical experience, particularly of groups in society subordinated or exploited in the development process,whether on the grounds of class, ethnicity or gender. In repressive or strife-ridden contexts, groups deprived of both national and international official resources for social development have felt this most profoundly. They have identified managerial and institutional structures based on self-reliance, with decentralized modes of decision-making. These have highlighted the close inter-relationship between social welfare, economic well-being and fundamental political and human rights.

Clearly, the relationship between the state and Third

World NGOs has become increasingly important over the past few decades, for political reasons as much as for economic and organisational ones. Whether this has equally been the case for women's organisations is the next important consideration.

Causes of Women to Organise

Whitehead has obviously shown, it is necessary to recognise that 'women' do not, and cannot, form a homogeneous category. Social relations between the genders vary from one society to another. Women experience significant variation in their situations in house wider areas of political, economic and social subordination and inequality which are not confined to the social relations of genders. These differences make it important to identify the basis for women's solidarity, collaboration and commonalty of interests.

Women are frequently divided on the basis of community, class, 'race' or religion. However, throughout history, in their gender-ascriptive roles they have informally organised together around a communality of interests relating to their practical gender needs. Women informally cooperate over such needs as child care, productive and reproductive labour, and credit. As the description women and community managing in Chapter 2 illustrated, women's daily support systems for shelter, food, employment and protection of their environment all provide a critical basis for protest and action. This is true, although women generally have not 'formalized' it within a organisational structure. External state influence has also been a critical determinant of the growth and success of women's groups. In Guayaquil, Ecuador, for example, a widely known procedure of petitioning services in return for votes by self-help committees exists. This provided a catalyst for initiating popular participation among newly settled communities. In formalizing this process an external donor, US President Kennedy's Alliance for Progress Programme, provide the greatest influence. The experience of local organisation gained from this programme was also then important for the formation of later groups. In Kenya, Moore (1988) convincingly argues that contemporary women's groups owe far more to the working of the modern state than to 'traditional' forms of mutual association and co-operation.'. One outstanding feature of the Kenyan state has been its mobilization of local populations through harambee ('let's unite') to participate in self-help development initiatives. Holmquist (1984) has identified this type of self-help as a hybrid phenomenon.

Although practical gender needs can provide the basis for female solidarity, they also can divide women. This obviously occurs when women prioritize different needs. However, it also can be based on kinship, class, 'race', ethnicity, age or patriarchy. Women's kinship networks, for instance, are frequently as important for the maintenance of links between male-based lineage groups as they are for women themselves. Particularly in contexts with scarce or very unequally allocated resources, such as land, food or water, antagonistic relations between different groups can often cause far greater divisions between women. Finally, the isolation woman experience when secluded within their own homes, both because of 'cultural' norms and their onerous work loads, often housemaid it difficult for them to organise, or to sustain organization. The privatisation of women's work in the domestic sphere, and the dispersal of female kinship groups, therefore, have both served to reduce the capacity of women for collective consciousness. Constraints such as these mean that community-level groups of women, such as those described in Ecuador and Kenya, typically do not move beyond articularting the need to meet practical gender needs. Yet women also share interests, as a gender, and it is these that relate to their strategic gender needs.

Historical documentation and oral histories of women themselves both show that the origin of Third World women's organisation around strategic gender needs are not new. Since the nineteenth century Third World feminism has been an important force for change. However, women have subsumed such struggles with nationalist and patriotic struggles, working-class agitation and peasant movements, rather than forming autonomous women's organisations. In the first half of the twentieth century struggle focused on legal, political and educational rights. Once achieved, most formal women's organisations in countries as diverse as India and Colombia along with their First World sisters, essentially 'sold out'. They turned themselves from reformist groups into social welfare organisations, concerned with practical gender needs. With their privileged, knowledgeable, middle and upper-class membership, they reinforced the tradition of 'taking responsibility for the plight of their less fortunate sisters'. Lacking any consciousness of their own oppression, they directed their attention at 'uplifting' lower-class women. Not only do such organisations fail to address strategic gender needs. In taking responsibility for social welfare provision, they comply and reinforce the state's attitude to social welfare as 'women's concern.'

This description of problems associated with women's organisations could lead to the conclusion that their capacity to become a powerful social and political movement is severely limited. Individually, women's NGOs frequently appear weak, under-financed and undirected. Yet in total their changing agenda may represents an important movement outside government for changing women's lives. A number of important questions require consideration. If women's organisations traditionally have been divided, co-opted and weak, why then did the opening of 'political space' provided by the UN Decade for Women (1976-85) result not only in a worldwide proliferation of small-scale groups operating outside government, but also in a new level of debate about their role in confronting government? Why is it that their policy agendas increasingly have included not only welfare and well-being but also improvement in the status and rights of women in society? Do women's NGOs have additional capacity beyond those of NGOs generally in terms of specific characteristics that unite or divide women? Is the current popularity of women's organisations simply a further extension of cheap labour and state control disguised under the media hype that currently surrounds NGOs generally? Do women's NGOs have the capacity not only to raise consciousness but also to engage in the planning process?

To answer questions such as these is critical, but also problematic, given the widespread hesitation to evaluate NGO capacity. In attempting to do so it is necessary to address three important issues: first, to 'unpac', categorise and desegregate with greater rigour such organisations; second to identify with greater candour the constraints that limit women's NGO capacity; and third, to identify with greater clarity the entry points for alliance and coalitions of women's NGOs to influence the planning process.

Women's NGOs, as much as NGOs generally, are not homogenous, with their classification sexually problematic. Most frequently women's NGOs are also distinguished in terms of their *institutional location, organisational composition or activity content*. Although this can usefully describe economic and organisational characteristics, it does not, however, distinguish the policy objectives of different organisations and their underlying political agendas. To date here have been few substantial classifications of women's NGOs, other than that undertaken by DAWN. This is done, not from the usual viewpoint of donor agencies that wish to know which groups are the most suited to receive funding.

Any classification is determined by its objectives. DAWN identifies the empowerment of women through organisation as the key to achieving the goals, of feminism —in other words, the emancipation of women. On this basis they identify six different types of women's organisations. These vary in their aims, funding and methods of operation, and their potential capacity to assist in the empowerment of women. The organisations identified fall into overlapping categories: outside initiated and small grassroots organisations identified in terms of their institutional location; worker-based and those affiliated to a political party identified in terms of organistional composition; finally, service-oriented and research type identified in terms of their activity content. To this list DAWN add a seventh, a coalition of organisations around specific issues.

Service-orientated organisations are the first type. These most frequently have welfarist approach. Their objective is to argument the role of social welfare agencies by meeting the practical gender needs of poor women relating to health, education and other services. They are essentially top-down, middle-class voluntary organisations with a low level of participation by local women limiting themselves to the objective of cost-sharing. Historically, service-orientated NGOs have been closely linked to the modernisation model of development. Now, however, they also include the neo-welfarist delivery models reappearing under recession and macro-economic models of structural adjustment. Such organisations take different forms, including middle-class women's clubs, such as Nigerian clubs (Enabulele 1985); those with an international affiliation, such as the YWCA, Women's Councils, Girl Guides and Ladies' Leagues (Lapido 1981; Lee 1985); and those originating from social reform movements or nationalist struggles.

As DAWN identifies, their weaknesses include the fact that they are elitist in bias. They employ top-down decision-making processes in which there is wide scope for empowerment. In addition, they have no clear theoretical understanding of gender subordination, or its links to other forms of oppression. Nevertheless, such organisations are important for several reasons. Because of their membership they often have both direct and indirect links to policy-makers. They command significant resources, and have systematic methods for transferring skills and building leadership (DAWN 1985). For many feminists, such organisations are anathema because of their role in the reproduction of class relations. However, given their significant power, in specific contexts, it may be constructive to learn from their ability to raise women's issues in the public arena. This includes the identification of appropriate strategies to co-opt them for specific strategic gender needs. Benepath (1982), for instance, argues that in the United States, older-established groups are often willing and motivated to co-operate with superficially more 'radical', newer groups. Such groups put contacts, expertise and financial resources at the disposal of more radical agendas.

In principle they have an equity approach, although in practice their policy approach is more likely to be either welfare or anti-poverty. If they achieve equity, the approach is top-down and does not involve the participation of women. However, such organisations may include the participation of women for the purpose of cost-sharing and efficiency. The structural position of these organisations is both their strength and weakness. By virtue of being within a party they potentially have space to raise women's issues at the highest level. Their autonomy to raise and address gender issues is questionable. There is a constant danger of co-option, with strategic gender needs subsumed to wider political goals. Very few political parties are explicitly feminist in orientation or internal structure. The co-option of female participation in order to further the wider aims of organisations that do not accord any genuine political status to women's struggle is a widespread phenonemon. It occurs in a diversity of politically aligned organisations. Nationalist struggles often highlight the problem. Here women's mobilization around gender needs, particularly strategic ones, may conflict with the more general aims of political struggle.

Worker-based organisations are a third type. These include trade unions of formal sector workers, as well as the organisations of low income, self-employed women, such as market sellers. DAWN makes a critical distinction between the two. In trade unions mainly male leadership makes decision, while women at the base participate in carrying out policy. In contrast, women's representation is much stronger in self-employed associations. The policy approach of worker-based organisations, in principle is equity. In practice, formal sector unions prioritize production concerns. They rarely consider as a priority the reproductive concerns of women workers such as child care, maternity leave and associated benefits. In contrast, all women workers' organisations, such as SEWA, whether of not they have in underlying empowerment approach or are explicitly aware of women's subordination, 'tend to be very successful in empowering poor women in their own personal life situations' (DAWN 1985:84). One important constraint for such organisations is their weak resources position, reflecting the poverty of their membership.

Organisations that have mushroomed recently, because of external funds, are the fourth type. DAWN identifies most outside-initiated organisations, with an underlying anti-poverty approach, as concerned with small income-generating projects. Primarily top-down in approach, the participation of local women is greatest at the implementation stage for effectiveness and cost-sharing. Both the funding source and the approach means that many such organisations lack a theoretical analysis of women's subordination and its links with broader economic, social and political issues. DAWN assesses them as among the weakest of the different types of organisations. With no previous organic history, and little independent organisational or resource base, they persist only as long as they generate outside funding.

Grass-roots organisations originate from the economic and material conditions women experience, and with their underlying policy approach, frequently empowerment. Such organisations focus on meeting practical gender needs relating not only to income but also to health and education. These are a means by which they raise consciousness to address strategic gender needs such as domestic violence, legal rights and political struggles. DAWN identifies that some of these groups are politicitly feminist in orientation. Their main weaknesses include an inadequate resource base and overwhelmingly middle-class, urban membership. Nevertheless, their focus on local-and household-level issues means that such organisations have a greater potential of empowering their membership than many other types of groups.

Research organisations focus on participator action research, women's studies associations and women's networks. When such groups are 'committed to using their findings to serve and empower the subjects of the research' they have an empowerment approach. Their research provides useful background to inform and back up political action by other organisations. However, the considerable potential that such groups have to influence public policy debate means that the can easily shift towards a less participatory equity approach. Research organisations need to develop structures and methods of accountability to both action organisations and the subjects of the research. Only then can they avoid the development of rifts between themselves and other groups.

Besides these types of organisations, DAWN identifies numerous women's movements. These encompass individuals, organisations and coalitions that have sprung up down the Decade around specific issues such as racism, political repression or sexual exploitation. As with issue-based organisations, their strength lies in their mobilization capacity, their weakness in a lack of clear organisational structure and ongoing commitment.

Some types of organisations have greater capacity than others to move from practical to strategic gender needs. Obviously, however, it is not enough simply to classify women's NGOs. Although DAWN's classification provides a useful starting point for upraising the capacity of different types of organisations to empower women, nevertheless it is limited in several significant respects. In the seven-year interval since first produced, important external political and economic changes have occurred. These have included the fall of the Berlin Wall and the break-up of the Soviet Union, the widespread adoption of economic structural adjustment measures throughout the Third World, and the continued resurgence of nationalism and religious fundamentalism. Such events high-hat the complexity of confronting and challenging the power of the forces of subordination at global, regional, national and local level.

Equally during this period women's NGOs have not remained static. Because of its wide usage, we have retained this six fold categorisation. However, convergence has become more explicit during the past five years. As resources have decreased, organisational processes of consolidation or fragmentation highlight underlying objectives with greater calrity. For instance, a tendency for convergence between worker-based and grass-roots groups can be observed, as well as a greater clarification of approach of outside-initiated groups. A diversity of internal and external constraints and opportunities that cut across organisational types determine the capacity of organisations to influence the planning process. While DAWN highlighted some, others have become more significant in the intervening period. In addition, organisations have begun to recognise that women's empowerment with in the confines of a project does not automatically lead to their emancipation in the planning process. This has resulted in a shift in emphasis towards coalitions and networks. These require greater compromise and more realistic understanding of both political and planning realities.

Empowerment and emancipation ultimately depend on multi-faceted inervention strategies, in which different types of organisations act at times individually, but also at other times collaboratively. To identify when, where and why politically appropriate entry points occur to shift the agenda requires the introduction of a more dynamic analysis. There is no one solution. In some contexts clearly defined 'voice' strategies can be successful to confront the issue. In other contexts the use of 'exit' and withdrawal as an alternative method of protest can be more appropriate. In the world of political power there are no easy technical rules and regulations. Nevertheless, general guidelines can be helpful. It highlights some of the main internal and external constraints and opportunities for women's NGOs to empower and emancipate themselves through the planning process.

Internal and External Constraints and Opportunities of Women's NGOs

One significant difference between many women's NGOs and other organisations relates to internal organisational and leadership structure. This presents comparative advantages and disadvantages. DAWN, for example, cites the search for non-hierarchical and non-formal organisational structures as problematical in an increasingly formalized and hierarchical world. It presents the establishment of clearly delineated relationships with complex and bureaucratic decision-making bodies, necessary to pressure them to carry out policies in the interest of women's NGOs. Such groups have a historical mistrust of the manner in which centralised power has been used as an instrument of subordination. This has led to innovative ways of sharing responsibility that do not reinforced existing relationships of domination. However, unstructured organisation and nuclear authority demarcation and defined responsibilities also can lead to a lack of internal commitment. This occurs especially among volunteers, and results in conflict, power struggles, and weakens 'voice'.

Managerial and organisational problems also become particularly problematical as organisations expand and grow. With the shift from a small grass-roots body to a large organisation, problems can easily arise. These concern when to set up new structures, where to place authority, and how to settle conflicts. Weak management structures are particularly open to inefficiency when women's NGOs expand their areas of commitment into inter-sectoral planning—reflecting women's different needs in health, services, water and transport. One obvious consequence of work overload is conflict and dissent.

Negotiation and Debate at the Intra-household Level

In many societies the starting point for the subordination of women is the family, one of the most powerful and pervasive mechanisms of control. The entry point for debate and negotiation at the intra-household level for women can come at an individual level from increased economic independence.

Moreover, the solidarity and support provided by local-level organisations can play a critical role in consciousness-raising and solidarity, as much as in opening economic opportunities and providing skill training and child care. Sen (1990) emphasises the importance of women's extra-household organisation for changing perceptions relating to women's perceived contritions of 'gainful' work, and their relative share to family entitlements. Local organisations also provide the entry point for community-level debate and action relating to more strategic intra-household issues such as domestic violence and fertility control. The establishment of rape crisis centres, battered women's homes and well women's clinics are all local planning solutions to help women have greater control of their bodies, and their lives.

One important debate relating to local community-level organisation concerns the composition of such groups, and whether they should be mixed or segregated. It there need for separate women's organisations to avoid the marignalisation so frequently experienced by women when integrated into mainstream groups? The disadvantages of mixed groups are well known. Male domination of the leadership, management and finance all tend to result in male priorities in terms of goal, policy and projects. This also results in a loss of funds for women's programmes, and a general pressure on women to conform to traditional roles with accompanying 'female' programmes of health and welfare. Opportunities for negotiation and debate at the level of civil society are constrained by the conflicts and difference in interests and needs between women based on class, 'race', religion or ethnicity. For middle-class women running welfare-service delivery organisations, this can be more a consequence of the air lack of comprehension of the problems experienced by poor women than their concern to preserve class interests. Working-class women preoccupied with practical gender needs are frequently unwilling or unable to support mobilizations or join organisations concerned with more strategic needs. As Chaplain so aptly states, 'Philanthrop provides a cross-cutting tie between the classes which masks the fact that their interests are opposed'.

Women's organisations, therefore, can only negotiate on issues where there is sufficient unity of interests due to gender, despite other causes of division. Over time, social and economic processes occurring in society influece this, with class transformations themselves often deciding what women's organisations can achieve. The Fakalakalaka Women's Movement provides an interesting example. This grass-roots network of self-help, income-generation women's groups was started in Tonga in 1978 by local Catholic nuns. Initially, it was an immensely successful, rapidly growing movement. By 1984, it had 400 groups involved in saving schemes, home-improvement projects and community-level activities. Small (1989) shows that initially the groups provided women with a means to negotiation at the intra-household level. This provided access to household funds they would otherwise not control. 'Individual women simply would never have been able to siphon off household income individually for development or home improvement. The would have had to contend with the demands of the household and kind in the use of household income' (1989:5). The gradual collapse of the movement was due to conflicts caused by growing class transformation in Tongan society. As better-off women wanted to spend group money on different things from poorer women, dissent grew over spending decision and the latter began to drop out. At the same time, wealthier women, who could afford more, increased membership fees, which accelerated the drop-out of poorer women. In contrast to this there are examples of organisations where women of different classes have effectively worked together. An example of an organisation to empower low-income women is the Center de Orientation de la Mujer (CPMO). a worker-based organisation in Mexico. Middle-class, educated women in Ciudad Juarez initially set up COMO in 1968. Its purpose was to assist in tackling the problems of working-class women factor workers in the *Maquiladoras* assembly plants. These included the provision of welfare services such as child care, better transport and counseling. By 1975 it had turned into a militant working-class women's movement, confronting plant management by pressing for reforms in working conditions. A highly participatory three-stage approach provided the basis for this shift; first, the increasing involvement of women workers in the organisation's work, through participation in community schemes, health, literacy and nutrition courses; secondly, skills training and local employment of women through COMO diploma courses in nursing, teaching, social work, secretarial work and English language; and thirdly, the development of other employment creation schemes for laid off women workers, such as worker-managed production co-operatives. In COMO, what began an a middle-class professional women's organisation shifted to a working-class women's movement, via participation and the empowerment of poor women. Here the participation of middle-class women was seen as an advantage, not a hindrance. Dr. Valdez, a women social psychologist and CIMO's leader, and other middle class members, had contacts to several Mexican presidents, the press and academic institutions. Therefore they had the necessary social position, connections and skills crucial to getting COMO off the ground (Yudelman 1987).

Negotiation and Debate at the State Level

Does the political or ideological orientation of a country determine the process of negotiation and debate for gender planning by women's NGOs? Jayawardena, in her historical analysis of women's organisations, writes that, 'women's movements do not occur in a vacuum but correspond to, and to some extent are determined by, the wider social movements of which they form part' (1986: 10). Simultaneously she shows that women's movements in Asia integrated into national liberation struggles against colonialism. After gaining liberation, however, they neglected women's issues, allowing them to fall into the background. Consequently, she argues, there is a need for autonomous women's organisations with their own goals, to avoid submergence in nation state goals. The extent to which the wider political context is a constraint that determines NGO capacity to empower and emancipate women is highly complex. It varies depending on different ideological interpretations of development, and their interrelationship not only to patriarchy and class, but also to race and religion. This in turn has important implications in terms of the composition of women's ogrganisations, as autonomous or integrated institutions.

Frequently, it is short-term coalitions on specific issues that provides the entry point for women's organisations to negotiate at the level of the state. One powerful interest to unite women, on the basis of gender, is the state's attitude, in theory and practice, with regard to the issue of rape. In India, a classic example occurred in 1972 when two policemen raped a fifteen-year-old tribal labourer, Mathura. The Supreme Court finally acquitted them on the greediness that since no. wounds were found on her body, it could be presumed she had not resisted and thus consented to sexual intercourse. This is a typical example of a rape victim being found guilty. It provoked a massive response only after four university law lecturers (two men and two women) wrote an open letter throughout India protesting against the case. In 1980 the protest and action provoked women's groups in Bombay to form a coalition, the Forum against Rape. A vigorous, organised campaign around local rape cases followed. A National Conference Against Oppression of Women then provided the basis for national-level debate on the rape issue. Coalition pressure to change the law led to a discussion in Parliament. In broadening its agenda, the coalition then changed its name to the Forum against the Oppression of Women (FAOW). Although this soon fractionalised, due to dissenting views, it nevertheless succeeded in getting the issue of rape on to the political and planning agenda. Many different organisations in the past decades have in turn reinforced this action.

Poignant but highly controversial coalitions between women can occur when they collaborate under conditions of conflict. Women's complicity against other women in the context of repression and war is a highly sensitive issue, as the experience in Nazi Germany showed only too clearly. However, women also can be at the forefront of conflict resolution, when their power is in non-political action. The Israeli Women in Black Movement protesting at the Intifada, Protestant and Catholic women's groups in Northern Ireland coming together over the rights of women prisoners, and black and white women in South Africa dealing with 'conflict creatively' provide only three examples of coalitions. Such coalitions form when women question their stereotyped roles as 'protectors of values and culture' and 'mothers of the nation'. They reject the ethics of 'preparing their sons to die for their countries', and demand to be 'part of the answer not the problem.' However, such coalitions are open to violence and abuse, particularly of a sexual nature with accusations of 'sleeping with the enemy'. The only defense women have is to recognise the 'they are god at not quitting' and that strength is in their 'steadfastness.'

Negotiation and Debate at the Global Level

The International Women's Decade provided the 'political space' for formal, 'top-down' coalitions at the superior-national level. A diversity of global networks, particularly within the UN and Commonwealth, remain an important forum for international debate on gender concerns. However, it has been an uphill struggle. The fact that even in 1992 not all countries have ratified the forward Looking Strategies suggests that for many it remains essentially a matter of lip-service.

'Bottom-up' coalitions to negotiate and debate global gender concerns have been more tentative and cautious, but also probably more realistic. Most women in both the North and South are caught up in their own parochial realities. Women in the North only too easily think that women in the South have to catch up. 'It may be that women in the UK can learn much from their better organised sisters in the Third World, who long ago learnt the limitations of relying on the state to reduce their dependence on men'.

Many activist, feminist women from the South are clear that there are more issues to divide them from their sisters in the North than there are to unite them. Not only have imperialism and colonialism left brutal scars. They identify the re-colonization of the Third World working through such instruments as GATT, and the loss of sovereignty and state legitimacy through structural adjustment programmes, as mechanisms that serve simply to reinforce the existing North-South divide.

Despite such difference, during the past decade, international and regional issue-based networks have proliferated. These encompass the full range of women's practical and strategic gender needs, from health to housing, and include institutions of every type, from trade unions to women's institutes. DAWN has been critical in identifying *global gender issues* for debate. These it identified in its analysis of the inter-locking crises of debt, food, energy and deterioration of social services, environmental degradation, political conservatism and religious fundamentalism and militarisation. This has been important in forging 'a close relationship between the work of the emerging internatioal women's movement and the socio-economic and political processes of the decade' (Antrobs 1989: 75). However, structural adjustment programmes essentially remain gender blind. This provides a salutary example of precisely how limited the impact of global networks has been to date, in shifting agendas relating to either practical or strategic gender needs in the context of economic reform. Negotiation and debate at the global level is the most difficult to accomplish, but the most important to achieve.

Bibliography

Atkins, E.C., N. Douglas, J.W.B., K.E. Kiernan, and M.E.J. Wadsworth, (1981), 'The 1946 cohort study', in S.A. Mednick and A.E. Baert (eds) *An Empirical Basis for Primary Prevention,* Oxford: Oxford University Press.

Bames, J.A., (1979), *Who Should Know What? Social Science, Privacy and Ethics,* Harmondsworth: Penguin.

Becker, H., (1967), 'Whose side are we on?', *Social Problems 14: 239-47.*

Blaxter, M., (1987), Alcohol Consumption', in B.B. Cox, A.W. Bucle, N.P. fenner, F.A. Hppert and M., Wichelow (eds) *The Health and Life Style Survey,* London, Health Promotion Research Trust.

Black, C., (1915), *Married Women's Work,* London, G. Bell and Sons.

Braddon, F.E.M., M.E.J. Wadsworth, J.M.C. Davies, and R.A. Cripps, (1988), 'Social and regional differences in food and alcohol consumption and their measurements in a national birth cohort', *Journal of Epidemiological and Community Health* 42: 341-9.

Branen, J. and Wilson, G. (eds.) (1987), *Give and Take in Families,* London: Allen & Unwin.

Bogunia, L., (1989), *Przerywanie Ciazy, Problemy Prawnokarne i Kryminologiczne* (Abortion, Penal and criminological Problems) Wrockaw.

Burgoyne, J. and Clark, D. (1986), *Making a Go of It.* London: Routledge.

Buxakowski, J., (1989), Wprowadzenie do dyskusji nad projeketem ustawy prawnej ochronie dziecka poczetego' (Introduction to the discussion of the draft act of legal protection of the unborn child), Lad No. 26 to 25 June.

Cohen, S. and Taylor, L., (1977), 'Talking about prison blues,' in C. Bell and H. Newby (eds) *Doing Sociological Research*, Allen & Unwin, London.

Clcoure, A.V., (1964), *Method and Measurenent in Sociology*, Free Press, New York.

Cunnison, S. (1986), 'Gender, consent and exploitation among sheltered housing wardens', in K. Purcell, S. Wood, A. Waton and S. Allen (eds) *The Changing Experience of Employment*, Macmillan, London.

Czynczyk, A. (1989), 'Ethicsand law on the first days of life' in A Sajo (ed.) *Modern Technology and Law*, Budapest.

Declaration on Abortion, Vatican (1974), *The Holy Congregation on Faith.*

Denzin, N.K., (1970), *The Research Act*, Chicago: Aldine.

Dominaan, J. (1965), *Marital breakdown*, Harmondsworth: Penguin.

Dunnell, K. (1980), *Family Formation 1976*, London: HMSO.

Eichler, M., (1980), *The Double Standard: A Feminist Critique of Feminist Social Science*, London: Croom Helm.

Eedelaar, J. and Maclean, M., (1986), *Maintenance after Divorce*, Oxford: Oxford University Press.

Finch, J. (1984a), 'The deceit of self help: Preschool Playgrounds and Working Class Women', *Journal of Social Policy, 13, 1:1-20.*

——, (1984b), "'It's great to have someone to talk to": the ethics and politics of interviewing women', in C. Bell and H. Roberts (eds) *Social Researching: Politics, Problems, Practice*, London: Routledge and Kegan Paul.

——, (1986), *Research and Policy: The Uses of Qualitative Methods in Social and Educational Research*, Brighton: Falmer.

Furstenberg, F. and Spanier, D. (1984), *Recycling the Family*, California:/ Sage.

Gilligan, C., *(1982), In a Different Voice: Psychological Theory and Women's Development*, Cambridge, Mass: Harvard University Press.

Graham, H. (1983), 'Do her answers fit his questions? Women and the survey method', in Gamarniknow, D. Moragan, J. Purvis and D. Taylorson (eds) *The Public and the Private*, Lodnon: Heinemann.

Guidobaldi, J., Cleminshaw, A., Perry, J.D. and Mclaughlin, C.G., 1987, 'Growing up in a divorced family', *Applied Social Psychology*, Annales 7, California: Sage.

Hanmer, J. and Saunders, S., (1984), *Well-Founded Fear: A Community Study of Violence to Women*, London: Hutchinson.

Harding, S., (1987), 'IntroductionL is there is feminist method?, in S. Harding (ed.) *Feminism and Methodology*, Bloomington: Indian a University Press.

Hart, N., 1976, *When Marriage Ends*, London: Tavistock.

Hordyniec, W., and Crabowska, T., (1982), 'spoleczna recepcja zjawiska przerywania ciazy i jej wplyw na system wartosoi u kobiet poddajacych sie temu zabietogwi', (Reception of abortion in society and its impact on the system of values of women who terminate a pregnancy), unpublished masters thesis.

Itzin, C. 1980, *Splittign Up*, London, Virago.

Jayarattne, T.E., (1983), 'the value of quantitative methodlogy for feminist research', in G. Bowles and R. Duelli Klein (eds) *Theories of Women's Studies*, London: Routledge & Kegan Paul.

Kelly, A., (1978),'Feminism and Research', *Women's Studies Inernational Quartely, 1:225-32.*

Kelly, J. and Corbin, J. (1986), 'Father-child relationships after divorce', *Family Law Quarterly* 20: 109-29.

Kiernan, K. (1986), Teenage marriage and marital breakdown', *Population Studies* 37:368-80.

Martin, J and Robers, C. (1984), *Women and Employment: A*

Lifetime Perspective, London: HMSO.

McLanahan, S., (1985), 'Family structure and the reproduction of poverty', *American Journal of Sociology* 90, 4: 873-901.

Maclean, and Wadswot, M.E.J. , (1987), 'Children's life chances and parental divorce', *International Journal of Law and Family* 2: 155-66.

Millar, J. and Glendinning, C. (1989), 'Gender and Poverty', *Joural of Social Policy* 18, 3: 363-82.

Oakle, A. (1981), 'Interviewing Women: A Contradiction in Terms', in H. Roberts (ed.) *Doing Feminist Research*, London: Routledge and Kegan Paul.

Pahl, J. (1984), 'The allocation of money within the household', in M. Freeman (ed.) *State, The Law and The Family: Critical Perspectives*, London: Tavistock Pember.

Reeves, M., (1913), *Round About a Pound a Week*, London: G. Bell & Sons.

Registrar General, Census of India.

Shapiro, J. (1981), 'Anthropology and the Study of Gender', in E. Langland and W. Gove (eds), *A Feminist Perspective in the Academy*, Chicago: University of Chicago Press.

Smith, D.E. (1974), 'Women's Persoective as a Radical Critique of Sociology', *Sociological Enquiry* 44, 1:7-13.

——, (1979), 'A Peculiar Eclipsing: Women's Exclusion from Man's Culture', *Women's Studies International Quarterly* 1, 4: 281-95.

Stanley, L and Wise, S. (1983), *Breaking Out: Feminist Consciousness and Feminist Research*, London: Routledge and Kegan Paul.

Ungerson, C. (1987), Policy is Personal: Sex, Gender and Informal Care, London: Tavistock.

Wise, S., (1985), "Becoming a Feminist Social Worker," Manchester University, Department of Sociology Studies in Sexual Politics.

Index

——□□□□——